THE MESSAGE OF JESUS

THE MESSAGE OF JESUS

JOHN DOMINIC CROSSAN AND BEN WITHERINGTON III IN DIALOGUE

ROBERT B. STEWART, EDITOR

Fortress Press
Minneapolis

THE MESSAGE OF JESUS

John Dominic Crossan and Ben Witherington III in Dialogue

Copyright © 2013 Fortress Press. All rights reserved. Except for brief quotations in critical articles or reviews, no part of this book may be reproduced in any manner without prior written permission from the publisher. Visit http://www.augsburgfortress.org/copyrights/ or write to Permissions, Augsburg Fortress, Box 1209, Minneapolis, MN 55440.

Cover image: Grunge background with Jesus Christ mosaic in Hagia Sophia © Shutterstock.com / Brian Chase

Cover design: Justin Korhonen

Library of Congress Cataloging-in-Publication Data
ISBN: 978-0-8006-9927-7

The paper used in this publication meets the minimum requirements of American National Standard for Information Sciences — Permanence of Paper for Printed Library Materials, ANSI Z329.48-1984.

Manufactured in the U.S.A.

This book was produced using PressBooks.com, and PDF rendering was done by PrinceXML.

For Gary Habermas

A philosopher seeking after Jesus

CONTENTS

Contributors — ix
Preface — xv
Acknowledgments — xix
Surveying the Quest of the Historical Jesus
   Robert B. Stewart — 1

1. The Message of Jesus
   A Dialogue
   John Dominic Crossan and Ben Witherington III — 33

2. The Place of Jewish Scripture in Jesus' Teaching
   Craig A. Evans — 79

3. Standard and Poor
   The Economic Index of the Parables
   Amy-Jill Levine, Myrick C. Shinall Jr. — 95

4. Everything in Parables
   On Jesus' Style
   Stephen J. Patterson — 117

5. How Matthew Helped Jesus Fulfill Prophecy
   Robert J. Miller — 127

6. Faith and the Historical Jesus
   Does A Confessional Position and Respect for the Jesus Tradition Preclude Serious Historical Engagement?
   Darrell L. Bock — 143

7. The Historical Jesus from the Synoptics and the Fourth Gospel?
   Jesus the Purifier
   Craig L. Blomberg — 165

8. Critical Blindness, Wise Virgins, and the Law of Christ
   Three Surprising Examples of Jesus Tradition in Paul
   David Wenham — 183

Index 205

Contributors

Craig L. Blomberg is Distinguished Professor of New Testament at Denver Seminary in Littleton, Colorado. He holds a PhD from the University of Aberdeen, Scotland; MA from Trinity Evangelical Divinity School, Deerfield, Illinois, and BA from Augustana College, Rock Island, Illinois. He has authored thirteen books and coauthored or coedited eight others, with over 130 articles and essays in print. His major publications are *The Historical Reliability of the Gospels; Interpreting the Parables; Matthew (New American Commentary); 1 Corinthians (NIV Application Commentary); Jesus and the Gospels: An Introduction and Survey; Neither Poverty nor Riches: A Biblical Theology of Possessions; The Historical Reliability of John's Gospel; Preaching the Parables; Contagious Holiness: Jesus' Meals with Sinners; From Pentecost to Patmos: An Introduction and Survey of Acts-Revelation; James (Zondervan Exegetical Commentary)*, with Mariam J. Kamell; *A Handbook of New Testament Exegesis*, with Jennifer Foutz Markley; and *Christians in an Age of Wealth: A Biblical Theology of Stewardship for Life*. He is a member of the Studiorum Novi Testamenti Societas, the Society of Biblical Literature, the Institute of Biblical Research, the Tyndale Fellowship, the Evangelical Theological Society, and the Committee on Bible Translation for the NIV.

Darrell L. Bock is Senior Research Professor of New Testament Studies at Dallas Theological Seminary in Dallas, Texas. He also serves as Executive Director of Cultural Engagement for the seminary's Center for Christian Leadership. His special fields of study involve hermeneutics, the use of the Old Testament in the New, Luke-Acts, the historical Jesus, gospel studies, and the integration of theology and culture. He has served on the board of Chosen People Ministries for almost a decade and also serves on the board at Wheaton College. He is a graduate of the University of Texas (BA), Dallas Theological Seminary (ThM), and the University of Aberdeen (PhD). He has had four annual stints of postdoctoral study at the University of Tübingen, the second through fourth as an Alexander von Humboldt scholar (1989–1990, 1995–1996, 2004–2005, and 2010–2011). He also serves as elder emeritus at Trinity Fellowship Church in Richardson, Texas, is editor at large for *Christianity Today*, served as President of the Evangelical Theological Society for the year 2000–2001, and has authored over thirty books, including a *New York Times* Best Seller in nonfiction. He is married to Sally and has two daughters (both married), a son, and two grandsons.

John Dominic Crossan is Emeritus Professor of Religious Studies at DePaul University and former co-chair of the Jesus Seminar (1985–1996). He is one of the most influential New Testament scholars in contemporary scholarship and has authored more than twenty bestselling books on the historical Jesus, early Christianities, and the historical Paul. He has authored many books on Jesus and Paul, including *The Historical Jesus: The Life of a Mediterranean Jewish Peasant* (1991), *Jesus: A Revolutionary Biography* (1994), *The Birth of Christianity* (1998), *God & Empire: Jesus Against Rome Then and Now* (2007). He also coauthored *Excavating Jesus* (2001) and *In Search of Paul: How Jesus's Apostle Opposed Rome's Empire with God's Kingdom* (2004), both with archaeologist Jonathan L. Reed. He has lectured to lay and scholarly audiences across the United States as well as in Ireland and England, Scandinavia and Finland, Australia and New Zealand, Brazil, Japan, and South Africa. He has been interviewed on more than two hundred radio stations, including National Public Radio's "Fresh Air" with Terry Gross. He has also been interviewed on numerous television shows such as ABC's *PrimeTime*, *Peter Jennings Reporting*, and *Nightline*, CBS's *Early Show* and *48 Hours*, NBC's *Dateline*, and Fox News's *The O'Reilly Factor*, and on cable programs such as A&E, History, Discovery, and the National Geographic Channel.

Craig A. Evans is Payzant Distinguished Professor of New Testament at Acadia Divinity College and Acadia University. Before his appointment at Acadia in 2002, he taught for twenty-one years at Trinity Western University, where he founded the Dead Sea Scrolls Institute. He has a BA degree from Claremont McKenna College, MDiv from Western Seminary, MA and PhD from Claremont Graduate University, and DHabil from Károli Gáspár Református University in Budapest. He has served as editor-in-chief of the *Bulletin for Biblical Research* and has served on the editorial boards of *Dead Sea Discoveries, Journal of Biblical Literature, Catholic Biblical Quarterly, New Testament Studies, Journal for the Study of the Historical Jesus*, and others. His recent books include *Matthew* (Cambridge), *Jesus and His World: The Archaeological Evidence* (SPCK/Westminster John Knox), *Guide to the Dead Sea Scrolls* (B&H), *Ancient Texts for New Testament Studies: A Guide to the Background Literature* (Hendrickson), *Jesus and the Ossuaries* (Baylor), and, with N. T. Wright, *Jesus,* *the Final Days* (SPCK/Westminster John Knox). Professor Evans has appeared in programs and documentaries that have aired on History Channel, BBC, and *Dateline NBC*. Evans and his wife Ginny live in Kentville, Nova Scotia, located in historic Annapolis Valley, and have two grown daughters and a grandson.

Amy-Jill Levine is University Professor of New Testament and Jewish Studies, E. Rhodes and Leona B. Carpenter Professor of New Testament Studies, and Professor of Jewish Studies at Vanderbilt Divinity School and College of Arts and Science. She is also Affiliated Professor, Centre for the Study of Jewish-Christian Relations, Cambridge, United Kingdom. Holding a BA from Smith College and MA and PhD from Duke University, she has honorary doctorates from the University of Richmond, the Episcopal Theological Seminary of the Southwest, the University of South Carolina–Upstate, Drury University, and Christian Theological Seminary. She has held office in the Society of Biblical Literature, the Catholic Biblical Association, and the Association of Jewish Studies. Her recent books include *The Misunderstood Jew: The Church and the Scandal of the Jewish Jesus* (HarperOne), *The Meaning of the Bible: What the Jewish Scriptures and the Christian Old Testament Can Teach Us* (coauthored with Douglas Knight; HarperOne), the edited *Historical Jesus in Context* (Princeton), and the thirteen-volume edited *Feminist Companions to the New Testament and Early Christian Writings* (Continuum). With Marc Brettler, she edited the *Jewish Annotated New Testament* (Oxford). A self-described "Yankee Jewish feminist," Professor Levine is a member of Congregation Sherith Israel, an Orthodox synagogue in Nashville, Tennessee, although she is often quite unorthodox.

Robert J. Miller is the Rosenberger Professor of Religious Studies and Christian Thought at Juniata College in Pennsylvania, where he teaches courses in Biblical Studies, World Religions, and the Philosophy of Religion. He received an MA in Religious Studies from the University of California at Santa Barbara and MA in Philosophy and PhD in Religion (New Testament) from Claremont Graduate University. He is the editor of *The Complete Gospels* (4th ed., 2010). His other publications include *The Jesus Seminar and Its Critics* (1999), *Born Divine: The Births of Jesus and Other Sons of God* (2003), and, with Arthur Dewey, *The Complete Gospel Parallels* (2012). He has served since 2004 on the program committee for the Historical Jesus Section of the Society of Biblical Literature. He is the editor of *The Fourth R*, a magazine sponsored by the Jesus Seminar for general readers. Bob has been a visiting professor at the Stockholm

School of Theology, Eden Theological Seminary, and Stanford University. He is also committed to adult education and has made over 250 appearances for various religious groups all across North America.

Stephen J. Patterson is the George H. Atkinson Professor of Religious and Ethical Studies at Willamette University in Salem, Oregon. From 1988 to 2010, he was Professor of New Testament at Eden Seminary in Saint Louis. His most recent book is *Beyond the Passion: Rethinking the Death and Life of Jesus* (Fortress, 2004). He is also the author of *The God of Jesus: The Historical Jesus and the Search for Meaning* (Trinity, 1998) and *The Gospel of Thomas and Jesus* (Polebridge, 1993) and coauthor of *The Q–Thomas Reader* (Polebridge, 1990), *The Search for Jesus* (Smithsonian Institution and Biblical Archaeology Society, 1994), *The Fifth Gospel: The Gospel of Thomas Comes of Age* (Trinity, 1998), and *The Apocalyptic Jesus: A Debate* (Polebridge, 2001). His many essays and reviews have appeared in the *Harvard Theological Review*, *Journal of Biblical Literature*, *Journal of Religion*, *Journal of the American Academy of Religion*, and *Theology Today*, among other publications both professional and popular.

Myrick C. Shinall Jr. is a PhD student in the New Testament and Early Christianity program in the Vanderbilt University Graduate Department of Religion and a resident physician in general surgery at Vanderbilt University Medical Center. He holds degrees from Harvard University (BA), Vanderbilt Divinity School (MDiv), and Vanderbilt Medical School (MD). He is a recipient of the H. William Scott Jr. Memorial Scholarship to fund his research. He has published work in several medical journals and has served as a guest editor for an issue of *Virtual Mentor: American Medical Association Journal of Ethics* on "Religion, Patients, and Medical Ethics." His primary research interest area is in issues of sickness, healing, and the body in New Testament and early Christianity and their impact on the contemporary experience of illness and death.

Robert B. Stewart (PhD, Southwestern Baptist Theological Seminary) is Professor of Philosophy and Theology at New Orleans Baptist Theological Seminary, where he is Greer-Heard Professor of Faith and Culture. He is editor of *The Resurrection of Jesus: John Dominic Crossan and N. T. Wright in Dialogue* (Fortress Press, 2006); *Intelligent Design: William A. Dembski and Michael Ruse in Dialogue* (Fortress Press, 2007); *The Future of Atheism: Alister McGrath and Daniel Dennett in Dialogue* (Fortress Press, 2008); and *The Reliability of the*

New Testament: Bart D. Ehrman and Daniel B. Wallace in Dialogue (Fortress Press, 2011). A contributor to the *Cambridge Dictionary of Christianity*, he has published articles or book reviews in numerous journals.

David Wenham (MA, Cambridge; PhD, Manchester) is Lecturer in New Testament Studies at Trinity College Bristol and Research Fellow at Bristol University (United Kingdom). Previously, he taught in Wycliffe Hall in the University of Oxford. He was until recently chairman of the New Testament Group of the Tyndale Fellowship for Biblical and Theological Research. His areas of specialization include the synoptic problem and gospel origins, the Jesus-Paul question, and the Sermon on the Mount. He was Director of the Gospels Research Project of Tyndale House in Cambridge, and editor or joint editor of the Gospel Perspectives series (JSOT, 1979–). He is author of *The Rediscovery of Jesus' Eschatological Discourse: Studies in the History of Gospel Traditions* (JSOT, 1984), *The Parables of Jesus: Pictures of Revolution* (Hodder/InterVarsity USA, 1989), *Paul: Follower of Jesus or Founder of Christianity?* (Eerdmans, 1995), *Exploring the New Testament*, vol. 1, *Introducing the Gospels and Acts,* jointly authored with Steve Walton (SPCK, 2001), *Paul and Jesus: The True Story* (SPCK/Eerdmans, 2002), and *Did St Paul Get Jesus Right? The Gospel According to Paul* (Lion, 2009). He has published widely in journals, Festschrifts, and other volumes, and is currently editing a volume on *Preaching the New Testament* (InterVarsity).

Ben Witherington III (MDiv, Gordon Conwell; PhD, University of Durham, United Kingdom) is Amos Professor of New Testament for Doctoral Studies at Asbury Theological Seminary and on the doctoral faculty at St. Andrews University in Scotland. Witherington has also taught at Ashland Theological Seminary, Vanderbilt University, Duke Divinity School, and Gordon-Conwell. He has written over thirty books, including *Jesus the Sage* and *Jesus, Paul and the End of the World*, plus a host of commentaries. Two of his books, *The Jesus Quest* and *The Paul Quest*, were selected as top biblical-studies works by *Christianity Today*. He also writes for many church and scholarly publications and is a frequent contributor to the *Beliefnet* website. Along with many interviews on radio networks across the country, Witherington has been seen on the History Channel, NBC, ABC, CBS, CNN, the Discovery Channel, A&E, and the PAX Network.

Preface

In March 2005, an interesting experiment began at New Orleans Baptist Theological Seminary. The experiment was the Greer-Heard Point-Counterpoint Forum in Faith and Culture. The intention of the forum was to have a respected Evangelical scholar dialogue with a respected non-Evangelical or non-Christian scholar on an important subject in religion or culture. The forum was intended to be a dialogue, rather than a debate. The hope was that the participants would speak to each other and not simply about the other's position. The goal was thus a respectful though uncompromising exchange of ideas. So often in our contemporary culture, the sorts of issues the forum was to address stoke the emotions, and consequently the rhetoric is of such a nature as to ensure that communication does *not* take place. There may be a place and time for such preaching to the choir, but minds are rarely changed as a result of such activity—nor are better arguments forthcoming. What frequently results, then, is that what passes for argument is really nothing more than a prolonged example of the straw-man fallacy. What made this experiment so interesting, however, was that it was taking place at a Southern Baptist seminary, a bastion of conservative Evangelical thought. Somewhat frequently, guests will comment to me that they are surprised that Southern Baptists are sponsoring such an "open-minded" sort of conversation. This just goes to show that one should not judge a book by its cover. The Greer-Heard experiment was made possible by a generous gift from Bill and Carolyn (née Greer) Heard. As such, the forum was originally a "five-year pilot program."

The first forum featured a dialogue between N. T. Wright and John Dominic Crossan on the resurrection of Jesus. The following year was the only year (so far) that the forum took place in a location other than New Orleans. Due to the New Orleans campus being flooded in the aftermath of Hurricane Katrina, the forum was moved to Marietta, Georgia, where Johnson Ferry Baptist Church became its temporary home. There could have been no better site for the event. The subject of the dialogue for that year was "Intelligent Design." Did I mention that Marrieta, Georgia, is in Cobb County, Georgia, the site of a very important court case involving Intelligent Design? The large size of the audience was no doubt due in part to the interest in the subject in Cobb County. The dialogue partners were William A. Dembski and Michael Ruse. In 2007, the forum returned to New Orleans and featured a dialogue between Daniel Dennett and Alister McGrath on the future of atheism. The next year featured a dialogue between Bart Ehrman and Dan Wallace on the textual reliability of the New Testament. The fifth year featured Paul Knitter and Harold Netland dialoguing on the subject of "Can Only One Religion Be True?"

The sixth year—yes, the experiment was deemed a success—featured the subject of this book: "The Message of Jesus." The scholars headlining the event were John Dominic Crossan and Ben Witherington III. Jesus remains the most interesting person who has ever lived. That books about Jesus continue to pour forth from publishing houses at breakneck pace demonstrates this. Surely, by any measure, Jesus is a worthy topic for discussion.

The forum continues and shows no signs of slowing down or ceasing to address relevant concerns. Each year, the Greer-Heard Forum has been well attended, and the spirit has been good—collegial and irenic, yet without requiring any compromise of one's convictions. As the chair of the forum, I must say that I am extremely honored to publish the fruit of the experiment with Fortress Press. All those at Fortress with whom I have worked have been creative and expert in every regard. What is more, Fortress is widely recognized as a publisher of excellence. The result is that readers with varying opinions and diverse backgrounds read the dialogues and accompanying papers from the forum. This has, indeed, been very satisfying to me.

The dialogue, "The Message of Jesus," took place Friday, February 26, 2010, in the Leavell Chapel on the campus of New Orleans Baptist Theological Seminary. The chapel was filled with an enthusiastic and appreciate crowd. Approximately 880 people heard the exchange. The discussion between Crossan and Witherington was spirited but civil, and very frequently witty and even humorous. Crossan and Witherington are passionately committed to their positions but also good friends with deep respect for the other's scholarship. Such was obvious. One of the consistent fruits of the forum has been a demonstration that disagreement does not have to be shrill or heated in nature, and that one does not have to check one's convictions at the door in order for respectful dialogue to take place. The following day, Saturday, February 27, 2010, papers were read by Craig A. Evans, Amy-Jill Levine, Darrell L. Bock, and Stephen J. Patterson on subjects related to Jesus and his message. After each paper, Dom and Ben briefly discussed the paper with each presenter.

Along with my introductory chapter, this book includes a transcript of the dialogue between Crossan and Witherington (including Q&A), as well as the papers presented the following day. In addition to the papers that were presented at the Greer-Heard Forum, other essays are included. Craig

Blomberg, David Wenham, and Robert Miller each contributes a chapter related to the message of Jesus.

While one could easily note issues that are still not addressed in this volume, or think of significant scholars who are not included, we believe these chapters make for a rich treatment of the issue. No doubt, readers will have to judge for themselves if this is in fact the case.

I am pleased to present to you the fruit of the 2010 Greer-Heard Forum. I trust that you will read it with an open mind and carefully consider what each author has to say. If you will, I have no doubt that you will be the richer for having done so.

Robert Stewart
September 24, 2012
New Orleans Baptist Theological Seminary

Acknowledgments

Thanking others in print always causes me a bit of anxiety, because I fear that I will fail to recognize someone who truly deserves a word of appreciation. But many deserve to be publicly thanked—and even praised—so I must go on. First of all, I must thank Bill and Carolyn Heard for their passion to have a forum where leading scholars can dialogue about important issues in faith and culture in a civilized manner and on a balanced playing field—and their willingness to fund such a project! Without them, the Greer-Heard Point-Counterpoint Forum in Faith and Culture would be a dream rather than a reality. As always, I thank New Orleans Baptist Theological Seminary (NOBTS) president, Dr. Chuck Kelley, for his support and encouragement.

I must thank my assistant at that time, Rhyne Putman. He did everything he was asked to do and more—and all of it with a cheerful attitude. As in past years, he maintained the Greer-Heard website. He also oversaw any number of other things that didn't fall under somebody else's job description. Tim Walker must also be thanked for the original transcription of the dialogue. I thank my present assistant, Andrew Bailey, and my son, Raymond Stewart, for producing the index.

The forum would never have come off successfully without the efforts of J. P. Cox and his staff at the Providence Learning Center. J. P. is a true professional. I also am grateful to Vanee Daure and her team for the work they did in media support. Sheila Taylor and the NOBTS cafeteria staff must be applauded for serving numerous meals of all varieties to large numbers. Without the high-quality graphic art and public relations work of Boyd Guy and Gary Myers, the task would have proven too great. Lisa Joyner of Johnson Ferry Baptist Church in Marietta, Georgia, deserves a word of recognition for her work in producing the conference programs and CD case covers.

I am appreciative of the Evangelical Theological Society for having their Southwest Regional Meeting on the NOBTS campus in conjunction with the Greer-Heard Forum. I especially thank Joe Wooddell, the southwest regional president at the time, for his efforts in publicizing the event.

I am grateful to NOBTS provost Steve Lemke for making it possible for several university groups to attend the event. His efforts, along with those of Archie England and Page Brooks and their respective staffs, were much appreciated.

The participants in the 2010 Greer-Heard Point-Counterpoint Forum, Dom Crossan and Ben Witherington, along with Craig Evans, Amy-Jill Levine, Darrell Bock, and Stephen Patterson, must all be thanked. Craig Blomberg was scheduled to deliver the regional Evangelical Theological Society plenary address on a related topic, but illness at the last moment kept him from being able to attend. Nevertheless, his paper was read at the conference (by Darrell Bock), and I am very pleased to have it as part of this book. I also thank David Wenham and Robert Miller for submitting additional chapters to the book.

I am especially grateful for Will Bergkamp. Without his support and encouragement, this project would never have been completed. Lisa Gruenisen, the project editor for this book, must also be thanked. Her cheerful attitude, eagerness to help in any way possible, and consummate professionalism are much appreciated.

As always, my wife, Marilyn, must be thanked. I suspect that she enjoys the rush and the fine meals that accompany an event like the forum, but she still makes numerous sacrifices. On top of that, the many hours at the office bringing the manuscript to completion surely take a toll. Yet she never complains; instead, she constantly encourages.

I am dedicating this book to my good friend Gary Habermas, a fellow philosopher who, like me, is intensely interested in the historical Jesus. Gary is a committed scholar, an astute historian, and a genuinely committed disciple of Jesus Christ. To recognize him in this way is the least I can do.

Surveying the Quest of the Historical Jesus

Robert B. Stewart

In the Gospel of Mark, Jesus is famously recorded as asking his disciples, "Who do men say that I am?" (Mark 8:27 RSV). This question can easily be translated into "Who do *scholars* say that I am?" Then it is only a small step to the question "What do they take my message to be?" Jesus' disciples answered, "John the Baptist; and others say, Elijah; and others one of the prophets" (Mark 8:28 RSV). The important thing to see is that, even at that stage, there were a number of opinions concerning who Jesus was and, by implication, about his message. Simply put, one cannot talk about Jesus without making some assumptions as to his message, and vice versa. Though the man and his message can be *distinguished*, they cannot be *divided*. This book features a dialogue about the message of Jesus, but lurking in the background (and sometimes coming out into the open, at times even moving to center stage) is always the question of who Jesus was. Attempts to answer this question are typically referred to under the rubric of the quest of the historical Jesus. This introductory essay will provide a flyover of some important moments in that quest.[1]

THE BACKGROUND OF THE QUEST FOR JESUS AND HIS MESSAGE

Nothing of historical significance takes place in a vacuum. There are no bare historical facts apart from a historical context. The quest for Jesus is not unique in this regard. In large part, the quest arose as a result of a seismic shift from one historical era to another. Its first rumblings were felt in the Renaissance, they continued on through the Reformation, and erupted with full force in the seventeenth century as part of modernity as a new way of thinking about both history and religion.

---

1. The amount of space that can be allotted to any individual in this section is limited. Some significant scholars will be overlooked entirely, a matter that is unavoidable. It is hoped, however, that enough of a sketch will be provided that one may make out the general features of historical-Jesus research over approximately the past 230 years.

The Renaissance is generally dated to the fourteenth century. One frequently hears of how the classical age was again appreciated in the Renaissance. No doubt this is true. This was due to the widespread recognition of just how different people in the fourteenth century were from those of Plato and Aristotle's time, as well as those of Jesus' age. Most importantly for our purposes, it marked a time when the pastness of the past was duly recognized, along with all that doing so entailed. The past was thus seen as both distant and different. These twin differences were fully appreciated in the fifteenth and sixteenth centuries. For our purposes, this may be seen primarily in two ways: first, in a willingness to revise what had previously been dogma;[2] and second, in a renewed interest in understanding ancient documents in light of their original languages and cultural contexts. This attitude ushered in a fresh breeze of skepticism about the old and openness to the new that birthed the disciplines of philology and textual criticism. Philology led to Lorenzo Valla's demonstration on historical and linguistic bases that the so-called Donation of Constantine could not be genuine. Textual criticism ushered in Desiderius Erasmus's publication of the received text of the Greek New Testament, which prompted a young German monk named Martin Luther to rock the Western church with his declaration that he would take his stand with sacred Scripture and evident reason over against tradition and authority.

The seventeenth century ushered in modernity in all its fury. The methodological skepticism of Rene Descartes's *Cogito* coupled with his rigorous logic and epistemological foundationalism led to a type of rational Christianity in which the concept of divine revelation was still *accepted* but no longer *required* for religious knowledge. This in turn led theologians to seek to ground Christian truth claims in reason rather than revelation. Fundamentally, this was a radically new way of conceiving religion, one in which reason came in practice to have priority over faith.

But perhaps the most significant role would be played by Baruch (Benedict) Spinoza. In many ways, inclusion of Spinoza seems a bit odd for an essay surveying research on the historical Jesus. After all, Spinoza died before H. S. Reimarus was even born. He was neither a biblical scholar nor a Christian. He was an excommunicated Jew and philosopher. Nevertheless, his *Tractatus Theologico-Politicus* would prove to be highly influential in the centuries to come. In it Spinoza proposes a new method of biblical interpretation. First, he

---

2. By dogma, I do not mean simply Christian doctrine but rather all historical conclusions, whether religious or political. Of course, I do certainly include religious belief and recognize that the two were far more closely connected—indeed, intertwined—before and during the fourteenth century than they are today.

insists that one make a thorough examination of the language of the Bible. Second, one should systematically classify the topics dealt with in the Scriptures, paying particular attention to the passages that are problematic or seem contradictory to other passages. Third, one should study each book and its background historically in order to identify its author and the context in which it was written, as well as its transmission history.[3]

Most controversially—and significantly for our purposes—he insisted that when properly conducted, biblical interpretation should be about discovering only the meaning of the biblical texts, not their truth. "The universal rule, then, in interpreting Scripture is to accept nothing as an authoritative Scriptural statement which we do not perceive very clearly when we examine it in the light of its history."[4] His basis for this contention was his abhorrence for religious oppression. So long as one view was seen as "correct," then dark periods in history, like the Inquisition (his family had relocated to France and then to the Netherlands to avoid the Inquisition in Portugal), could be justified. Publicly, Spinoza insisted that faith was primarily a moral matter, and so far as morality was concerned, there was little if anything in Scripture that was controversial. So faith would remain unscathed.

At first glance, his method seems fairly innocuous. In addition to these three steps, however, Spinoza also claimed that "the method of interpreting Scripture does not widely differ from the method of interpreting Nature—in fact it is almost the same."[5] He furthermore stated (some would say overstated) the difficulties in reading biblical Hebrew and challenged the transmission of the Old Testament text. In short, in part at least, his treatise was a broadside across the bow of the established theology and a forceful defense of reason over against faith, or as he saw it, superstition.[6] Though it would take some time for his thoughts to bear fruit (and for it to be known that they were his thoughts—he published anonymously), in time his conclusions would be widely accepted. As such, his pioneering work in biblical criticism, even if primarily with regard to the Old Testament, would eventually bear fruit in modern forms of biblical criticism, which would affect the quest for the historical Jesus.

All these factors, as well as others of some significance that space does not permit mention of, played a role in bringing about a time in which Jesus could

---

3. Baruch Spinoza, "Of the Interpretation of Scripture," in *The Philosophy of Spinoza*, ed. and trans. Joseph Ratner (New York: Modern Library, 1954), 15–24.
4. Ibid., 15.
5. Ibid., 13.
6. Ibid., 26–35.

be sought for as a historical figure. And this led to Jesus' message as well as his person, interrelated as they are, being critically assessed.

A Brief History of Jesus Research

James D. G. Dunn writes, "The key issue in any attempt to talk historically about Jesus of Nazareth has been and continues to be the tension between faith and history, or more accurately now, the *hermeneutical* tension between faith and history" (italics added).[7] This introductory chapter will thus pay particular attention to hermeneutical issues and their influence upon certain key thinkers in the history of historical Jesus research. Significant thinkers and their methods in the history of Jesus research thus need to be briefly examined to understand more fully how they affected Jesus research, particularly with regard to how they understood the message of Jesus.

The Original Quest

Albert Schweitzer dates the beginning of the quest of the historical Jesus to 1778, when G. E. Lessing's edition of Hermann Samuel Reimarus's essay "On the Aims of Jesus and His Disciples" was published.[8] Prior to Reimarus, there were many harmonies of the gospels,[9] but there had been no scholarly attempt to study the gospels as historical documents.[10] All of that changed with Lessing's posthumous publication of Reimarus's work in a series Lessing named *Fragmente*

---

7. James D. G. Dunn, *Jesus Remembered*, vol. 1, *Christianity in the Making* (Grand Rapids: Eerdmans, 2003), 125. Space and focus do not allow me to interact with Dunn's work. For a prolonged examination of Dunn that includes a response from Dunn, see Robert B. Stewart and Gary R. Habermas, *Memories of Jesus: A Critical Appraisal of James D. G. Dunn's Jesus Remembered* (Nashville: B&H Academic, 2010).

8. A. Schweitzer, *The Quest of the Historical Jesus: A Critical Study of Its Progress from Reimarus to Wrede*, trans. W. Montgomery. New York: Macmillan, 1968; repr., Baltimore: Johns Hopkins University Press, 1998), 15. Cf. H. S. Reimarus, "Concerning the Intention of Jesus and His Teaching," in *Reimarus: Fragments*, ed. C. H. Talbert, trans. R. S. Fraser, 59–269, Lives of Jesus Series, ed. L. Keck (Philadelphia: Fortress Press, 1970).

9. Cf. Schweitzer, *The Quest of the Historical Jesus*, 13–15; W. B. Tatum, *In Quest of Jesus*, 2nd ed. (Nashville: Abingdon, 1999), 39–40.

10. Schweitzer briefly mentions a life of Jesus that predated Reimarus and was written in Persian by the Jesuit Hieronymus Xavier, a missionary to India for a Moghul emperor. Schweitzer concludes that it was a "skilful falsification of the life of Jesus in which the omissions, and the additions taken from the Apocrypha, are inspired by the sole purpose of presenting to the open-minded ruler a glorious Jesus, in whom there should be nothing to offend him." Schweitzer, *The Quest of the Historical Jesus*, 13–14.

eines Ungenannten (*Fragments from an Unnamed Author*), commonly referred to today as the *Wolfenbüttel Fragments*.[11]

Reimarus was consumed with answering one basic question: "What sort of purpose did Jesus himself see in his teachings and deeds?"[12] Reimarus concluded that there was a theological rupture between the New Testament gospels and the New Testament epistles. He insisted that Jesus' disciples had intentionally changed the message of Jesus and that one cannot use the epistles to interpret the gospels. Therefore, it is in the gospels, not the epistles, where one finds the historical Jesus:

> However, I find great cause to separate completely what the apostles say in their own writing from that which Jesus himself actually said and taught, for the apostles were themselves teachers and consequently present their own views; indeed, they never claim that Jesus himself said and taught in his lifetime all the things that they have written. On the other hand, the four evangelists represent themselves only as historians who have reported the most important things that Jesus said as well as did. If now we wish to know what Jesus' teaching actually was, what he said and preached, that is a *res facti*—a matter of something that actually occurred; hence this is to be derived from the reports of the historians. . . . Everyone will grant, then, that in my investigation of the intention of Jesus' teaching I have sufficient reason to limit myself exclusively to the reports of the four evangelists who offer the proper and true record. I shall not bring in those things that the apostles taught or intended on their own, since the latter are not historians of their master's teaching but present themselves as teachers. Later, when once we have discovered the actual teaching and intention of Jesus from the four documents of the historians, we shall be able to judge reliably whether the apostles expressed the same teaching and intention as their master."[13]

Reimarus defined the essence of religion as "the doctrine of the salvation and immortality of the soul."[14] This generic liberal description of the essence of

---

11. See Reimarus, "Concerning the Intention of Jesus and His Teaching." At the time of publication, Lessing was librarian to the Duke of Brunswick at the ducal library in Wolfenbüttel, hence the name of the series.
12. Ibid., 64.
13. Ibid., 64–65.
14. Ibid., 61.

religion masks Reimarus's eventual conclusions concerning Jesus. He concluded that Jesus: (1) was a pious Jew; (2) called Israel to repent; (3) did not intend to teach new truth, found a new religion, or establish new rituals; (4) became sidetracked by embracing a political position; (5) sought to force God's hand; and (6) died alone, deserted by his disciples. What began as a call for repentance ended up as a misguided attempt to usher in an earthly, political kingdom of God.[15]

Reimarus was significantly influenced by deism. That influence may be seen in his attempt to ground understanding of the historical Jesus in deistic reason (*Vernunft*). He also posited that after Jesus' failure and death, his disciples stole his body and declared his resurrection in order to maintain their financial security and ensure themselves some standing.[16] In typical deistic fashion, Reimarus insisted that there are "no mysteries" or "new articles of faith" in the teachings of Jesus.[17] This view grew out of his conviction that Jesus was essentially Jewish, not Christian. The uniquely Christian doctrines that one finds in the New Testament originated with the apostles, not Jesus. Reimarus rightly maintained that Jesus' mind-set was eschatological in nature. He correctly discerned that the historical Jesus is never to be found in a non-Jewish setting, but wrongly saw early Christianity as discontinuous with Judaism.

Reimarus explicitly rejected the twin pillars of traditional Christian apologetics concerning the deity of Jesus: miracles and prophecy.[18] Accordingly, Jesus' message could not have been prophetic, and in his preaching, Jesus could never have referred to performing miracles or casting out demons. The historical Jesus called Israel to repentance and spoke much of the coming kingdom, but he was in no sense a supernatural figure. Reimarus accepted the basic historicity of the gospels but reasoned away their supernatural elements through the use of deistic explanations. In short, his rejection of portions of the gospels is not the result of literary criticism, but rather of a prior commitment to the deistic worldview. In this sense, his project could be said to be pre-critical. Reimarus is critical of supernaturalism and the miracle stories in the gospels, but he did not read the gospels critically as literature.

Friedrich Daniel Ernst Schleiermacher is best known for his pioneering contributions to modern theology, *Der christliche Glaube: Nach den Grundsätzen der evangelischen Kirche im Zusammenhange dargestellt* (*The Christian Faith: Outlined Systematically According to the Principles of the Protestant Church*) and

---

15. Ibid., 61–150.
16. Ibid., 243–50.
17. Ibid., 71–76.
18. Ibid., 229–37.

Über die Religion: Reden an die Gebildeten unter ihren Verächtern (*On Religion: Speeches to Its Cultured Despisers*).[19] He was, however, also a pioneer in hermeneutical theory and life-of-Jesus research. Schleiermacher was the first scholar to lecture on the historical Jesus in a university. Although he never wrote a book on the Jesus of history, the notes from his class lectures, along with the comments of five of his students, were edited by K. A. Rütenik and published in 1864, thirty years after Schleiermacher's death.[20]

Schleiermacher divided the exegetical task into two subcategories: higher and lower criticism. Higher criticism was concerned with establishing the New Testament canon, while lower criticism was concerned with arriving at an accurate original understanding of a particular text. In other words, he practiced something approaching canonical criticism and textual criticism.[21] For Schleiermacher, the Old Testament was not normative in the same way as the New Testament. It was the Scripture of Judaism, not Christianity. It could serve to help one understand New Testament texts but could not serve as the basis for Christianity, which was, in his estimation, an entirely new faith. Furthermore, the Christian interpreter was prone to read foreign ideas and concepts into the Old Testament and thus to obscure its original historic sense. Nevertheless, he concluded that it could be a useful appendix in Christian Bibles, rather than part of the Christian Scriptures.[22]

According to Schleiermacher, hermeneutics, as opposed to exegesis, consists of two parts: the grammatical (universal) and the psychological (particular). The former focuses upon the syntactical structure of a text, while the latter addresses the intentions of the author. In practice, though, the two are interwoven in a spiral. The role of the interpreter is first to recognize distinctive markings of a particular biblical author. This is the comparative reading of a text. The second role of the reader is to intuit or divine the thought processes involved in writing the text.[23]

Schleiermacher primarily focused on Jesus' proclamation and the time period of his public ministry. He considered issues such as the virgin birth,

---

19. F. D. E. Schleiermacher, *The Christian Faith*, ed. H. R. Mackintosh and J. S. Stewart (Edinburgh: T. & T. Clark, 1928); idem, *On Religion: Speeches to Its Cultured Despisers*, ed. and trans. R. Crouter (Cambridge: Cambridge University Press, 1996).

20. J. C. Verheyden, introduction to Friedrich Schleiermacher, *The Life of Jesus*, ed. J. C. Verheyden, trans. S. M. Gilmour, Lives of Jesus Series, ed. L. E. Keck (Philadelphia: Fortress Press, 1975), xv–xvi.

21. D. DeVries, "Schleiermacher, Friedrich Daniel Ernst," *Major Biblical Interpreters*, ed. D. K. McKim (Downers Grove: InterVarsity, 1998), 351.

22. Ibid. It is thus not difficult to see how Schleiermacher is hesitant to situate Jesus within Judaism.

23. Ibid., 352.

crucifixion, and resurrection unhistorical. For Schleiermacher, what mattered most in interpretation was the intention of the writer, and with historical reports, the intention of the historical person written about. He thus inquired of Jesus' intentions and his perfect God-consciousness.[24] As a result, Schleiermacher insisted that Jesus placed himself at the center of his teaching. But he explicitly denied that Jesus ever saw himself as "actually the one described by the prophets."[25] The gospel that Jesus preached had to do most of all with faith, particularly with placing one's faith in Jesus himself and, through his preaching (and the preaching about him), coming to an awareness that God was saving the world through Jesus.[26] Therefore, in good romanticist style, Schleiermacher was most concerned with intuiting Jesus' intentions and religious consciousness.

David Friedrich Strauss wrote three best-selling books about Jesus (or perhaps three different versions of one book). Each of the three was different. In retrospect, his first book has proven to be most significant.[27]

In his first *Life of Jesus*, Strauss sought to apply Hegel's historical dialectic to understanding Jesus. Accordingly, he applied the concept of myth to the gospels, something his teacher, F. C. Baur, had already done in Old Testament studies. Jesus understood mythically is the synthesis of the thesis of supernaturalism and the antithesis of rationalism. As a committed Hegelian (at least at this point), Strauss maintained that the inner nucleus of Christian faith was not touched by the mythical approach:

> The author is aware that the essence of the Christian faith is perfectly independent of his criticism. The supernatural birth of Christ, his miracles, his resurrection and ascension, remain eternal truths, whatever doubts may be cast on their reality as historical facts. The certainty of this alone can give calmness or dignity to our criticism, and distinguish it from the naturalistic criticism of the last century, the design of which was, with the historical fact, to subvert also the religious truth, and which thus necessarily became frivolous. A dissertation at the close of the work will show that the dogmatic significance of the life of Jesus remains inviolate: in the meantime let the calmness and *sang-froid* with which in the course of it, criticism

---

24. Schleiermacher, *The Life of Jesus*, 87–123.
25. Ibid., 246.
26. Ibid., 248–49.
27. David Friedrich Strauss, *The Life of Jesus Critically Examined*, ed. P. C. Hodgson, trans. G. Eliot, Life of Jesus Series, ed. L. E. Keck (Philadelphia: Fortress Press, 1972).

undertakes apparently dangerous operations, be explained solely by the security of the author's conviction that no injury is threatened to the Christian faith.[28]

One can easily see then that, at least at this time, Strauss intended not to destroy the Christian faith; his intention was instead to critique the gospels historically.

Strauss emphasized not the events (miracles) in the gospels (although the book is structured as an analysis of Jesus' miracles), but the *nature* of the gospels. Unlike Reimarus, he was not primarily interested in explaining (away) how events in the gospels took place. Neither was he interested in uncovering the sequence in which the gospels were produced. His interest lay in revealing the nature of the gospels as literature. By focusing on the literary nature of the gospels, he anticipated several crucial issues and advances in twentieth-century New Testament studies.

Strauss's work initiated a paradigm shift in gospel studies. Whereas Reimarus had proposed two possibilities, natural or supernatural, Strauss proposed two different categories for interpreting the gospels: mythic or historical. Unlike Reimarus, Strauss did not attribute the nonhistorical to deliberate deception on the part of the apostles, but to their unconscious mythic imagination.[29] Strauss maintained that the biblical narratives were written well after they occurred and were embellished through years of oral retelling and religious reflection.[30] Strauss thus insisted that the key to understanding Jesus historically was being fully aware of the differences between then and now.[31] The gospel stories, according to Strauss, are poetic in form, not historical or philosophical.[32] They tell us about the religious experience of their authors but nothing historically about Jesus or his message. Simply put, the message of Jesus was not to be found in the gospels.

Although Strauss was certainly critical in questioning the supernatural events one finds in the gospels, he was not methodologically "critical" in the sense of questioning the order or authorship of the gospels. Ben Meyer comments that Strauss's first *Life of Jesus* is consistently less a literary discovery

---

28. Ibid., lii.
29. Ibid., 39–92.
30. Ibid., 49.
31. Ibid., 39–44.
32. Ibid., 53.

than a Hegelian deduction.³³ This is doubtless one reason he ignored the synoptic question.

Strauss's *Life of Jesus* was immediately a source of controversy. Upon its publication, Strauss was forbidden to teach theology any longer. When he took a post at another school, the controversy was so great that he was terminated before even beginning his teaching duties. In his second book on Jesus, *Das Leben Jesu: für das deutsche Volk* (*The Life of Jesus: For the German People*),³⁴ Strauss abandoned Hegelian categories for moral categories. Eventually, Strauss repudiated entirely any attachment to Christianity and died a committed materialist.³⁵

In summary, Reimarus, Schleiermacher, and Strauss all played important roles in life-of-Jesus research. All of them, however, ignored what became the most consuming question for a generation of Jesus scholars to follow: in what order were the gospels written?

Concerning the synoptic problem, Stephen Neill writes, "The first scholar to approach the correct solution of the problem on the basis of careful observation of the facts seems to have been Karl Lachmann."³⁶ In 1835, Lachmann wrote an article proposing that Mark was the earliest of the four canonical gospels.³⁷ The philosopher Christian Hermann Weisse soon echoed Lachmann's opinion on the matter.³⁸ Yet both Lachmann and Weisse were approaching the matter apart from a clearly stated and justified methodology. It was left to Heinrich Julius Holtzmann to treat the matter in a systematic fashion. Contra Strauss, he was adamant that to understand Jesus historically, one must first undergo a thorough investigation of the synoptic gospels. Holtzmann understood the primary problem in historical-Jesus research to be the order of sources. Therefore, the primary task was solving the synoptic problem. In *Die Synoptischen Evangelien: Ihr Ursprung und geschichtlicher Charakter* (*The*

---

33. Ben F. Meyer, *The Aims of Jesus* (London: SCM, 1979), 34. Cf. Strauss, *The Life of Jesus Critically Examined*, 779.

34. D. F. Strauss, ed., *Das Leben Jesu: fur das deutsche Volk. Bearb. von David Friedrich Strauss* (Leipzig: F. A. Brockhaus, 1874).

35. R. Morgan, "Strauss, David Friedrich," in McKim, *Major Biblical Interpreters*, 367.

36. S. Neill and N. T. Wright, *The Interpretation of the New Testament, 1861–1986* (Oxford: Oxford University Press, 1988), 116–17.

37. K. Lachmann, "*De Ordine Narratorionum* in *Evangeliis Synopticis*," *Theologische Studien und Kritiken* 8 (1835): 570.

38. C. H. Weisse, *Die evangelische Geschichte kritische und philosophisch bearbeitet Leipzig*, 2 vols. (Leipzig: Breitkopf and Hartel, 1838); idem, *Die Evangelienfrage in ihrem gegenwärtigen Stadium* (Leipzig: Breitkopf und Härtel, 1856).

Synoptic Gospels: Their Origin and Historical Nature), Holtzmann proposed that two written sources containing sayings of Jesus, *Urmarcus* and *Urmatthäus*, were available to the evangelists.[39] It was in these sources that the message of Jesus was to be found.

To the degree that Holtzmann shared the basic presuppositions of nineteenth-century German liberalism, he represents the mainstream of the first quest. Behind the fascination with sources lay the liberal presupposition that the theological elements in the gospels were later accretions from the early church. It was assumed, therefore, that the further back one goes, the less theological and the more historical the picture of Jesus becomes. Behind this expectation lay the liberal presupposition that Jesus preached a timeless ethic.[40] They fully expected to find that Jesus was a teacher of moral truths who had a unique awareness of God working through him. They also thought that, by determining the order of the earliest sources, they could discern a noticeable shift in the personality of Jesus.[41] It is not going too far to say that the first quest, the liberal quest, was based in large part upon an unwarranted optimism concerning how much historical knowledge of Jesus and his message one could acquire from the proper application of source criticism. Neither is it going too far to say that the message of Jesus they expected to find—and thus did find—was an ethical message concerning the kingdom of God.

Similarly, Albrecht Ritschl and Adolf von Harnack understood Jesus primarily in ethical terms. Ritschl insisted that to grasp who Jesus was and what he taught, one must focus upon the observable experience of the church, because the gospels become "completely intelligible only when we see how they are reflected in the consciousness of those who believe in Him."[42] He also believed not only that the kingdom of God and the message of Jesus were ethical in nature, but also that Jesus was the bearer of God's ethical Lordship over humanity:[43] "The delineation of the ethical connection between the sufferings and the vocation of Christ already give place to *the religious view* of the same, apart from which Christ Himself was not conscious of His unique and independent vocation among men. The business of His vocation was the establishment of the universal ethical fellowship of mankind, as that aim in the

---

39. H. J. Holtzmann, *Die Synoptischen Evangelien: Ihr Ursprung und geschichtlicher Charakter* (Leipzig: Wilhelm Engelmann, 1863), 64–67.
40. Ibid., 470.
41. Ibid., 1–9.
42. A. Ritschl, *The Christian Doctrine of Justification and Reconciliation: The Positive Development of the Doctrine*, ed. H. R. Mackintosh and A. B. Macaulay (Clifton, NJ: Reference Book Publishers, 1966), 1.
43. Ibid., 385–484.

world which rises above all conditions included in the notion of the world."[44] For von Harnack, Jesus' message of the kingdom emphasized: (1) the kingdom of God and its coming; (2) God the Father and the infinite value of the human soul; and (3) the higher righteousness and the commandment of love.[45]

Meyer comments that most Jesus scholars of that day coupled the liberal emphasis upon ethics with an equally liberal "hermeneutic of empathy."[46] In turn, a host of imaginative theses were put forward in an effort to understand more fully the nature of Jesus' religious experience by tracing out the psychological development of Jesus' messianic awareness.[47] Doing so allowed authors to write something akin to a biography of Jesus.[48] The weakness of this approach lay in the fact that it was dependent more upon intuition and/or imagination than historical method. Concerning this, Otto Pfleiderer writes:

> We may never forget how much, with the poverty of the ascertained historical materials is left to the uncontrolled power of combination and divination; in other words, to the imagination, which at best can do no more than roughly and approximately arrive at the truth, while it may no less easily go far astray. . . . Yet this advance is manifestly attended by the temptation to sacrifice the caution of historical criticism to the production of a biography as rich in detail and as dramatic in movement as possible, and to represent things as the ascertained results of critical examination, which are really nothing more than subjective combinations of the writers, to which a certain degree of probability will always remain, that the actual facts were something quite different.[49]

In 1901, William Wrede published *Das Messiasgeheimnis in den Evangelien* (The Messianic Secret in the Gospels).[50] Wrede insisted that the psychological

---

44. Ibid., 449.

45. A. Harnack, *What Is Christianity?*, trans. T. B. Saunders (New York: Harper & Row, 1957), 19–78.

46. Meyer, *The Aims of Jesus*, 40.

47. T. Keim, *The History of Jesus of Nazara*, 2 vols., trans. A. Ransom (London: Williams and Norgate, 1876); K. Hase, *Geschichte Jesu Nach Akademischen Vorlesungen* (Leipzig: Breitkoph und Härtel, 1876); K. H. Weizsacker, *Untersuchungen über die evangelische Geschichte, ihre Quellen und den Gang ihrer Entwicklung* (Leipzig: Gotha, 1864); B. Weiss, *Das Leben Jesu*, 2 vols. (Berlin: Wilhelm Hertz, 1882).

48. The first truly significant biography of Jesus was E. Renan, *La Vie de Jesus* (Paris: Michel Lévy Frères, 1863).

49. O. Pfleiderer, introduction to David Friedrich Strauss, *The Life of Jesus Critically Examined*, trans. G. Eliot (London: Swan Sonnenschein, 1902), xxiv–xxv.

theories of nineteenth-century life-of-Jesus work were derived from somewhere other than the text:

> And this is the malady to which we must here allude—let us not dignify it with the euphemism 'historical imagination.' *The Scientific study of the life of Jesus is suffering from psychological 'suppositionitis'* which amounts to a sort of historical guesswork. For this reason interpretations to suit every taste proliferate. The number of arbitrary psychological interpretations at the same time form the basis for important structures of thought; and how often do people think that the task of criticism has already been discharged by playing tuneful psychological variations on a given factual theme![51]

Wrede further maintained that the gospels were not to be understood as biographies. The issue that he directly addressed was how best to explain the presence of the messianic secret in the gospels. For Wrede, this messianic secret was best understood as a creation of the evangelist that reflected his attempt to harmonize two streams of thought in the early church concerning the truth that was clearly perceived in the post-Easter church. That truth was that Jesus was the Messiah but that nobody had heard him declare that prior to his death. He believed that the early church understood historically that Jesus was *made* Messiah at his resurrection, not that he was *revealed* as Messiah through the resurrection.[52] The idea that Jesus was the Messiah before his resurrection was merely the result of the early church's theological reflection on his then-evident messiahship.[53] Simply put, the messianic secret was Mark's attempt to harmonize history with theology.[54] While Wrede allowed that Jesus' words and actions might have caused some to question if he might be the Messiah prior to his death and resurrection, he would not allow that Jesus ever taught that he was the Messiah.[55] The messianic secret was the product of a theological idea, not historical facts.[56]

---

50. W. Wrede, *Das Messiasgeheimnis in den Evangelien*, 3rd ed. (Gottingen: Vandenhoeck & Ruprecht, 1963). For English, see *The Messianic Secret: Forming a Contribution Also to the Understanding of Mark*, trans. J. C. G. Greig (Cambridge: James Clarke, 1971).

51. Ibid., 6.

52. Ibid., 216–19.

53. Ibid., 219–30.

54. While Wrede insisted that Mark is not alone responsible for the content of his gospel in that it reflects the theology of the early church, he does nevertheless saw Mark as providing a distinctive touch. Ibid. From this, one can see how both form criticism and redaction criticism are well in line with Wrede's skepticism.

According to Wrede, one must distinguish between historical and literary-critical questions, and literary-critical questions should be dealt with before historical ones. In this way, Wrede was able to point to messianic passages in the gospels as support for his hypothesis, and problematic texts were thus neatly excised in the interest of historical tidiness. The result was predictable: truncated gospels resulted in a truncated picture of Jesus. Wrede's Jesus lacked both messianic consciousness and theological creativity. But Wrede's conclusions have been influential in both form and redaction criticism. Consistent with the emphasis of the *Religionsgeschichtliche Schule* (the history of religions school), of which Wrede is a representative, the result of Wrede's work was to shift the focus from Jesus—and his message—onto the communities the evangelists represent. Discerning the nature of the tradition behind a text thus became the focus of biblical interpretation. Not only do truncated gospels result in a truncated picture of Jesus, they also result in a truncated message of Jesus.

On the same day in 1901 that Wrede published his book on the messianic secret, Albert Schweitzer published *Das Messianitats-und Leidensgeheimnis: Ein Skizze des Lebens Jesus*.[57] In this brief sketch of Jesus' life, Schweitzer pictured Jesus as thoroughly conscious of his messianic role. In fact, it was this messianic consciousness that motivated Jesus to do all that he did. In contrast to Wrede, Schweitzer understood Jesus as a messianic hero, along the lines of Nietzsche's cult of the hero (*Übermensch*).[58] Schweitzer's Jesus is a heroic figure, seeking to usher in the kingdom through his decisive sacrifice of himself. Schweitzer saw the messianic themes, which Wrede took to be later creations, as central to any understanding of Jesus. According to Schweitzer, one could not begin to understand Jesus without correctly perceiving that his messianic consciousness drove him to do all that he did.[59] Tragically, although the idea of resurrection

---

55. Ibid., 230. H. Rollmann mentions a letter from Wrede to Harnack, written shortly before Wrede's death, in which Wrede writes that he had changed his mind concerning Jesus' messianic consciousness but saw no point in abandoning his tradition-historical approach to interpretation. Hans Rollmann, "Wrede, William," in McKim, *Major Biblical Interpreters*, 397.

56. Wrede, *The Messianic Secret*, 67.

57. Albert Schweitzer, *Das Messianitats-und Leidensgeheimnis: Ein Skizze des Lebens Jesus* (Tubingen: J. C. B. Mohr, 1901). For English, see *The Mystery of the Kingdom of God: The Secret of Jesus' Messiahship and Passion*, trans. Walter Lowrie (New York: Macmillan, 1950). Originally, Schweitzer's *Mystery* was part 2 of his *Das Abendmahl im Zusammenhang mit dem Leben Jesu und der Geschichte der Urchristentums* (Tubingen: Mohr, 1901). (English translation: The Last Supper in Connection with the Life of Jesus and the History of Early Christianity.)

58. Schweitzer wrote of his philosophy of reverence for life as a superior version of Nietzsche's concern for life lived to fullest degree. A. Schweitzer, *The Philosophy of Civilization*, trans. C. T. Campion (London: A. & C. Black, 1946), 174–76.

is clearly in the mind of Schweitzer's Jesus, his summary concludes, "On the afternoon of the fourteenth of Nissan, as they ate the Paschal lamb at even, he uttered a loud cry and died."[60]

Schweitzer's first offering was not overly well received.[61] This prompted him to publish *Von Reimarus zu Wrede: eine Geschichte der Leben-Jesu-Forschung* (*From Reimarus to Wrede: A History of Life of Jesus Research*; English title: *The Quest of the Historical Jesus*) in 1906.[62] Eventually, this work became the standard by which all other histories of life-of-Jesus research would be measured.

Schweitzer is often cited as one who advocated the end of historical-Jesus research. Such is not the case. Schweitzer did not intend to end the quest, but to redirect it. Although Schweitzer did maintain that one could not use history to write a biography of Jesus, he believed that historical research could destroy false constructs of Jesus, including the most monstrous one of all—Jesus as a modern man. For Schweitzer, Jesus was the product of first-century Jewish apocalyptic expectation, not Enlightenment rationalism. In short, although Schweitzer believed that knowledge of the historical Jesus could not afford one a foundation upon which to ground Christian faith, he saw historical-Jesus research as useful in destroying the fictional platforms that had been built by ecclesiastical dogma and/or Enlightenment historicism. The value of historical knowledge of Jesus was to be found in the recognition of one's inability to know him through investigation. Instead, Jesus is known most fully in decisive individual commitment. Indeed, for Schweitzer, the message of Jesus was quite simple: "Follow me."[63] Again the voice of Nietzsche is heard in the conclusion of *The Quest of the Historical Jesus*:

---

59. Schweitzer was not the first to advocate an eschatological Jesus. Johannes Weiss, Ritschl's son in law, had previously written that Jesus' proclamation of the kingdom of God was eschatological in nature. J. Weiss, *Jesus' Proclamation of the Kingdom of God*, trans. and ed. R. H. Hiers and D. L. Holland, Lives of Jesus Series, ed. Leander E. Keck (Philadelphia: Fortress Press, 1971). The primary difference between Weiss and Schweitzer is that while Weiss understood eschatology as the central motif of Jesus' teaching, Schweitzer saw it as the key to Jesus' personality and ministry.

60. Schweitzer, *The Mystery of the Kingdom*, 173. Following Schweitzer's summary of the life of Jesus, there is a one-page postscript that focuses upon recognition that the nature of Jesus is bound forever to be a mystery to modern man, and that modern culture can be revived only by grasping the nature of his conscious sacrifice for others. It fittingly concludes with a sentence reminiscent of Nietzsche: "Only then can the heroic in our Christianity and in our *Weltanschauung* be again revived." Ibid, 174.

61. For a thorough treatment of the response to Schweitzer's work, see W. P. Weaver, *The Historical Jesus in the Twentieth Century, 1900–1950* (Harrisburg, PA: Trinity Press International, 1999), 31–38.

62. Schweitzer, *The Quest of the Historical Jesus*. For German, see *Von Reimarus zu Wrede: eine Geschichte der Leben-Jesu-Forschung* (Tübingen: Mohr, 1906).

He comes to us as One unknown, without a name, as of old, by the lake-side, He came to those men who knew Him not. He speaks to us the same word: 'Follow thou me!' and sets us to the tasks which He has to fulfil for our time. He commands. And to those who obey Him, whether they be wise or simple, He will reveal Himself in the toils, the conflicts, the sufferings which they shall pass through in His fellowship, and, as an ineffable mystery, they shall learn in their own experience Who He is.[64]

From the standpoint of biblical criticism and interpretive method, Schweitzer's work was simplistic. For one as concerned with critical history as he was, his approach to interpreting Scripture was surprisingly noncritical. In contrast to his predecessors, he was not especially concerned with answering source-critical questions. He accepted the general synoptic narrative as historical and interpreted the gospels in light of his one guiding principle: thoroughgoing eschatology.

The Abandoned Quest

It is often assumed that Schweitzer's *Quest* ended the first phase of historical-Jesus research, but such a position is simplistic. While it is true that Schweitzer offered up a devastating critique of the liberal quest, it was left to others to provide a positive diversion from liberal historical-Jesus research. Several factors contributed to bringing the first quest to an "end."

In 1896, Martin Kähler argued that "the entire Life-of-Jesus movement is a blind alley,"[65] because the necessary sources were not available. His basic premise was that the certainty of faith could not rest on the unavoidable uncertainties of history. He declared that the accuracy of Scripture cannot be based "on the success or failure of the inquiries of historical research; for these are always limited and only provisionally valid, that is, their validity endures only until new sources of knowledge appear on the horizon."[66] Instead of

---

63. Those familiar with the story of Schweitzer's life will immediately see that Schweitzer himself was no ivory tower academic content to study life but never live it. He heard the call to Lambaréné and faithfully followed Jesus.

64. Ibid., 403. Those familiar with Schweitzer's life and philosophy will immediately see that this was for Schweitzer not simply a pithy phrase, but a credo for life.

65. M. Kähler, *The So-Called Historical Jesus and the Historic Biblical Christ*, ed. and trans. C. Braaten (Philadelphia: Fortress Press, 1964), 46.

66. Ibid., 111.

searching for the *historical* Jesus, one should seek the *historic* Jesus, the one who has molded history and contributed to it.⁶⁷

Also, in addition to Schweitzer's critique of the liberal historical-Jesus project, there was the influence of the *Religionsgeschichtliche Schule*. Two names often associated with the history of religions school are Ernst Troeltsch and Wilhelm Bousset.

Troeltsch served as the philosopher for the movement. He insisted that Christianity was not historically unique. Like all religions, it was a historical phenomenon within its own time. Consequently, Jesus was no different from any other figure in history. To insist, as Kähler did, that faith in Jesus is not subject to historical critique is simply naive, according to Troeltsch.⁶⁸ The historian is bound to explain movements in terms of causal events in the natural world.⁶⁹ Therefore, the historian's role in relation to Christian origins is simply to explain how Christianity came to be, not to answer theological or metaphysical questions concerning Jesus. The hermeneutical result of applying this principle to the study of Christian origins was that the referent of the gospels became the early church, not Jesus. Therefore, the question changed from "Who was Jesus?" to "How did the early church come to think of Jesus in this way?"

Bousset's answer in *Kyrios Christos: Geschichte des Christusglaubens von den Anfängen des Christentums bis Irenaeus* (*Christ the Lord: A History of the Christian Faith from the Beginning to Irenaeus*) was that the church came to deify Jesus through a historical process of transformation due to its encounter with Hellenism, an encounter in which alien ideas were grafted into Christianity. He maintained that the earliest traditions concerning Jesus contained nothing miraculous and did not proclaim Jesus to be divine.⁷⁰

The shadow of Rudolf Bultmann falls over any attempt to understand New Testament theology in the twentieth century. Along with K. L. Schmidt and Martin Dibelius, he pioneered New Testament form criticism.⁷¹ He understood

---

67. Ibid., 63.

68. E. Troeltsch, *Die Bedeutung der Geschichtlichkeit Jesus für den Glauben* (Tübingen: Mohr, 1929), 34. For an insightful discussion of Troeltsch's significance for biblical interpretation, see A. C. Thiselton, *The Two Horizons: New Testament Interpretation and Philosophical Description* (Grand Rapids: Zondervan, 1992), 69–74.

69. E. Troeltsch, *Gesammelte Schriften* (Tübingen: Mohr, 1912–25), 2:734. Troeltsch is particularly critical of Christian theologians who attempt to use part of the historical-critical method but reject the presuppositions of it. Ibid., 2:730.

70. W. Bousset, *Kyrios Christos: A History of Belief in Christ from the Beginnings of Christianity to Irenaeus*, trans. J. E. Steely (Nashville: Abingdon, 1970).

the gospels as collections of fragments edited together that addressed particular needs of the early church, not as single documents chronicling the life of Jesus. Therefore, Bultmann understood the primary purpose of form criticism to be the discovery of the origin of the particular units of oral tradition that lay behind the written pericopes of the gospels, not simply identifying different forms of gospel sayings.[72] In *Jesus and the Word*, he declared, "I do indeed think that we can now know almost nothing concerning the life and personality of Jesus, since the early Christian sources show no interest in either, are moreover fragmentary and often legendary; and other sources about Jesus do not exist."[73] Bultmann posited that the early church was filled with controversy and infighting between Hellenistic Jewish believers and Palestinian Jewish believers. This resulted in a situation where sayings were attributed to Jesus that he did not utter. This led Bultmann to declare, "One can only emphasize the uncertainty of our knowledge of the person and work of the historical Jesus and likewise of the origin of Christianity."[74] The result was not only that form criticism, like the history of religions school, focused on something other than Jesus, the *Sitz im Leben* of the early church, but also that its foremost proponent announced that historical-Jesus research could not succeed.

Bultmann's objections to historical-Jesus research were not only methodological, but also philosophical and theological. Influenced as he was by Kierkegaard and Heidegger, as well as the early Karl Barth,[75] Bultmann thought historical knowledge of Jesus' personhood (*Persönlichkeit*) was secondary in importance to existential knowledge of his word.[76] Bultmann's approach demanded that one first recognize that the New Testament is mythological in nature and then demythologize the New Testament myths. Bultmann openly drew upon Heidegger's categories of existence and being to interpret the New Testament. But what often is missed in his method is that he adopted

---

71. C. Brown, "Historical Jesus, Quest of," in *Dictionary of Jesus and the Gospels*, (Downers Grove: InterVarsity, 1992) 334.

72. R. Bultmann, *The History of the Synoptic Tradition*, trans. J. Marsh (Oxford: Basil Blackwell, 1963), 3–4.

73. R. Bultmann, *Jesus and the Word*, trans. L. Pettibone Smith and E. Huntress Lantero (New York: Scribner's, 1958), 8.

74. R. Bultmann, "The Study of the Synoptic Gospels," in *Form Criticism: Two Essays on New Testament Research*, ed. R. Bultmann and K. Kundsin, trans. F. C. Grant (n.p.: Willett Clark, 1934; repr., New York: Harper Torchbook, 1962), 17.

75. Other influences on Bultmann include Luther, Collingwood, and the history of religions school, as well as the liberal theology of his teacher, Harnack. For a general discussion of influences upon Bultmann, see Thiselton, *The Two Horizons*, 205–51.

76. Bultmann, *Jesus and the Word*, 9–12.

these categories because he believed that the New Testament demanded to be demythologized—that such was the intention of the authors.[77] Therefore, encountering Jesus existentially was what mattered most. And although the voice of Jesus is rarely heard in the New Testament gospels, through the proper application of form criticism and Bultmann's demythologizing hermeneutic, the message of Jesus—the kerygma—can still be heard.

Bultmann thus contributed to a decline in historical-Jesus research in several ways. First, his form-critical method shifted the emphasis from Jesus onto the early Christian communities. Second, his form-critical conclusions led to a sense of pessimism concerning historical-Jesus research in general. In addition, his demythologization shifted the emphasis from history to anthropology. And finally, his commitment to existentialism assigned historical knowledge of Jesus to a secondary status and thus undermined the entire project in general.

In summary, several factors were influential in the abandonment of the original quest of the historical Jesus. Among them were Wrede's skepticism, Schweitzer's critique of nineteenth-century lives of Jesus, the influence of Martin Kähler, the influence of the history of religions school, the rise of form criticism, Bultmann's demythologizing hermeneutic, and the influence of existentialism upon dialectical theology.

THE NEW QUEST OF THE HISTORICAL JESUS

The movement in historical-Jesus research that is commonly called the "New Quest of the Historical Jesus" began in 1953 with a speech by Ernst Käsemann to a group of Bultmann's former students.[78] Käsemann agreed with Bultmann about the earlier quest: it was largely impossible and at least partially irrelevant. Käsemann also insisted that the primary interest of the primitive church was not historical verification of facts concerning Jesus, but rather the proclamation of the kerygma. He held that the primitive church sought to rescue historical facts from obscurity through appeal to the reality of their present experience of Jesus as Lord. Käsemann concluded that this not only was the experience of the primitive church but also is the task of Christians today.[79] But he also insisted that to disregard Jesus entirely as a historical figure was to lapse into Docetism.[80]

---

77. Bultmann, "New Testament and Mythology," in *Kerygma and Myth*, ed. H. W. Bartsch, trans. R. Fuller, 11–12 (London: SPCK, 1953).

78. E. Käsemann, "The Problem of the Historical Jesus," in *Essays on New Testament Themes*, trans. W. J. Montague, 15–47 (London: SCM, 1964).

79. Ibid., 20.

Käsemann thus argued for a new type of historical inquiry concerning Jesus, one that recognizes that mere history apart from hermeneutics is insignificant:

> For mere history becomes significant history not through tradition as such but through interpretation, not through the simple establishment of facts but through the understanding of the events of the past which have become objectified and frozen into facts. . . . . Mere history only takes on genuine historical significance in so far as it can address both a question and an answer to our contemporary situation; in other words, by finding interpreters who hear and utter this question and answer. For this purpose primitive Christianity allows mere history no vehicle of expression other than the kerygma.[81]

Historical inquiry is thus more difficult than either the supernaturalists or the rationalists imagined it to be. Käsemann's solution was to focus on the language of Jesus by separating the authentic from the inauthentic in the preaching of Jesus by applying the criterion of dissimilarity to his preaching.[82]

Although Käsemann was the initiator of the New Quest, James M. Robinson was the popularizer and historian of the movement. His 1959 book, *A New Quest of the Historical Jesus*,[83] gave the label *New Quest* intelligibility in the vocabulary of contemporary historical-Jesus research. Robinson was primarily concerned to answer the question of how Jesus the proclaimer became Jesus Christ the proclaimed.[84] Also recognized with Käsemann and Robinson as participants in the New Quest are Günther Bornkamm, Norman Perrin, Hans Conzelmann, Ernst Fuchs, and Gerhard Ebeling.

Redaction criticism was primarily developed by Bornkamm and Conzelmann.[85] Although redaction criticism presupposes the results of source and form criticism, it also differs in several respects. It focuses upon whole gospels as well as the individual pericopes. It stresses the role of the evangelist over that of the community or tradition. In doing so, it seeks to answer the

80. Ibid., 46.
81. Ibid., 21.
82. Ibid., 37.
83. J. M. Robinson, *A New Quest of the Historical Jesus and Other Essays* (London: SCM, 1959; repr., Philadelphia: Fortress Press, 1983).
84. Ibid., 22–25.
85. G. Bornkamm, G. Barth, and H. Joachim Held, *Tradition and Interpretation in Matthew*, trans. P. Scott (Philadelphia: Westminster, 1963); H. Conzelmann, *The Theology of St. Luke*, trans. G. Buswell (New York: Harper & Row, 1960).

question "What is the theology of this gospel?"[86] The hermeneutical effect of redaction criticism is to focus on how the gospel stories relate to one another, which leads to reading the gospels as whole stories, not just as disparate fragments. The introduction of this method led to a renewal of interest among biblical scholars in theology. But as seen before with form criticism and the history of religions school, the focus was still not upon Jesus, but upon the theology of the editors of the gospels. The voice of Jesus was not heard in the gospels; rather, the one speaking was the evangelist.

The effect of the New Quest of the historical Jesus was to focus upon the language of Jesus and the theological intentions of those who edited his message for later readers. Through it all, the New Quest continued to maintain Bultmann's existential concerns and was relatively short-lived because it was perceived to be much the same in nature as the Bultmannian "No Quest."

The Present State of the Quest

Less than a century ago, the historical quest for Jesus was widely believed by many to be, if not dead, at least at a dead end. Even when I began seminary in the mid-1980s, the quest was still thought of largely in terms of the "New Quest," and that quest was viewed as a relatively small group of scholars working with post-Bultmannian presuppositions run low on steam. Such is clearly not the case today. There has never been more activity and variety in the field of historical-Jesus research than there has been in the past thirty years. I do not think it is going too far to say the past thirty years have been the most fruitful in all the years of scholarly investigation of the historical figure of Jesus. In other words, more significant work from a wider array of perspectives has been produced in the past three decades than at any time since Reimarus's fragments were first published. We are truly living in the golden age of research on the historical Jesus. In large part, this is because of the variety of historical and interpretive methods that are used today in New Testament scholarship.

In the last part of his *Quest*, Schweitzer concluded that there were only two live options for those wishing to find the historical Jesus: Wrede's thoroughgoing skepticism or his own thoroughgoing eschatology.[87] Wrede's approach led to historical skepticism and non-Jewish, modernist conclusions concerning Jesus, based in large part upon Wrede's willingness to treat

---

86. G. R. Osborne, "Redaction Criticism," in *New Testament Criticism and Interpretation*, ed. D. A. Black and D. S. Dockery, 199–224 (Grand Rapids: Zondervan, 1991).

87. Schweitzer, *The Quest of the Historical Jesus*, 398.

messianic texts as inventions of the early church. Schweitzer's approach, in contrast, led to wholly eschatological, Jewish conclusions concerning Jesus, due in large part to his refusal to assign messianic statements to the early church.

N. T. Wright holds that Schweitzer's words, written at the beginning of the twentieth century, have proven prophetic in that most who are seeking the historical Jesus may be grouped into two camps: those who have followed Wrede (thoroughgoing skepticism) and those who have followed Schweitzer (thoroughgoing eschatology). In recognizing these two distinct groups, Wright distinguishes between the Third Quest and the Renewed New Quest.[88] The Renewed New Quest has adopted the thoroughgoing skepticism of Wrede concerning the gospels as sources and has sought to discover a non-Jewish Jesus. The Third Quest has sought to ground Jesus within the Judaism of the first century and has been far less skeptical than the Renewed New Quest concerning the value of the canonical gospels as sources for the life of Jesus. The most obvious expression of the Renewed New Quest is the Jesus Seminar, led by the late Robert Funk. Some prominent advocates of the Third Quest include Wright, E. P. Sanders, John P. Meier, the late Ben F. Meyer, James D. G. Dunn, and Ben Witherington III. This does not mean, of course, that all contemporary parties in historical-Jesus research fit neatly into one of these two categories. But recognition that these two overarching categories are not perfect does not render them useless.

While recognizing the validity of Wright's observations concerning Wrede and Schweitzer, I would note that skepticism and eschatology are not mutually exclusive categories. One can be skeptical about the chances of significant success in discovering a historical basis for knowledge of Jesus and still hold that Jesus had an eschatological orientation (e.g., as Bultmann did). Still, recognizing the diversity of approaches in present-day Jesus scholarship, one must provide some way to measure or classify various approaches that different authors take in seeking him. To this end, I suggest we think in terms of "modern" approaches on the one hand and "postmodern" on the other, recognizing that these two overarching categories are somewhat ill-defined and that the terms are more broadly descriptive than specifically definitive.

Historians adopting an essentially modernist approach seek to be as scientific and as objective as possible in the doing of history. They are thus

---

88. N. T. Wright, *Jesus and the Victory of God*, Christian Origins and the Question of God, vol. 2 (Minneapolis: Fortress Press, 1992), 28–124. Wright coined the term *Third Quest*. Neill and Wright, *The Interpretation of the New Testament, 1861–1986*, 363. For a prolonged evaluation of Wright, see my *The Quest of the Hermeneutical Jesus: The Impact of Hermeneutics on the Jesus Research of John Dominic Crossan and N. T. Wright* (Lanham, MD: University Press of America, 2008).

optimistic about the possibility of discovering what history can tell us concerning Jesus, although they may be somewhat pessimistic about how close history can take us to the actual person of Jesus of Nazareth. A modern approach insists that some pictures of Jesus are right and others are wrong, or at the very least that some pictures of Jesus more accurately describe the historical figure of Jesus than do others. The modern approach also insists that there is a right way to conduct historical research and read texts about Jesus, although different scholars disagree about historical method and/or how texts should be read or what they mean.

Postmodern historians are pessimistic about the possibility of ever engaging in historical research with a sufficiently objective mind-set. Furthermore, they doubt that any historian can arrive at a single picture of Jesus that is correct, or better than any other picture. Texts about Jesus are thus essentially open. The postmoderns say Jesus is now, and forever has been, a construct—and that this is not a bad thing for historians, because we live in a world that is composed of stories and symbols. While modernist historians see history as being essentially a scientific task, postmodern historians view it either as a literary task or perhaps as a quest for self-realization, better suited to the school of humanities than the science department.

The projects of John P. Meier and E. P. Sanders serve as good examples of an essentially modern approach to the quest. Meier optimistically declares that he hopes to find the Jesus that a symposium composed of a Roman Catholic scholar, a Protestant scholar, a Jewish scholar, and an agnostic scholar could agree upon.[89] On the other hand, he pessimistically declares, "By the Jesus of History I mean the Jesus whom we can 'recover' and examine by using the scientific tools of modern historical research"[90] and "Both method and goal are extremely narrow and limited: the results do not claim to provide either a substitute for or the object of faith."[91]

Sanders also brings an essentially modernist approach to the task. Sounding like a scientist, he spends a great deal of time talking about evidence, facts, and hypotheses.[92] He seeks to be as objective and impartial as possible. In doing so, he intends not to raise questions or provide answers of theological significance

---

89. J. P. Meier, *A Marginal Jew: Rethinking the Historical Jesus*, vol. 1, *The Roots of the Problem and the Person* (New York: Doubleday, 1991), 1.

90. Ibid., 25.

91. Ibid., 30–31.

92. E. P. Sanders, Jesus and Judaism (Philadelphia: Fortress Press, 1985), 3–13.

but to be *purely historical*.⁹³ Finally, he intends to focus on "facts" about Jesus, rather than "sayings" of Jesus.⁹⁴

The postmodern end of the continuum is ably represented by John Dominic Crossan.⁹⁵ Crossan has no illusions about being objective. He forthrightly declares, "I am concerned, not with an unattainable objectivity, but with an attainable honesty. My challenge to my colleagues is to accept those formal moves or, if they reject them, to replace them with better ones. They are, of course, only *formal* moves, which then demand a *material* investment."⁹⁶ He further sees a plurality of equally valid positions concerning the historical Jesus (although his own reconstruction presents Jesus as a peasant, Jewish cynic).⁹⁷ Recognizing that there will be differing valid responses to, and readings of, Jesus does not in any way lead him to be pessimistic about either history or faith or to conclude that the historical Jesus is not relevant to Christian faith: "But there is not in my work any presumption that the historical Jesus or earliest Christianity is something you get once and for all forever. And that is not because Jesus and Christianity are special or unique. No past of continuing importance can ever avoid repeated reconstruction. . . . In every generation, the historical Jesus must be reconstructed anew, and that reconstruction must become by faith the face of God for here and now."⁹⁸

Many have commented, however, on the apparent contradiction between Crossan's seemingly objective evaluation of sources and his postmodern preference for perspectivalism.⁹⁹ Simply put, in my estimation, Crossan's seemingly objective manner of treating sources is subjectively colored by his

---

93. Sanders, Jesus and Judaism, 2.

94. Ibid., 3–13.

95. For a prolonged evaluation of Crossan, see my *The Quest of the Hermeneutical Jesus*.

96. J. D. Crossan, *The Historical Jesus: The Life of a Mediterranean Jewish Peasant* (San Francisco: Harper & Row, 1991), xxxiv.

97. Crossan, *The Historical Jesus*, 423; and Crossan, "The Historical Jesus in Earliest Christianity," in *Jesus and Faith: A Conversation on the Work of John Dominic Crossan*, ed. Jeffrey Carlson and Robert A. Ludwig (Maryknoll, NY: Orbis, 1994), 3–4.

98. J. D. Crossan, *Four Other Gospels: Shadows on the Contour of the Canon* (Minneapolis: Seabury, 1995), 7–11.

99. See especially N. T. Wright, "Taking the Text with Her Pleasure: A Post-Post-Modernist Response to J. Dominic Crossan's The Historical Jesus: The Life of a Mediterranean Jewish Peasant," Theology 96, no. 2 (July/August 1993): 303–10; Paul Rhodes Eddy, "Response by Paul Rhodes Eddy," in The Resurrection: An Interdisciplinary Symposium on the Resurrection of Jesus, ed. S. T. Davis, D. Kendall, and G. O'Collins, 285–86 (New York: Oxford University Press, 1997). For an evaluation of the impact of Crossan's postmodern hermeneutic on his Jesus research, see my *The Quest of the Hermeneutical Jesus*, 27–75.

idiosyncratic selection of which sources belong to which historical strata. Yet Crossan is happy to allow others to reach their own conclusions regarding who they believe the historical Jesus was, so long as they seek him, are confronted by him, and respond appropriately to the Jesus they find. In the 2005 Greer-Heard Point-Counterpoint Forum dialogue between Crossan and N. T. Wright on the resurrection of Jesus, Crossan repeatedly declared that the *mode* of Jesus' resurrection was secondary in importance to the *meaning* of his resurrection.[100] In other words, the living message of Jesus, which is collaborative eschatology, open commensality, and nonviolent resistance to empire and other domineering powers, takes priority over historical facts.[101]

So, what does Crossan take to be the message of Jesus? Jesus' message, according to Crossan, can be summed up in two words: magic and meal. Magic refers to Jesus healing individuals of their illnesses. Meal refers to Jesus sharing meals with outcasts. These two practices of Jesus symbolize his view of the kingdom of God. Together, magic (free healing) and meal (common eating) make for "a religious and economic egalitarianism that negated alike and at once the hierarchical and patronal normalcies of Jewish religion and Roman power."[102] When Crossan speaks of magic or free healing, one should not suppose he believes that the historical Jesus actually performed miracles in which diseases were cured or dead people returned to life. Instead, following Arthur Kleinman and Lilias Sung, he distinguishes between *disease* and *illness*. Disease refers to malfunctioning biological or psychological functions, while illness refers to "the secondary psychological responses to disease, e.g., how the patient, his family, and social network react to his disease."[103] The historical Jesus, according to Crossan, healed people of their illnesses, not their diseases. In fact, Jesus did not and could not cure any disease in a medical sense. Simply put, stories that speak of Jesus healing, exorcising, or even raising the dead proclaim that brokered systems, be they political or religious, are invalid.[104] In this way

---

100. N. T. Wright and John Dominic Crossan, "The Resurrection: Historical Event or Theological Explanation, a Dialogue," in *The Resurrection of Jesus: John Dominic Crossan and N. T. Wright in Dialogue*, ed. Robert B. Stewart, 16–47 (Minneapolis: Fortress Press; London: SPCK, 2006), esp. 27–29.

101. John Dominic Crossan, "Appendix: Bodily-Resurrection Faith," in Stewart, *The Resurrection of Jesus*, 171–86.

102. Crossan, *The Historical Jesus*, 422.

103. Crossan, *The Historical Jesus*, 336. Cf. Arthur Kleinman and Lilias Sung, "Why Do Indigenous Practitioners Successfully Heal?," *Social Science and Medicine* 13B, no. 1 (1979): 7–8; and Leon Eisenberg, "Disease and Illness: Distinctions between Professional and Popular Ideas of Sickness," *Culture, Medicine and Psychiatry* 1 (1977): 11.

104. Crossan, *Jesus: A Revolutionary Biography* (San Francisco: HarperSanFrancisco, 1994), 96.

the slave or the leper is empowered to take back control of his or her own body.[105]

Jesus' meals with their open table fellowship highlight his rejection of the bounded social order of his day, based as it was on honor and shame. Crossan refers to Jesus' disregard for social boundaries related to meals as "open commensality." Commensality (from the Latin *mensa*, meaning table) is vital to Crossan's reconstruction because meals, like bodies, represent far more than individual events. Meals follow the rules of an elaborate social order based upon honor and shame. Crossan defines commensality as "*the rules of tabling and eating as miniature models for the rules of association and socialization.*"[106]

The message of Crossan's Jesus is that of a peasant's protest against unjust hierarchical structures. He was a champion of radical equality. But peasants do not openly revolt; instead, they use subtle means that are more thoroughgoing than revolution. They practice a type of social banditry.[107] The means of this social banditry is twofold: parables and performance. For Jesus, as an egalitarian preacher, it was appropriate to teach in parables: "A parable empowers rather than dominates an audience. It challenges them to think and judge for themselves. It is the most appropriate teaching technique for a Kingdom of God in which God empowers rather than dominates, challenges rather than controls."[108]

Through magic and meal, Jesus performed the kingdom of God. In the same way that his parables and his aphorisms announce a kingdom that is unexpected, his actions reverse the expectations of his brokered society. He lived out his parables.[footnote] Crossan, *Jesus: A Revolutionary Biography*, 66–70. Through his actions as well as his words, Jesus rejected brokered hierarchies and pictured them as condemned by God.[109]

In summary, Jesus proclaimed a message that undermined the political, social, and religious hierarchies of his day. He announced this message through parables and aphorisms that empowered his hearers. He performed it through open meals, free healings, and symbolic actions of judgment.

---

105. Crossan, *Jesus: A Revolutionary Biography*, 93–95. There is an irreconcilable tension at points in that Crossan insists at the same time both that many of these stories were later inventions and that they nevertheless reveal something about the proclamation of the historical Jesus. Ibid., 87–95.

106. Crossan, *Jesus: A Revolutionary Biography*, 68. Crossan builds here on the cross-cultural anthropology of Peter Farb and George Armelagos on eating. See Peter Farb and George Armelagos, *Consuming Passions: The Anthropology of Eating* (Boston: Houghton Mifflin, 1980).

107. Crossan, *The Historical Jesus*, 304–5.

108.

109. Ibid., 130.

Ben Witherington III maintains that Jesus cannot be understood simply in the airtight categories that modern scholars find so attractive. He carefully asserts:

> I should repeat from the outset that I do not think any one term or title fully captures the truth about the historical Jesus. . . . I believe that some combination of several different approaches and insights best represents who Jesus thought he was. I am quite convinced, for instance, that Jesus was indeed a healer, was seen as a prophetic figure and did prefer the term *Son of Man* to refer to himself. I also believe that he saw himself in some sort of messianic light. . . . But if we ask what heuristic category comes closest to explaining the most about who Jesus thought he was and what he said and did, what comes closest to explaining why early christological thinking about Jesus developed as it did, then we must come to grips with sages and wisdom.[110]

One can see a development in Witherington's thought in this regard. In his first study on the subject, *The Christology of Jesus*, Witherington concluded that the case for Jesus seeing himself as "Wisdom incarnate, the very embodiment of the mind and plan of God for God's people," was more speculative than the case for believing that Jesus understood himself as Messiah, God's Son, and the Son of Man. Still, he granted that it had merit.[111] In his next book touching on the subject, *Jesus the Sage: The Pilgrimage of Wisdom*, Witherington argued more strongly for this view: "Jesus usually sapientialized whatever he said, often expressing prophetic or apocalyptic ideas in some sort of Wisdom form of speech. It is for this reason that calling Jesus a sage is heuristically the most all-encompassing and satisfying term. It explains not only the form of the vast majority of his sayings, but also the content of some of these sayings."[112] Again he states:

> What is especially daring about the idea of Jesus taking the personification of Wisdom and suggesting that he was the living embodiment of it, is that while a prophet might be seen as a *mashal*

---

110. Ben Witherington III, *The Jesus Quest: The Third Search for the Jew of Nazareth* (Downers Grove: InterVarsity, 1995), 185.
111. Ben Witherington III, *The Christology of Jesus* (Minneapolis: Fortress Press, 1990), 274.
112. Ben Witherington III, *Jesus the Sage: The Pilgrimage of Wisdom* (Minneapolis: Fortress Press, 2000), 201.

or prophetic sign, no one, so far as one can tell, up to that point in early Judaism had dared to suggested [sic] that he was a human embodiment of an attribute of God—God's Wisdom. . . . Some explanation for this remarkable and anomalous development must be given, and the best, though by no means the only, explanation of this fact is that Jesus presented himself as both sage and the message of the sage—God's Wisdom.[113]

Witherington points out that Jesus' teaching style was unique. Though Jesus was called a rabbi, he was certainly no traditional rabbi and did not establish a formal rabbinic school. He held the Torah in high regard but was not a commentator per se, nor did his preaching typically consist of interpreting Scripture. Nor was he a Galilean *hasid*, or charismatic teacher, though there were some obvious similarities between Jesus and the *hasidim*. Witherington rejects Vernon Robbins's hypothesis that Jesus was some sort of Jewish itinerant teacher à la Greek philosophers and also Gerald Downing's conclusion that Jesus was a type of popular Cynic preacher:[114]

> Thus, there are no comprehensive paradigms or parallels to Jesus as a teacher. . . . One needs to reckon with the fact that Jesus the teacher was, if not *sui generis*, nonetheless a complex combination of influences, and no one parallel model is adequate to categorize him. It seems clear that although there may have been Hellenistic influences on Jesus' teaching style, content, and lifestyle, nonetheless these were mediated to him through early Judaism, which had been affected in various ways by Hellenization. In short, the primary matrix for understanding Jesus as a teacher is the constellation of Jewish parallels. But if we admit that to some degree Jesus was a unique teacher, we should not be surprised that even the Jewish parallels fall short of describing the nature of Jesus as a pedagogue.[115]

So, what was Jesus' message, and how did he declare it? In reverse order, the message of Jesus was declared via Wisdom forms such as parables, riddles, and aphorisms. But he also declared it through miracles (healings and exorcisms). Unlike Crossan, Witherington believes that Jesus did physically heal people and supernaturally delivered individuals from demon possession. Through his

---

113. Ibid., 204.
114. Witherington, *The Christology of Jesus*, 179–84.
115. Ibid., 184–85.

miracles, Jesus declared that the eschatological dominion of God was breaking into the world through his actions: "Jesus sees his miracles as bringing about something unprecedented—the coming of God's dominion."[116] Jesus believed he was on "a mission to fulfill God's promises concerning the final state of God's people."[117] But more than simply announcing good news, Jesus put himself at the center of the story. "Jesus came to preach and bring the eschatological blessing of God; how one reacts to Jesus determines whether or not he will be blessed by these activities."[118] Again, Witherington states:

> Notice that how one reacts to Jesus and his actions now will affect one's status at the last judgment. This saying, like the previous two we have examined suggests that Jesus saw his miracles as evidence of the inbreaking dominion of God that should lead people to humble themselves before their God. Jesus, then, is the one who brings the final decisive action of God upon God's people. How one responds will determine one's final status with God. This suggests that Jesus saw himself as the final and decisive mediator between God and God's people.[119]

More to the point, Jesus saw himself as human and divine: "The question that begs to be asked is, 'What kind of person thinks he can personally reign forever—not him and his offspring but just him?' Or again, what sort of person thinks he can bring the eschatological saving reign of God upon the earth, the one that eclipses and replaces all previous human attempts at dominion? My answer is, 'A person who thought he was both human and divine.'"[120] Witherington is aware that many historians shy away from trying to answer the question of whether Jesus was divine, or saw himself as such. Still, following Raymond Brown, he states, "One must then ask questions like, What did Jesus imply when he left the suggestion that he should be seen as David's Lord? I think he implied that he should be seen not merely as a greater king than David but in a higher and more transcendent category. What Jesus implied about his self-conception is as important as what he publicly claimed."[121]

116. Ibid., 165.
117. Ibid., 165.
118. Ibid., 165.
119. Ibid., 167.
120. Ben Witherington III, "Jesus the Seer," in *Contending with Christianity's Critics: Answering the New Atheists and Other Objectors*, ed. William Lane Craig and Paul Copan (Nashville: B&H Academic, 2009), 104.
121. Witherington, *The Christology of Jesus*, 276.

According to Witherington, Jesus came declaring good news of the inbreaking of God's kingdom and that God's people should humble themselves before God. Jesus' message was also eschatological but not in Schweitzer's apocalyptic sense of an imminent end of the space-time world, but rather in the sense of bringing "human history to a climax, however long the denouement after the crucial events occur."[122] Witherington insists that it is not improbable that Jesus proclaimed the coming of "a messianic age that precedes 'the end of the world,' an age that in the relevant Jewish literature can last for a considerable period of time before the 'end of the world' (cf. *Syr. Baruch* 24-30, 4 Ezra 7.29f., *1 Enoch* 91-93)."[123]

In summary, for Witherington, Jesus' message was that of a prophet, Israel's Messiah, God's son, the Son of Man, and Wisdom incarnated. Most significantly, by implication, Jesus taught that he was in some sense divine.

At each and every point along the way, the quest for Jesus and his message have been affected not only by various cultural settings and philosophical presuppositions, but also by different critical and hermeneutical methods. The conclusions and methods of Reimarus, Strauss, and Schleiermacher were affected by their differing philosophical presuppositions. The historical Jesus of the first quest (after Schleiermacher) was the product of liberal theology coupled with source criticism. The (non)historical Jesus of the No-Quest period was the product of Kähler's dogmatic critique of the historical Jesus, the history of religions school, Bultmann's existentialism, and form criticism. The Jesus of the New Quest was the result of the post-Bultmannian emphasis upon the language of Jesus coupled with redaction criticism's concern to discover the theological motivation of the evangelists. Similarly, contemporary quests of Jesus, whether of the Renewed New Quest or Third Quest variety, modern or postmodern variety, are at least in part the product of the philosophical trends of our day and contemporary critical methods brought to bear upon historical data concerning Jesus. This is the way historians have always worked and, I suspect, always will.

Both Dom Crossan and Ben Witherington have crafted bold positions concerning the historical Jesus and his message. Both have many supporters and also many critics, and are widely respected within the guild of New Testament scholars. More importantly, both are gentlemen-scholars who are willing to dialogue with each other on important issues on which they disagree—but not disagree disagreeably.

I know that I have learned much from each of them—and will continue to do so, because thankfully, they are both still quite active as scholars. Their

---

122. Witherington, *The Christology of Jesus*, 193.
123. Ibid., 193.

dialogue is lively and assertive without ever coming close to the edgy sort of sound-bite, petty rhetoric that is so frequently mistaken for dialogue in our contemporary culture. If you pay close attention to their conversation and the essays by our other contributors, I'm confident that you will learn something valuable. Grace and peace to you!

1

The Message of Jesus
A Dialogue

John Dominic Crossan and Ben Witherington III

Opening Statement
By John Dominic Crossan

Prologue: History and Tragedy

The Bardo Museum in Tunis contains the world's greatest collection of Roman mosaics, and the greatest of the greatest is one that was excavated at Sousse on the Gulf of Hammamet about ninety miles south of the capital. It dates—probably—to the early third century and depicts Virgil with a scroll on his lap as he starts to write his *Aeneid*, that gospel of Roman imperial theology published in 19 BCE after his own death and by order of Augustus.

Virgil's left hand holds a scroll on his lap, and his right holds the stylus aloft as he stares meditatively into the distance. He is starting his epic poem and has just written these words: *"Musa, mihi causas memora, quo numine laeso quidve . . ."* We know them as book 1, lines 8-9a: "O Muse, recall the causes for me why—wounded by sacrilege or [angered by sorrow]," Hera, Queen of the Gods, made Aeneas' life so difficult as he journeyed from the doomed city of Troy to found the Roman race and Julian dynasty in Italy.

You immediately hear—as you are meant to hear—the echo from the opening line of the *Odyssey*, where Homer starts with, "Tell me about the man, O Muse." Tell me about Odysseus, that earlier and archetypal sea-wanderer trying amid great travail to reach his home. But that parallelism only increases your surprise when you see not just one but two of the nine Muses standing one on either side of Virgil. They are the goddess-spirits of artistic creativity, but while only one is invoked, two are present. Just for symmetry? Not really.

To Virgil's right stands Clio, the Muse of History, identified by her scroll of record. On his left, then, you expect to see Calliope, Muse of Epic Poetry, identified by her writing tablet. But what you see is Melpomene, the Muse of Tragedy, identified by the tragic mask worn in Greek drama. History and Tragedy stand on either side as Virgil composes his Roman imperial manifesto and Roman theological masterpiece.

Finally, it is all clear. Of course. You are in Carthage, that great city destroyed by Rome, not just as a military defeat but as a ruthless vengeance for Hannibal's incursions into Italy. From the off-again, on-again hundred years' war for control of the Mediterranean between the mid-third and mid-second centuries BCE, that mosaic sends out this message: *What the victors record as history, the vanquished know as tragedy.*

So, therefore, before you ever hear or even imagine the "message of Jesus," on which side of Virgil do you find yourself standing? And do you think it might make a difference to your interpretation?

EMPIRE AND ESCHATON

The God of the biblical tradition opposes empire. That is repeatedly clear—from the Egyptians in Exodus, through the Assyrians in Nahum, the Babylonians, Medes, Persians, and Greeks in Daniel, on into the Romans in Revelation. What is not so clear is why exactly. What is wrong with those empires, that is, with imperialism itself as the normalcy of human civilization across the last six thousand years?

Is it that they are all pagan, rather than Jewish (in the Old Testament) or pagan rather than Christian (in the New Testament)? Is it that they are distributively unjust, and the biblical God is a God of distributive justice? Or, more deeply, is it that distributive injustice is maintained only by the act or at least threat of violence? Does the biblical God stand against injustice and/or against violence? Put another way, is the biblical God violent or nonviolent? For Christians, that question means, is the God revealed in Jesus violent or nonviolent? Again, is the "message" incarnated and embodied in Jesus one of violence or nonviolence against violence itself?

Terms like *background* and *foreground*, or even *text* and *context*, often obscure the necessarily interactive mode of those words. Imagine thinking that American racism was simply background that could be avoided or context that could be omitted from the "message" of Dr. Martin Luther King Jr. But since we have often or even usually done that with the "message" of Jesus, I prefer the solitary term *matrix* to designate the interactive context of Jesus. That matrix sees Jesus as a homeland Jew turning Jewish eschaton against Roman *imperium*. It is not, in other words, a clash between Christianity and Judaism, but between Christian (that is, Messianic) Judaism and Roman imperialism.

The best place to see that matrix in operation is Daniel 7 from the 160s BCE. IN THAT CHAPTER, IMPERIALISM IS SUMMED UP BY THE BABYLONIANS, MEDEANS, PERSIANS, AND MACEDONIAN GREEKS. THE FIRST THREE OF THEM ARE NOT TRULY HUMAN BUT ARE RATHER BEASTS "UP OUT OF THE SEA," FERAL THRUSTS FROM THE CHAOS OF THE LAND-THREATENING OCEAN (7:3). THE BABYLONIAN EMPIRE "WAS LIKE A LION AND HAD EAGLES' WINGS"; THE MEDEAN EMPIRE "LOOKED LIKE A BEAR"; AND THE PERSIAN EMPIRE "APPEARED LIKE A LEOPARD" (7:46).

No wild-animal comparison, however, is adequate to describe the fourth imperial kingdom of the Macedonian Greeks. Alexander's terrible war machine—with its heavy infantry as anvil and heavy cavalry as hammer, with its twenty-foot two-handed pikes so that five ranks of lethal points intruded into the killing zone—can only be described as "different," and Daniel does so three times (7:7, 19, 23).

Those imperial kingdoms are animal-ified (not person-ified!) "like a beast" from the disorder of the sea's fury. By contrast, the fifth kingdom is personified "like a son of man" from the order of God's heaven. That phrase is, by the way, simply Semitic male chauvinism for "like a human being." That fifth kingdom, that kingdom of God, is brought down from heaven to earth by this transcendental Human One who has been entrusted with it by God, the transcendent Ancient One (7:9-13). Once again, Daniel mentions that three times (7:14, 18, 27).

Furthermore, imperial kingdoms come and go, rise and fall. But God's kingdom was already emphasized as an "everlasting" one in earlier chapters of Daniel: "His kingdom is an everlasting kingdom, and his sovereignty is from generation to generation" (4:3); "His sovereignty is an everlasting sovereignty, and his kingdom endures from generation to generation" (4:34); "His kingdom shall never be destroyed, and his dominion has no end" (6:26). That theme is repeated in those just-cited quotations from 7:14, 18, 27.

Imperial kingdoms (plural) are confronted with eschatological kingdom (singular) here below upon our human earth. *Empire* is one people or nations using other peoples or nations unjustly and violently. *Eschaton* is an ordinary Greek word for "the end"—but the end of what? Negatively, it is not—emphatically not—about the end of the world. We moderns can, of course, do that in several different ways, but God would never annul the creation declared in Genesis to be "good" in each part (1:4, 10, 12, 18, 21, 25) and "very good" in its entirety (1:31) . The eschaton is not about the destruction of the world but about its transformation into a place of justice and nonviolence. It is not about the annihilation of the earth but about its transfiguration into a location of freedom and peace. Daniel's vision of the kingdom of God coming down from heaven to earth was an eschatological vision, and my own term for that is the Great Divine Cleanup of the World.

That Cosmic Cleanup is described as a worldwide reforging of weapons of war into implements of peace in Micah 4:3-4 = Isaiah 2:4 and as a banquet for all the earth in Isaiah 25:6-8. It is described—at the time of Jesus—as a moment when "the earth will belong equally to all, undivided by walls or fences.... Lives will be in common and wealth will have no division. For there will be no poor man there, no rich, and no tyrant, no slave. Further, no one will be either great or small anymore. No kings, no leaders. All will be equal together" (*Sibylline Oracles* 2.319-24).

In Daniel 7, God replaces beastlike kingdoms with a humanlike kingdom, earth-born kingdoms with a heaven-born kingdom, and as earlier in Daniel, transient kingdoms with an everlasting kingdom. It replaces—as throughout the biblical tradition—empire(s) with eschaton. But we are not told exactly how this kingdom of God is *internally* different from those kingdoms of empire. They are given external qualifications but not internal descriptions. The confrontation is quite emphatic, but what, beyond name-calling, is the intrinsic difference in content? In other words, what was the message of Jesus about the kingdom of God "as in heaven so on earth," in the Greek word order of the Lord's Prayer in Matt. 6:10?

ANTIPAS AND TIBERIAS

Deep below our geological earth are giant tectonic plates that grind against one another along fault lines and produce, at very specific times and in very specific places, the surface disturbances of volcanoes, earthquakes, and tsunamis. Deep below our historical world are those tectonic plates of empire and eschaton, and their clash was promised but not yet performed in Daniel 7. How was it then that—to keep my metaphor—those plates created a seismic disturbance not just in Israel or even Galilee but precisely on the northwest quadrant of the Lake of Tiberias in the 20s of the first century CE?

Here are some other ways to ask that same constitutive and generative question. Why did two popular movements, the baptism movement of John and the kingdom movement of Jesus, happen in territories ruled by Herod Antipas in the 20s of that first common-era century? What did Antipas do at that time and in that place to create resistance after a quiet rule of a quarter century? Why did Jesus leave Nazareth, "make his home in Capernaum by the Sea" of Galilee (Matt. 4:13)? Why are there miracles with an abundance of fish (Mark 6:43; Luke 5:6; John 21:6)? Why are the most important disciples all from different fishing villages—Mary from Magdala (Luke 8:2); Peter, Andrew, and Philip from Bethsaida (John 1:44); James and John from Capernaum (Mark 1:16)? And why was their vocation to become "fishers" and not, say, "farmers" of people? Jesus in Galilee is seldom far from lake and boat and net and fish. Why?

In the generation before Jesus, Rome replaced the Hasmoneans with the Herodians and made Herod the Great "King of the Jews." On the one hand, to ensure approval from his imperial masters, he built the great port of Sebastos—Greek for Augustus—and its adjacent city of Caesarea as a world-class all-weather port on Israel's mid-Mediterranean coast. He also built temples to "Roma et Augustus"—the divine couple at the center of the new world order at that coastal Caesarea, at Sebaste in Samaria, and at what would later be called Caesarea Philippi. On the other hand, to ensure approval from his Jewish subjects, he married a Hasmonean princess, Mariamme—whom he later executed. He also magnificently expanded the temple plaza to the size of fifteen football fields in another world-class construction project.

When you survey all those huge building projects, you suddenly realize that Herod the Great skipped or ignored Galilee, which was, of course, under his control. This means that the process of Romanization by urbanization for commercialization struck Galilee forcibly not in the generation of Herod the Great but in that of his son, Herod Antipas. That was also, of course, the generation of both John and Jesus.

Herod Antipas ruled the disconnected territories of Galilee (west of the Jordan) and Peraea (east of the Jordan) from 4 BCE until 39 CE, that is, under three separate Roman emperors. I use what happened under the first and third to interpret what happened under the second.

In 4 BCE, he went to Rome under Augustus to become King of the Jews over the entire Jewish homeland and returned not as "monarch" of the whole but simply "tetrarch" of a part. In 39 CE, he went to Rome to try again under Caligula and ended up in permanent exile as Herod Agrippa I became the next and last Rome-appointed King of the Jews. In between Augustus and Caligula was the emperor Tiberius, who ruled from 14 to 39 CE. That was when Antipas (as I interpret his actions) made his second major attempt to become Rome's designated King of the Jews—like his father and with his father as model.

On the one hand, to ensure approval from his Roman masters, he had to increase his tax revenues without forcing his subsistence-level peasantry into violent rebellion. His solution was to commercialize the lake by building on its shores a new capital city, naming it Tiberias after the emperor, and creating a fishing industry geared to commercial export rather than local consumption. He had already learned how to multiply the loaves in the valleys around his old capital of Sepphoris. He would now do the same for the fishes in the "Sea [now] of Tiberias" (John 6:1; 21:1).

On the other hand, to ensure approval from his Jewish subjects, he divorced his Nabatean wife and married the divorced wife of one of his half-brothers. This was Herodias, the granddaughter of the popularly beloved Mariamme, and intended a deliberate Harmonean-Herodian connection. Criticism of that marriage from both John (Mark 6:18) and Jesus (Mark 10:11-12) was, therefore, not just moral complaint but political obstruction.

By the 20s CE, Tiberias was open for business, and fishing rights on the lake changed drastically. There would have been taxes on each step of the process, and at the end, fishers would have had to sell to Antipas's fish factories making dried and salted fish for export sale. Think of that first-century boat nursed by excellent workers with inadequate materials until it could not hold up anymore and was sunk offshore to be discovered and restored two thousand years later. "The Galilee at this time was economically depressed," according to Shelley Wachsmann, "the timbers used in the boat's construction are perhaps a physical expression of this overall economic situation,"[1] but, I would add, not so much "depressed" as oppressed.

Here, then, is where John and Jesus enter the picture. And why? If "the earth is the Lord's and all that is in it, the world, and those who live in it" (Ps. 24:1), whose is the lake and all of its fishes? That was the question of cosmic justice and covenantal righteousness as lake became microcosm of world. Was it God's lake and God's world, or was it Rome's lake and Rome's world? It was never about just *fish*. It was always about *just* fish. This is why eschaton opposed empire, the kingdom of God opposed the kingdom of Rome, John and Jesus opposed Antipas—as a seismic disturbance—in Peraea for John and Galilee for Jesus in the 20s CE.

JOHN AND JESUS

In contrasting the message of John with that of Jesus, I emphatically do not intend any cheap exaltation of the latter over the former. Indeed, I am

---

1. Shelley Wachsmann, *The Sea of Galilee Boat: An Extraordinary 2000 Year Old Discovery* (New York: Plenum, 1985), 358.

convinced that Jesus learned powerfully from John—learned what to believe but also what not to believe, especially about God. Furthermore, the execution of one popular prophet, John, may have protected that other one, Jesus, for a given amount of time under Herod Antipas's prudent rule in Galilee. But I am sure that their messages were different for two main reasons.

First, even those who opposed both of them recognized that they were different from one another. "For John came neither eating nor drinking, and they say, 'He has a demon'; the Son of Man came eating and drinking, and they say, 'Look, a glutton and a drunkard, a friend of tax collectors and sinners!'" (Matt. 11:18-19 = Luke 7:33-34). I bracket the name-calling but accept fasting versus feasting as an accurate insight into two different visions, missions, and messages.

Second, Jesus was certainly baptized by John. I say certainly because of the acute embarrassment in the New Testament gospels about that event—with Mark accepting it (1:9-10), Matthew protesting it (3:13-16), Luke hurrying it (3:21), and John omitting it completely (1:29-34). Yet, later, when Jesus speaks with his own voice, he distances himself—but respectfully so—from John: "Truly I tell you, among those born of women no one has arisen greater than John the Baptist; yet the least in the kingdom of heaven is greater than he" (Matt. 11:11 = Luke 7:28).

In other words, the baptism movement of John was changed into or, better, replaced by the kingdom movement of Jesus—even though Matthew equates them with the same message from John (3:2) and Jesus (4:17). Next, then, I contrast them under two rubrics: the imminence or presence of the kingdom of God and the violence or nonviolence of the God of kingdom.

GOD'S KINGDOM: IMMINENT OR PRESENT?

John the Baptist was an *apocalyptic* eschatologist, a prophet with an apocalypse (Greek for a revelation) about the Great Divine Cleanup of the World. In theory, his message could have had any revelatory content about God's kingdom. But in practice, when centuries of empires had climaxed with Rome as the strongest of them all, a first-century apocalyptic revelation had better be about the kingdom's advent: about "how soon?"; about "if not now, when?"; and about "if not now, why?"

So John's message was about the *imminent* advent of God's kingdom. It was not, by the way, about—as it later became in our gospels—the imminent advent of Jesus as God's Messiah. But since a future-but-imminent event is easy enough to proclaim, why did so many accept and follow John's movement and message?

John believed that only sin held up God's transformative intervention (Deuteronomy 28). So he created a great sacramental and penitential renewal of the exodus. His followers were first brought out into the Peraean desert east of the Jordan and were then brought back into the Jewish homeland through that river. As they passed through it, repentance purified their souls, just as water washed their bodies. Thereafter, they were received into the promised land as a reborn people. Then, surely, said John, God would come, any day now. For surely, said John, once a critical mass of purified people were ready, God would have no further excuse for delay.

John's program was as persuasive as it was apocalyptic. When enough people "were baptized by him in the river Jordan, confessing their sins," then God would arrive: "The one who is more powerful than I is coming after me; I am not worthy to stoop down and untie the thong of his sandals. I have baptized you with water; but he will baptize you with the Holy Spirit" (Mark 1:5, 7-8). That, of course, was not originally about the coming of Jesus but of God.

What came, however, was not the kingdom of God but the cavalry of Antipas, and what happened was not an eschatological life for the world but a lonely death for John. At that point, Jesus could have taken up the fallen banner of the Baptist—as Elisha to his Elijah—and proclaimed the same message with "soon" still holding firm. But instead, Jesus performed a paradigm shift, a tradition swerve, a disruptive innovation within his contemporary apocalyptic eschatology. He proclaimed not the imminence of eschaton, but its presence, not the future-soon but the present-already of God's kingdom "as in heaven so on earth"—here and now. For example: "The kingdom of God is not coming with things that can be observed; nor will they say, 'Look, here it is!' or 'There it is!' For, in fact, the kingdom of God is among you" (Luke 17:20-21; see also Luke 16:16 = Matt. 11:12-13; Luke 11:20 = Matt. 12:28; Luke 10:23b-24 = Matt. 13:16-17; Mark 2:19-20 = Matt. 9:15-16 = Luke 5:34-35; Mark 1:14b-15 = Matt. 4:17).

It is hard, however, to realize how absurd that proclamation must have sounded to its first hearers. Where, they would have asked Jesus, is God's transfigured world to be seen? Are not Tiberius still emperor of Rome, Antipas still tetrarch of Galilee, and Pilate still prefect of Judea? How has anything changed in a world of peasant poverty, local injustice, and imperial oppression?

In answer, Jesus proclaimed another—and necessarily concomitant—aspect of his paradigm shift within contemporary eschatological expectation. You have been waiting for God, he said, while God has been waiting for you. No wonder nothing is happening. You want God's intervention, he said, while God wants your collaboration. Kingdom is here, but only insofar as you accept it, enter it, live it, and thereby establish it. Collaboration with God, Jesus might have said, is but another word for covenant with God.

That is why Jesus did not settle down at Nazareth or Capernaum and have his companions bring others to him. Instead, he sent them out to do exactly what he himself was doing: heal the sick, eat with the healed, and demonstrate the kingdom's presence in that reciprocity and mutuality (Mark 6:6-13; Matt. 10:1-14; Luke 9:1-6; 10:1-12). God's Great Cleanup of the World does not begin, cannot continue, and will not conclude without our divinely empowered participation and transcendentally driven collaboration. That is the message and challenge of Jesus.

GOD'S CHARACTER: VIOLENT OR NONVIOLENT?

John's message involved the imminent advent of an avenging God of retributive justice. Recall his metaphors of the swinging ax and the falling tree (Matt. 3:10 = Luke 3:9) or the winnowing fork and the burning chaff (Matt. 3:12 = Luke 3:17). Indeed, Luke had to balance that "wrath to come" language (Matt. 3:7 = Luke 3:7) with his own more gentle ethical insert (3:10-14).

But John was wrong, terribly, tragically wrong. He announced the immediate advent of an avenging God, and what came was the immediate advent of an avenging tetrarch. Herod Antipas, the Rome-appointed governor of Galilee, arrested and executed John. And God did nothing—no intervention and no prevention. John died in lonely isolation in Antipas's southern fortress of Machaerus east of the Jordan. And God did nothing—no intervention and no prevention. And in my interpretation, Jesus watched, Jesus learned, and Jesus changed.

Jesus called for eschatological collaboration—not, however, with a God of violent retributive justice but with a God of nonviolent distributive justice. Recall the reason Jesus gave for nonviolent resistance to evil: "Love your enemies and pray for those who persecute you" (Matt. 5:44) or "Love your enemies, do good to those who hate you, bless those who curse you, pray for those who abuse you" (Luke 6:28). But why? "So that you may be children of your Father in heaven; for he makes his sun rise on the evil and on the good, and sends rain on the righteous and on the unrighteous . . . . Be perfect, therefore, as your heavenly Father is perfect" (5:45, 48). Like God, like Jesus, we are called to nonviolent resistance to the violent normalcy of civilization. We are called, *with* God, to take back God's world, *for* God.

Internally, we can see Jesus' earliest followers struggled with that absolute nonviolent mode of resistance to evil. It meant not only no attacks but also no defenses! You can see, for example, how the peasant vision struggled between "staff" (Mark 6:8) and "no-staff" (Matt. 10:10 = Luke 9:3) or the aristocratic vision struggled between "sword" (Luke 22:35-38) and "no sword" (Luke 22:49-52). To all of that, Jesus said, "Enough of this!" and "No more of this!" (Luke 22:38, 51).

Externally, and universally, the strongest witness to Jesus' message of nonviolent resistance to violence is the judgment of Pilate, Rome's governor of Israel. Paula Fredriksen built her 1999 book, *Jesus of Nazareth, King of the Jews*, around the "incontrovertible fact" that, "though Jesus was executed as a political insurrectionist, his followers were not."[2] I do not interpret that crucial insight to mean that Pilate thought Jesus was completely innocent but that, while guilty of nonviolent resistance, he was innocent of violent intentions.

Compare, for example, that parable about Barabbas who "was in prison with the rebels who had committed murder during the insurrection" (Mark 15:7). Jesus met the precise fate of public but nonviolent resistance to Roman law and order. In terms of his imperial mandate, Pilate was quite correct: public execution for Jesus but no communal arrest for his companions.

That was illustrated powerfully in another parable about the interaction between Pilate and Jesus in John's gospel. "My kingdom," said Jesus in 18:36a, "is not of this world" (KJV) or "is not from this world" (NRSV). We often cite the sentence only up to that point and thereby make it extremely ambiguous. Does it mean not about present but future? Not about earth but heaven? Not about politics but religion? Not about the exterior but the interior life?

Jesus continued, however, and made all those preliminary interpretations irrelevant: "If my kingdom were from this world, my followers would be fighting to keep me from being handed over to the Jews. But as it is, my kingdom is not from here" (18:36b). I leave aside John's standard prejudice about "the Jews" to emphasize the structure of that sentence. That repeated "if [= not] . . . from this world" and "not from here" frame what cannot and did not happen. The followers of Jesus did not "fight," did not use violence even to attempt his release.

The difference between God's kingdom and Rome's empire, between Jesus and Pilate, between Jesus' companions and Pilate's followers is nonviolence as opposed to violence. Violence cannot be used even to protect or free Jesus. The coming of God's kingdom, the dawn of eschatological transformation, the Great Divine Cleanup of the World—by whatever name—is nonviolent and so also is our God-empowered participation in it and God-driven collaboration with it.

2. Paula Fredriksen, *Jesus of Nazareth, King of the Jews: A Jewish Life and the Emergence of Christianity* (New York: Vintage, 1999), 9; see also ibid., 11, 240, 255.

That is, for me, the message of Jesus. It was summed up far better than I have just done by two African bishops who lived at either end of that continent and almost a millennium and a half apart. First, Augustine of Hippo in a sermon of 416: "God made you without you. He doesn't justify you without you." Then, Desmond Tutu of Cape Town in a sermon of 1999 and in a magnificent misquotation: "St. Augustine says, 'God, without us, will not; as we, without God, cannot.'"

Opening Statement
By Ben Witherington III

Sometimes in the study of the message of Jesus, we have all been guilty of missing the forest due to the overanalysis of interesting individual trees. I am reminded of the famous saying of John Muir the naturalist, who once suggested that we look at life from the back side of a beautiful tapestry. Normally, what we see are individual loose ends, knots, threads here and there. But occasionally, when the light shines through the tapestry, it dawns on us that there is a larger design, a weaving together of darks and lights with purpose, pattern, rich color. My presentation here will focus not so much on individual sayings of Jesus but rather on the storied world, the narrative thought world which generated all of his teachings.

It was G. B. Caird who said that Jesus was the starting point and goal of New Testament theology. He meant this in several ways. For one thing, in the thought world of the earliest Christians, there is continuity between the Jesus of history and the Christ of faith, and between Jesus and the risen Lord. Caird put it this way: "Without the Jesus of history the Christ of faith becomes a Docetic figure, a figment of pious imagination who, like Alice's Cheshire cat, ultimately disappears from view."[3] Unfortunately, that happens all too regularly in Christian discussions of Jesus, which is why I am starting this discussion with an examination of Jesus' narrative thought world, which most certainly influenced that of his earliest followers, who, like him, were Torah-loving Jews. It was Caird's view (and I think he is right) that human experience is the point at which theology is grounded in history.[4] It was the experiencing of the risen Lord or the experiencing of conversion to Christ that led to the Copernican revolution in the thinking of those Jews who became Christians after Easter. Later, it was the worshiping of Christ that led to rethinking his significance and

---

3. G. B. Caird, *New Testament Theology*, ed. L. D. Hurst (Oxford: Oxford University Press, 1994), 346.
4. Ibid., 347.

how to tell his story.⁵ These sorts of things caused the earliest Christians to go back and reevaluate what the historical Jesus had said and done, and particularly to reevaluate his own teaching. What sort of worldview had undergirded and been articulated in Jesus' teaching?

Without question, Jesus was one of the great sages of all time, and that included being a great storyteller. Whether we consider his original parables or his creative handling of Old Testament stories, he was quite the improviser, to say the least. He lived out of and spoke into a rich storied world, and he told his own and others' tales in light of the dawning eschatological realities. Not surprisingly, his storied world is populated chiefly by Old Testament figures and stories, alluded to, retold, and recycled in various ways, but also his storied world involves the spinning out of new tales, often in the form of parables or visionary remarks (e.g., "I saw Satan fall like lightning from the sky"; Luke 10:18). The function of Jesus' discourse was not merely to inform but also to transform, and that transformation was to involve not merely the audience's symbolic universe but also its behavior in relationship to God as well as in relationship to each other. In other words, there was both a theological and an ethical thrust to Jesus' teaching. The stories were meant to transform not only the religious imagination of the audience but also their praxis, giving them samples and examples of how to believe and behave in the light of the inbreaking dominion of God.

If there is a difference in thrust in the way Jesus articulated his eschatological worldview from that of his predecessor John the Baptizer, it is that Jesus, even in his more apocalyptic sayings, tended to emphasize the good news about the coming of the dominion of God on earth. "The object of winnowing is not to collect enough chaff to have a glorious bonfire; it is to gather the wheat into the granary; the bonfire is purely incidental."⁶ Thus, Jesus set about to rescue the perishing and to free Israel from its various forms of bondage. In this, Jesus is not trying to be Israel, any more than the Twelve were set up initially to be Israel. All of them were trying to free Israel through a mission of preaching, teaching, and healing. There was, however, urgency and corporate focus to what they did. "The disciples were not evangelistic preachers sent out to save individual souls for some unearthly paradise. They were couriers proclaiming a national emergency and conducting a referendum on a question of national survival."⁷ The storm of judgment was looming on

---

5. On which, see Larry Hurtado, *Lord Jesus Christ: Devotion to Jesus in Earliest Christianity* (Grand Rapids: Eerdmans, 2003).

6. Caird, *New Testament Theology*, 360.

7. Ibid., 361.

the horizon for the Jewish faith centered on temple, territory, and Torah. God was intervening in Jesus and his followers before this disaster happened, just as he had already intervened through John the Baptizer. It is this context of social unrest and sense of impending doom that we must keep in view when considering the way Jesus articulates his thought world and the urgency with which he stresses certain things.

This line of discussion raises the issue of the relationship of Jesus to Israel. I suggest that Jesus presents himself not as Israel but rather as the Son of Man, and as the Son of Man, he is Adam gone right. That is, the scope of his messianic ministry is much broader than fulfilling the promise of being the ultimate Son of David, restoring Israel and its reign in the Holy Land. That is a part of what Jesus is about, but only a part. The temptation scenes make clear that something more wide-ranging and more cosmic is at stake, for Jesus is tempted as Son of God, not as Israel or Son of David. The issue is what sort of Son of God was Jesus to be. Was it one that comported with his being the true Son of Man of Danielic prophecy or not?

Of course, Jesus spoke to a different audience than did his later Christian followers. Every single one of the New Testament documents is written for Christians, even if in some cases written for Christians to use in some form with outsiders. Jesus, on the other hand, was addressing Jews, even when he was addressing his disciples, and so he was able to presuppose the storied world of the Old Testament as something that he and his audience shared. This perhaps explains why Jesus was able to simply allude to figures such as the queen of the South (Matt. 12:41-42 par.), or Noah (Matt. 24:36-41), or a widow in Zarephath (Luke 4:26) and expect the audience to know who he meant. It is no surprise that many of the figures from the past that Jesus spoke of, including both the queen of the South and Noah, were associated with judgments past and future. According to Matt. 12:38-40 (cf. Matt. 16:1-4; Luke 11:29-32), the only "sign" that a wicked generation would get out of Jesus was the sign of Jonah, that reluctant crisis intervention specialist called upon to warn the people of Nineveh of impending disaster if they did not repent. Jonah 3:4 says the Ninevites were warned that if they did not repent, destruction would fall upon them within forty days. Jesus offers a similar warning in Mark 13, except that the clock is set to forty years. Luke, in his relating of this sort of teaching, makes it all the more explicit that Jesus meant the destruction of Jerusalem by human armies, namely, Roman armies (Luke 19:41-44; 21:20-24; 23:27-31).

It is interesting, however, that most of the stories Jesus told were of his own making, stories about contemporaries and contemporary things, such as the coming of God's eschatological saving activity. As we read through even just the narrative parables, we find anonymous human figures providing examples of various sorts. Only the parable of the Rich Man and Lazarus presents a story about a named individual human being (Luke 16:19-31). Even more interesting is the fact that God is portrayed as an actor in various of these parables: he is the owner of the vineyard in the parable of the Wicked Tenants (Mark 12:1-11) and the forgiving father in the parable of the Prodigal Son (Luke 15:11-32). Most importantly, we discover that Jesus provides an example of how to do theology and ethics in story form, for these stories are about both divine activity and human responses of various sorts.

There is also a dark edge to the stories that Jesus tells, when it comes to the evaluation of his own people. By this, I mean that they are portrayed as lost (see Luke 15), and their leaders as those who reject God's emissaries the prophets and even his Son (Matt. 23:29-39). The eschatological situation is portrayed as drastic, with all sorts of unexpected persons trying to race through the narrow gate into the kingdom, while the invited guests have snubbed the host and either have refused to come or have come late and without the appropriate attire. Pious Jews are going away from temple prayer unjustified while tax collectors are being accepted. There is some sort of drastic reversal of normal expectations happening as the dominion breaks into human history, and it does not bode well for the faithful elder brothers of the family, it would appear. God is busy vindicating the oppressed, liberating the lost, enfranchising the least and last, and changing the guest list at the messianic banquet. These are stories about the upsetting of a highly stratified world, about the changing of the guard, about new occasions teaching new duties, about both judgment and redemption catching Jews by surprise, and perhaps most of all about the need for repentance by one and all as God's divine saving activity is happening in their midst, and yet many are blind to it.

The storied world that Jesus tells of has not only a dark edge but also a strangeness. Good shepherds do not normally leave ninety-nine sheep to rescue one straggler. People do not plant a weed such as a mustard bush, as it only attracts the wrong sort of birds and attention. God is not like an unjust judge who has to be forced into vindicating a persistent widow. We could go on. Jesus is offering new perspectives on old images and ideas and, in some cases, new perspectives on new vistas and horizons that are coming into view.

N. T. Wright rightly senses what is going on in Jesus' ministry when he says, "The crucial element in his prophetic activity was the story, both implicit and explicit, that he was telling and acting out. It was Israel's story reaching its climax: the long-awaiting moment has arrived! . . . To say 'the kingdom of God is at hand' makes sense only when the hearers know 'the story thus far' and are waiting for it to be completed."[8]

And precisely because Jesus is operating in the Jewish ethos of *eretz Yisrael* (land of Israel), he can presuppose a storied world context that most of the writers of the New Testament cannot presuppose. This may well explain why indeed we find no parables outside the Gospels. It is because we are no longer speaking into Jesus' specific world, a world where sapiential Jewish thinking with an eschatological twist made sense.

In its own context, then, how would Jesus' articulation of his vision in stories have been heard? Again Wright helps us: "It would clearly *both* challenge some prevailing assumptions within that Jewish context *and* retain a special focus which would be characteristic only of Jesus' career, not the work of his post-Easter followers. It must be set within Judaism, but as a challenge; it must be the presupposition for the church, but not the blueprint."[9]

Just so, and this means that it is crucial to get the balance right between continuity and discontinuity when it comes to assessing the storied world of Jesus and of his post-Easter followers. And again, the point of the parables is to reorder the thinking of Jews: "The parables offer not only information, but challenge; they are stories designed to evoke fresh praxis, to reorder the symbolic world, to break open current understandings and inculcate fresh ones."[10]

A good example to examine closely is the parable of the Sower in Mark 4:1-9. Here, as Wright observes, we have the revolutionary notion that Jesus is the person who is bringing the story of Israel to a climax in his own ministry. "If we fail to see how profoundly subversive, how almost suicidally dangerous, such a claim was," it is because we have tended to turn Jesus' counter-order wisdom speech into innocuous sermon illustrations.[11] It is right to say that when we are dealing with the narrative parables, we need to follow the narrative logic of the story, not assume that these are thinly veiled allegories of history in detail. At the same time, there are allegorical elements in Jesus' parables, and especially perhaps this one. Modern distinctions between parable and allegory are not all that helpful when it comes to ancient Jewish storytelling.[12] Who, then, is the

---

8. N. T. Wright, *Jesus and the Victory of God*, vol. 2 of *Christians Origins and the Question of God* (Minneapolis: Fortress Press, 1996), 226.

9. Ibid., 226.

10. Ibid., 229.

11. Ibid., 235.

12. On which, see Ben Witherington III, *Jesus the Sage: The Pilgrimage of Wisdom* (Minneapolis: Fortress Press, 1994); idem, *Jesus the Seer: The Progress of Prophecy* (Peabody, MA: Hendrickson, 1999).

sower in this parable? Along with most commentators, I agree that it is Jesus, assuming a divine role here of planting God's word about the dominion in surprising as well as familiar places.

There are some surprising results of following this narrative logic. For one thing, Jesus is not sanguine that most of those who hear him will respond positively in the long term. He is unlike the naive and overly optimistic preacher of today. But what is perhaps most telling about this parable is that Jesus expects rejection and ephemeral positive responses. He expects too much competition to allow his message to grow in the hearts of many. He expects absolute, hard-hearted rejection. And yes, in the good soil he expects good, long-lasting results.

This is an odd message for a person who saw himself in a messianic light, as one who had come to rescue Israel from disaster. In a sense, it is a message about the end of one thought world and the unexpected beginnings of another out of the ashes of the first one. In Jesus' view, his world is hell-bent, not heaven bound, and he, like John the Baptizer, is here to try to rescue a few of the perishing before the dark night of judgment falls. This parable differs considerably from the one in Mark 12:1-11 about the wicked tenants, as that is a commentary on Jewish leadership in the vineyard, not about the state of the Jewish vineyard in general. But both parables presuppose that things are coming to a climax, and that God's last-ditch efforts to rescue his people are culminating in the ministry of Jesus, who seeks to reclaim God's land, his vineyard, before it produces nothing but the grapes of wrath.

Along with Wright, I think the aforementioned parables in Mark 4 and Mark 12 would have been seen as echoing or alluding to Isaiah 5–6. In this light, there can be no question but that the vineyard is Israel, and Jesus sees himself as fulfilling a prophetic role like that of Isaiah, dealing with hard-of-hearing Israel. But what is most telling when we closely read Isaiah 5–6 and then think of these two parables of Jesus is that, already in Isaiah, the theme of impending judgment and the exile of God's Jewish people is clear. In this context, the use of parables reflects and indeed presupposes the hard-heartedness of the audience and their refusal to listen. They will not hear and understand unless they turn or repent. Listen to some of Isaiah's Song of the Vineyard:

> What more could have been done for my vineyard
> than I have done for it?
> When I looked for good grapes,
> why did it yield only bad?
> Now I will tell you

what I am going to do to my vineyard:
I will take away its hedge,
and it will be destroyed;
I will break down its wall
and it will be trampled.
(Isa. 5:4-5, author's translation)

The song is a lament that goes on to bemoan the injustice and bloodshed in Israel.

Here is where I say that this all comports nicely with Jesus' prediction of the demise of the temple and Jerusalem in Mark 13. In Jesus' view, as his prophetic sign-act in the temple showed, this temple was the temple of doom, one that God would judge within a generation. And indeed, exactly one biblical generation after Jesus died in ad 30, the temple fell in Jerusalem to the Romans. Jesus was no false prophet any more than Isaiah was in regard to the demise of Jerusalem and exile in his own era. In light of all this, it is interesting that the later Christian followers of Jesus not only continued to evangelize Jews and see God as promising them much, but also, as a text such as Romans 11 shows, continued to believe that God, though he might temporarily break off from his people those who did not accept Jesus as their messiah, would not replace an unresponsive Jewish people with a more responsive Gentile one. This is surprising only to those who do not know the regular pattern in the Old Testament prophetic oracles of redemption of Israel after and indeed as a result of judgment on Israel (see, e.g., Hosea, Amos, and of course, Isaiah). Perhaps most radically and paradoxically, Jesus was suggesting in Mark 4 that God's radical rescue of his people would come not by means of military action or a warrior-messiah but rather through the call and response of Jesus' preaching of the good news.

This brings us to the other seed parables in Mark 4. Jesus seems to think there will be some "seedy" characters—indeed, some characters that Jews would consider "for the birds" (cf. Dan. 4:20-22) in the dominion—to the surprise of the longtime dwellers there. Hence, Jesus tells the parable of the Mustard Seed, a seed that no Jewish farmer would ever plant in a garden. The parable of the Mustard Seed is a parable of contrast between small beginnings and large, if noxious and surprising, outcomes, but it is also a parable that tells us what sort of persons are going to end up in the vineyard: the wild birds from afar, which should probably be seen as an allusion to Gentiles.

The parable of the Seed Growing Secretly tells us something about the method by which the dominion is coming: secretly, under the radar, without a lot of human effort, and certainly without violence. This parable can be fruitfully compared to the parable of the Leaven in the Dough (Matt. 13:33 // Luke 13:20-21) in that both suggest a sort of automatic process, one without human aid that produces the result. The hiddenness theme is also evident in the parables of the Pearl of Great Price and the Treasure in the Field (Matt. 13:44-46). There are apocalyptic overtones to all these parables as they emerge from a world of opacity, of secrets that require teasing the brain into active thought to figure out, of God producing a crop and a harvest or a treasure as if by sleight of hand. The harvest theme is a dead giveaway that Jesus believed that the eschatological scenario was already in play.

And here precisely is where I differ strongly with Wright. These are not parables about return from exile. If anything, they are parables about the surprising presence of God's saving activity in the midst of occupation and oppression in the Holy Land, a very different message indeed. Jesus did not come to meet the audience's messianic expectations; he came to meet their needs. But ultimately, that task could be consummated only through a sacrifice on a cross and its sequel. Redemption would not come on the cheap or even just by a spiritual revival of good preaching accompanied by some miracles. The sin problem would not be dealt with or overcome by those means alone. And this brings us to another crucial point.

Did Jesus tell stories about himself? One could argue that Jesus appears in some of the parables. For example, in Mark 4, he seems to be the sower, and in Mark 12, it seems clear enough that he is the Son who is rejected, killed, and thrown out of the vineyard. We could perhaps also suggest that in the parable of the Lost Sheep, he is the shepherd, or in the parable of the Lost Coin, he is the woman seeking the coin (see Luke 15:3-10). But these parables in the main are not about the king Jesus; they are about the coming of the kingdom of God.

When Jesus referred to himself, he chose a phrase that we do not find in any of the parables: the "Son of Man." A close examination of his use of this term shows that, at least a good bit of the time, he was alluding to the story of that enigmatic "one like a son of man" in Dan. 7:13-14, the one who would be given a kingdom by God and would rule and judge the earth forever. This is especially clear in a saying such as that in Mark 14:62, but it is also in evidence in other Son of Man sayings, even in the Johannine tradition (see John 1:51; 3:13; 8:28). Jesus, it appears, exegeted his own career, purpose, existence, and importance out of various Old Testament stories, and I suggest that this influenced the various christological hymns that his earliest followers created after Easter. The link between the proclaimer and becoming the one proclaimed becomes clearer when we realize that Jesus also exegeted himself out of the story of Wisdom. This is especially clear in various places in Matthew 11, especially Matt. 11:19, where Jesus calls himself Wisdom directly. Then, too, we must point to a text such as Mark 12:35-37, where Jesus cleverly intimates in his interpretation of Psalm 110 that the Messiah is in fact not just David's son, but even greater than that, he is David's Lord; and in either case, he is alluding to himself here. Jesus himself, then, provided the catalyst for interpreting and exegeting his significance out of the prophetic and wisdom literature of early Judaism.

Jesus is not merely telling a story or carrying a story already in play forward to its logical climax. This becomes quite clear in, for example, his "yoke" saying (Matt. 11:28-30), where it is Jesus' yoke that his disciples are to take upon themselves with rigor and vigor, not the yoke of the Mosaic law. The Mosaic law, having been fulfilled in the Christ event, would not provide the ethical script for all Christian conduct going forward; rather, the law of Christ would do so. Of course, this would be confusing, because some elements of the Mosaic law would be renewed or reaffirmed or intensified by Christ—for example, the Great Commandment—and thus would be part of the binding contract known as the New Covenant. But Christ's followers would do these things because they were part of Christ's yoke, which he commanded his disciples to take up, called, paradoxically, a light burden. They would not merely continue the story of obedience (and disobedience) of Israel to Moses' law.

However subversive or paradoxical the later Christian message may have seemed or have been, and however much Christian preachers may have relied on Jesus' message, even his message about himself, they did not by and large follow Jesus' methodology of preaching. They told the story straight. Partly this had to do with ethos and social context, since most audiences outside Israel were not well schooled in Jewish sapiential literature. Partly also, however, this had to do with the change in symbolic universe from before to after the death and resurrection of Jesus. The proclaimer had become the universally proclaimed, and this because of the way his life turned out. Apparently, it was felt that the message about a crucified and risen Messiah was paradoxical enough in itself, and required enough explaining in itself, that an evangelistic religion needed to tell the story in a clear and straightforward way. While some of the themes of the "good news" song and part of the tune remained the same, the lyrics needed to be less enigmatic and more singularly focused on Jesus himself and his redemptive work.

It was the Frenchman Alfred Loisy who famously once said Jesus preached the kingdom, but it was the church that showed up. What Loisy did not really grasp, it would appear, is that what Jesus was preaching was the divine saving intervention of God through his own ministry and that of his disciples, and in this sense, it certainly did show up both during and after the life of the historical Jesus. Without the coming of the Son of Man, there would have been no good news of the kingdom, and without his death, resurrection, and return, there would have been no completion to the arc of the story Jesus believed he was living out of—the story in Daniel 7 of the one like a son of man who came down from heaven to rule forever on earth and to be worshipped by every tribe and tongue and people and nation. In Daniel 7, we see the harmonic convergence in the key elements in Jesus' message: kingdom of God and Son of Man, and it was, and is, and ever shall be only the latter that brings the former on earth, as it is in heaven.

I would like to close with a story. Shelly Jackson, a gifted contemporary writer, has set out on a remarkable project to enflesh a story of hers, quite literally. The story has 2,095 words and is entitled "Skin." She has asked for volunteers from all over the world to have exactly one word of the story tattooed on some readily visible part of their skin. Not only has she had some takers, she has had more takers than she needs to tell this story in the flesh, to incarnate this story on living human beings.

What if the message of Jesus can only be truly and fully understood not only when it is set in the larger context of Jesus' own narrative thought world, but when it is incarnated in us, and only together as a living group can we make sense of it, with each one of us having but one piece of the puzzle to contribute to that understanding of the story? What if the message of Jesus can only be understood and believed when it is experienced and lived out in *koinonia*, in community, in love, in self-sacrifice, in service to others? I suspect that since Hurricane Katrina, those of you who live in New Orleans and have participated in the recovery efforts may well have gotten a glimpse of how true that is. We are not, or at least ought not to be, merely witnesses as the saints go marching in. Rather, we have or should become part of "that number," part of the Grand Narrative, a story in which we become what we admire, we become like the one we emulate, and so when the story is lived out through us, we come to understand and believe in the Son of Man and his kingdom, and so reflect his indelible image, renewed in us.

Dialogue

Witherington: I completely agree with you about that; if you want to call him a nonviolent revolutionary, I'm good with that. But the question is, what is he fighting against? He's not mainly fighting against the Roman Empire.

He knew the stories in Daniel. Beastly empires come, and beastly empires go, and the Son of Man is the one who replaces all those inhuman and inhumane empires. He's not so much an eschatologist that he believes he's bringing the final, human empire. And the best way to do that is by doing the positive thing of rescuing the perishing. So I don't think the focus is one eye on Rome and . . . I think the focus is on rescuing the least, the last, and the lost, etc. If that has implications for the Roman Empire, so be it.

Crossan: I think that is right. Jesus has a positive vision. (I'll get to Daniel 7 in a minute.) Jesus definitely, absolutely—I'm embarrassed to have to say it—has a positive vision. It is not as if he is just against Rome, and if Rome went away, everything would be fine. But from the time of the Exodus, that positive vision has been against empire—every time you find an empire mentioned right up to Daniel—Egyptians, Assyrians, and the whole dreary line. The Romans are the last, and empires are getting stronger. Empires are not getting weaker; they are getting stronger. So I think it would be profoundly naive of Jesus, since he emphatically has a positive vision and knows what happened to John the Baptist, not to recognize the danger of his own mission. The Baptist also had a positive vision; he wasn't just against Antipas. But Antipas knew he needed to be executed, so somehow his positive vision is against a positive alternative.

Witherington: I guess the other thing that struck me is that I don't want to marginalize or neglect the evidence of Roman presence in Galilee or anywhere else. I don't think that that's all about what day-to-day Jewish life was like in those places. Whether you go to Yodfat or go to the new synagogue in Migdal, they were getting on with their own positive Jewish religious life. It was profoundly religious, and you know that the evidence of an impressive temple domination system that's sort of taken over the land, or you've got these large estate owners who have wrung everybody dry—I just don't hear that in Jesus' parables very much. I think there's something to that with Herod Antipas, but I don't really think it's the heart of the matter.

Crossan: In the 150 years from, say, the death of Herod, there were four violent revolts against the Romans—three in the Jewish homeland and one across North Africa. In that same period, there were at least four major nonviolent resistance movements: I am thinking of Judas the Galilean in the time of the census; I am thinking of the disputes with Pilate, about the iconic standards and the aqueduct expenses, probably around 26 CE; and I'm thinking of what Philo and Josephus tell us about Caligula's statue and the nonviolent resistance of tens of thousands of devout Jews. So both violent resistance and nonviolent resistance were going on before, during, and after Jesus, at least up to ad 41. I don't think everyone was quietly going about business as usual.

Another important matter is that, about the time Jesus was born, a legion was burning down the nearby city of Sepphoris, according to Josephus. I am here using some presuppositions from my own Irish tradition, that when the imperial forces—legions or dragoons—have been in your neighborhood, your little villages remember it for several generations. I cannot imagine that Jesus, growing up in Nazareth, would not find the day the Romans destroyed Sepphoris to be a major topic of conversation in his young life. I cannot imagine it!

Witherington: Jesus never mentioned Sepphoris or Tiberius whatsoever. I'm not saying that the presence isn't there; I'm not saying that over a cup of gruel or whatever they were eating, they might not have discussed these matters. I'm certainly not saying that there were no Jewish Zealots. I'm saying that the Zealot party didn't represent the majority of Jews. They were one part of Judaism, and it's not clear to me that most Jews were in sympathy with all of the Zealots, or at least with their violent tactics. How do we explain that the city of Jerusalem goes from 50,000 to 500,000 during pilgrim season, and they're involved in the temple at length? These folks are not like the Qumranites. They think that it's OK; the temple may not be perfect, and the rulers may be bad, but how's that different from America now? The political system may be somewhat broken, but they're getting on with their religion, and that has everything to do with celebrating Passover and the other feasts, and for them, this is a positive thing.

Crossan: I am not talking about either the temple authorities or the Zealots. I am talking about ordinary everyday life, and I think actually that the first century in the Jewish homeland was a pressure cooker. Of course they went about their life—people do that even in the most horrible situations we can imagine—but to leave out the whole Roman presence just doesn't make sense. Let me put it this way: If Jesus had lived, did everything we know he did, and just died in his own bed, he must have been talking only about the interior life, because Rome is not paying attention, no one is bothered by it. If Rome ignored Jesus, then his message can't have to do with who controlled the earth. So I am, I suppose, starting Jesus' life with the destruction of Sepphoris in 4 CE, and if I took that out, I could easily be persuaded the Romans were just background and nobody was paying attention.

Witherington: I think the issue is getting the balance right and getting the tensions right. I have no hesitation saying that Jesus was crucified by the Romans. They are responsible for his death, and why that didn't spring up in Christianity later as a type of anti-Italianism, I don't know. But Jesus was not crucified by Jews, and so it is certainly the case then that the question becomes why? Jesus either made, or they made for him, some messianic claims, and he didn't reject those messianic claims. This was sure to look like treason to a frustrated Pilate, who was an anti-Semite anyway. So maybe he didn't want to do it during the Passover season, but he certainly did. He was ruthless enough to have done it at any point really. So, yes, there is absolutely a clash between Jesus and his kingdom, which is not of this world, and Pilate, who's all about kingdom in this world. There is no doubt about that, but I don't see that as either characterizing or defining the teaching and message of Jesus over and over again. Nor do I think he mainly defines kingdom over against the Roman Empire. I think he defines it in light of his understanding of the sacred Scriptures.

Crossan: But I would simply say that Jesus' life focused Scripture against empire. Let me go back to Daniel and emphasize what was mentioned in Daniel 7. You know as well as I do that Daniel 7 starts off with those "beastly" empires. We really get that: the Babylonians, Medes, Persians, Macedonians (they don't have a beast for Alexander—he's just totally "different"—no feral beast is adequate to represent the horrors of Alexander's war machine), and Syrians. But they are all judged by God in heaven, and for me, that means that imperialism itself is condemned. And then you get the Son of Man to whom the kingdom of God is given to bring it down to earth. I would precisely take Daniel 7, if I'm looking for a text, as a major matrix—Daniel 7, and then of course Mark, when Mark talks about the Son of Man being already on earth. I don't know how Mark could possibly say that unless he is thinking that the kingdom of God is already here as well. So not everything depends on how you translate the Greek of "has come near" in Mark 1:15. If the Son of Man is already on earth, the kingdom of God is already here.

Witherington: I agree.

Crossan: But the empires are there, too. I don't want to leave out one or the other.

Witherington: Well, OK, I'm all right with that, but it seems to me that one of the issues here is a profoundly theological issue: In what sense did an early Jew like Jesus believe in the sovereignty of God? It seems to me that if Jesus is not a Zealot, if he's a nonviolent revolutionary, then he believes that God can work all things together for good. So how is he going to get on with the project of bringing the kingdom on earth? He is going to gather disciples, he is going to teach them, he is going to present a positive message, and he's going to go forward that way. And he's not going to spend most of his time worrying about the Roman Empire or critiquing it. He's going to be getting on with the positive task of ministry at hand because he believes that it's in God's hands.

I'm not talking about somebody who's withdrawn to a monastery in order simply to be pious. I believe there are absolutely social implications to what Jesus says—radical social implications to some of things he says. No question. It is not just about theology. It's about praxis, but the praxis that he's enunciating and that they carried over the divide of Golgotha into the early church, looks very much like what the early Christians were doing in Jerusalem, according to Acts 3 and 4 and 5 and 6: they were a movement wishing to proclaim the Jewish Messiah first to Jews, then to others, and they believed that way to change the world.

Crossan: I get nervous about terms like *social implications*, because I think the core issue is, to whom does the earth belong? Any Roman would have said it belongs to us. If you like it in theological terms, they might say, our Jupiter took it from your Yahweh, and it's still ours. But what if you refuse that imperial claim and actually believe that the earth belongs to God and the Land of Israel belongs to God? But of course, for a Josephus, it's no problem at all. It's not the slightest problem that the Romans are in charge of the world—under God. But if you actually take the biblical God seriously, then it creates this issue for you: Who's in charge of the world, and how should it be run? I don't want to talk about social implications; I want to talk about God and God's world.

Witherington: You know I would not want to paint an image of Jesus as sort of a Jewish version of the Amish: let's withdraw from the world and create our own little pious, glorious anachronism and call it good. No. I don't think that's what Jesus is about, nor do I think Dick Horsley is right that Jesus was running around creating little base camps all over Galilee for you to have a sort of ferment that would be like yeast and to create a society that would be anti-Roman. I don't see him doing that either, so it's hard to get how we can say that there were always social dimensions for the teaching of Jesus, rather than social implications to the teaching of Jesus. The question is what kind?

Crossan: I suppose my problem is that we've always talked as if there were a social gospel over here . . .

Witherington: Right.

Crossan: . . . but there is some kind of other gospel over there.

Witherington: Right.

Crossan: If there were the social gospel distinct from the other gospel, one could say, "Well, I do the other gospel." But what I am trying to say is that the good news, as I see it, is that the world belongs to God. I don't know any empire that really would accept that statement. If you say the church belongs to God, no problem. But, if you say that the world belongs to God, that immediately raises issues about how the world should be run. That's why I am trying not to put any sort of division between the "social dimensions" of Christianity and Christianity itself. I realize the language problem we have created by talking of a "social gospel" (I myself never use that redundancy). There is only one gospel, and it is, at once, religious and political, theological, social, and economic.

Witherington: My own spiritual forebearer, John Wesley, said there is no spiritual gospel without the social gospel, and equally, there is no social gospel without spiritual gospel. These are two parts of the one and singular gospel of Jesus, and I believe that wholeheartedly, and I certainly don't believe Jesus was so heavenly minded that he was no earthly good. I certainly don't believe that. So I guess where the conversation needs to go forward is, what's that look like? What is Jesus actually doing in terms of his praxis that it is a game changer in terms of the social milieu? Maybe you could ask it that way.

Crossan: I think that would get close to it. Because what we are really saying, as I see both of us, is that Jesus' vision is radical. Now, I would be horrified if somebody said that Jesus is simply against the Romans, as though if the Romans went away, then everything would be just fine.

Witherington: No.

Crossan: And then we'd have a Christian Empire or something. It simply isn't true. Rome happens to be the current incarnation of the alternative that the world belongs to imperial power. So Jesus is not just negatively against Rome, and again I couldn't agree with you more on that point. Jesus has a positive vision—if Rome weren't there, the positive vision would still be there—but it seems to me that a positive vision of divine sovereignty really is an affront to the normalcy of civilization (if I can use that term), because the normalcy of civilization has been imperial for at least six thousand years.

Witherington: What we're struggling against—and, Dom, I think you would probably agree with this—is the privatization of sin, making sin a purely individual matter that has nothing to do with the structures of society, nothing to do with governments, etc. The problem where we are—living in the most radically individualistic country in human history—is that we have this huge disconnect. For most people, when they hear the gospel of Jesus, they think it's all about Jesus and their pea-pickin' heart being saved. The truth of the matter is that, of course, that's part of what Jesus is dealing with, and it's certainly what one part or the other of the New Testament writers are dealing with, but it's about saving of the world, not just individuals, from sin. And that doesn't mean that there isn't a critique of the structures of society. That does mean that there are various things you're doing to work for change in society, but it's going to be done in a nonviolent way.

Crossan: I was asked about Satan. A lot of people think that evil is only individual and personal, but there are also satanic structures and systems that are sort of mysterious—you don't quite know where they come from. They are a line item in the budget that guarantees that six months from now, some people who don't vote are going to get very badly hurt. Those are satanic structures. I agree with you wholeheartedly that we have swung over to a privatization and individualization with both sin and Satan.

Witherington: And would you agree as well with this? I try to emphasize that although the gospel is a deeply personal matter, it's never a private matter. One of the problems in America with the separation of church and state is that we also have what I would call a postmodern situation that is increasingly gnostic, i.e., we have a separation of the spiritual from the physical, and the spiritual from the historical. And I see that as a very dangerous move either within or outside of Christianity in terms of spirituality.

Crossan: I cannot even imagine anyone in the biblical tradition thinking any of this is private. It is, of course, personal. But you cannot be personally holy and socially unholy. And you probably cannot be socially holy, I suspect, without being personally holy. So that's another matter we have to think about dialectically. They are two sides of a coin; you can distinguish them, but you can't separate them. I don't think it's possible to be personally holy in God's world without being socially holy.

Witherington: Yes, and that has to be a community project, not an individual crusade.

Crossan: Was there anything else that you heard from what I said?

Witherington: I missed the best bits with the jokes.

Crossan: I would say this goes back to William Herzog's book *Parables as Subversive Speech*.[13] The appropriate term for that would be what I call collaborative discourse. Parables are a way of luring people into thinking for themselves and to collaborating in participatory actions. It's probably a mouthful to say it, but parables are participatory pedagogy. Don't try that from the pulpit. But I think it goes with thinking about why Jesus would speak in parables. It seems to me to be inevitability correct if he is really talking about collaborative eschatology.

Witherington: But the other thing that we are facing, Dom, is anti-intellectualism. Many in the church see the intellectualizing of the faith as spirit-killing in various ways. One of the things we have to overcome is the idea that you have to check your brain at the door to talk about or believe these things that we're talking about and believing in. And so one of the important purposes of this dialogue is to make clear that we need both sound and keen minds thinking about these things as well as more parties to embrace the truth. That's something we have to overcome. My grandmother's advice to me when I went off to seminary—she had no more than an eighth-grade education—was "Don't be so open-minded that your brains fall out." *(Laughter)*

Crossan: There's a subtle difference between baptism and lobotomy, I suppose. *(Laughter)*

---

13. William R. Herzog II, *Parables as Subversive Speech: Jesus as Pedagogue of the Oppressed* (Louisville: Westminster John Knox, 1994).

Witherington: All right then.

Crossan: I think we are probably done.

Witherington: We are done.

Friday-Night Q&A

Amy-Jill Levine: Dom, I don't understand where justice fits into your eschatology. Where is justice for all the others, the others who were crucified but didn't come back? Where is the justice for the mothers whose babies were killed by those soldiers? Do you envision some sort of sheep-and-goats model, or is justice simply the hope that Rome doesn't win in the end?

And Ben, what exactly is your earthly ethics? You talked about various ways you worked with society. You talked about Jesus being radical, but I don't see exactly what that looks like. If it is love of God and love of neighbor, we already got that in Leviticus. If it is Jesus giving his life as sacrifice, good—but how exactly does that transform Christian life in terms of things like family structures or a debt economy or land ownership? What does it look like on the ground?

So Dom, eschatological justice; Ben, earthly ethics.

Crossan: I am profoundly impressed by Eastern Christianity's vision of the resurrection, which does not simply show Jesus coming out of the tomb *alone*, as we do in the Western tradition. I think that an individual resurrection of Jesus could be called, by any Jew in the first century, nepotism or filiotism—God taking care only of God's own Messiah or Son. They would ask exactly this question: Jesus is not the first Jew, nor will he be the last Jew, to die on a Roman cross, so where is God's justice for them? I think that the Jewish vision of communal or corporate resurrection is better preserved within the Eastern Christian tradition, where Jesus is coming out with all the just behind him—especially Adam and Eve, but also Abel, the first martyr of the Old Testament, and John the Baptist, the first martyr of the New Testament.

I cannot, by the way, take that vision literally. I wish it could be taken literally. But I think what it means is that when we finally talk about divine justice for the future, we have to have a cosmic peace-and-reconciliation commission for the past. That is how I would describe what I call the Eastern resurrection tradition, which is much closer, I think, to Judaism's vision of resurrection than our Western one. So yes, they will die; their names we will not know. But if we ever speak of justice for the future, we will have to admit injustice of the past. We can't expect God to be just for the future but not for the past.

Witherington: I would say I do believe in the justice that is coming in the future with the resurrection of the dead in the body when Jesus returns. And if justice is not done and seen to be done on the earth, then it is not done. And it will be done. So I just add that as a footnote.

To AJ's question to me, my answer would be, among other things, that the earth is the Lord's and the fullness thereof. What that means to me is that none of us are owners. We are all stewards. And what that means—this cuts equally well against communism and capitalism, frankly, or socialism, take your pick—is that God is the owner of it all. We didn't bring it with us. And even if you are buried with your pink Cadillac, you can't take it with you. The truth is that we are simply stewards of God's property. For me, that is profoundly important. That affects the way I do my budget, I spend my money, etc. And that is far more than a theology of tithing. It belongs to God, and we have to take that very seriously.

Darrell Bock: I want to put on the table two ideas to get into the conversation you all are having. And two elements are the Great Commandment and the New Covenant. And what the New Covenant gives us is forgiveness, which points to acceptance, and enablement, which points to the Spirit. So I want you to comment on this statement in putting this all together: Jesus goes for the heart to form a different kind of community that he calls "kingdom," that needs Spirit in order to function, that relates people to one another in love, which subsumes justice, in order to bring peace to the world. Or if I can say this with a Southern accent, y'all need to relate better to God so y'all can love each other better, and we will all have a better world, and God will be honored. So Spirit and Great Commandment.

Crossan: What I would say, Darrell, is that I would want to know and be clear on what Spirit I am dealing with.

Bock: The Holy Spirit.

Crossan: Holy Spirit, right. But what makes the Holy Spirit holy, as far as I am concerned, is that it is nonviolent. I don't want the spirit of a violent

God. I really don't; I prefer not to have it. On the one hand, I do not think we can have justice on earth—because it is far too radical for us—without the Holy Spirit. But for me, that is the Spirit of the nonviolent God. I don't think it is holy if it is the Spirit of a violent God, because then we are back again with the standard imperial program of religion, war, victory, peace. The alternative for Rome's empire is God's kingdom, and its program is religion, nonviolence, justice, peace. But you still use the word *kingdom*. That is the word we can't get around.

Of course, Jesus says to love God and love your neighbor—I think, historically, yes, but let me put it this way: if you think of a human being as a body and soul, when they are separated, you get a corpse. You've separated justice and love. And I think justice is the flesh of love, and love is the spirit of justice. You can distinguish them, but I don't think you can separate them. So I always want to know what's the content of this love. I think the content of the love is justice, but I don't think you can get the one without the other. They strike me as two sides of the same coin. You can distinguish them, but if you split the coin, you don't get two coins, you get neither. So I want justice as the spirit of love.

Witherington: I just want to make a distinction here: Justice is when you get what you deserve. Mercy is when you don't get what you deserve. And grace is when you get what you don't deserve. Honestly, at the end of the day, even though there are lots of reasons to cry for justice, and there is a righteous anger that deserves to be heard—no question about that—there are several sides to justice. If it is true that all have sinned and fallen short of the glory of God, then it's important that what the Bible says about God be recognized, which is "Justice is mine, I will repay. Vengeance is mine, I will repay."

I think the need, Darrell, is to focus on the forgiveness side of this. I am so struck by the way it is presented in Matthew, when Peter says, "Lord, should I forgive my neighbors seven times when they sin against me?" And Jesus says, "Not seven times, but seven times seventy" (that's probably how the text reads). What is striking to me about that is that it is the reverse of what Genesis says Lamech said. Lamech said, "I am going to take vengeance seven times seventy." Jesus is deliberately reversing the polarity and saying we are going to forgive that much. I think Jesus' followers, including Paul, got that. Paul says, "Love keeps no record of wrongdoing." However hard it may be, forgiveness is at the heart of this gospel, and that's a game changer in itself.

Stephen Patterson: Dom and Ben, I would like to hear you both speak a bit about the social location of the historical Jesus. I am rather biblical in my view of his social location. That means I take him as a peasant who was a handworker, which in my estimation places him fairly low on the social food chain. It means that he has a fairly limited worldview. It means that he has no access to education. You kind of see where I am going with this.

Dom, how do you imagine Jesus as socially located in such a way that he can engage questions of empire? And at what level does he engage the whole question? He doesn't have a Virgil's understanding of the empire and how it works. He has never been to Rome. He doesn't know what the senate is. He probably has very little understanding of the Roman army. What does he understand about the empire, given his social location?

And Ben, for you, the social location of Jesus will dictate what we can imagine him as able to do in terms of engaging the tradition. I think, perhaps, Matthew has Lamech in his head. I'm not sure Jesus does. So how do you imagine him with cultural resources where you could propose the kind of engagement with the tradition that you want to propose?

Witherington: I'll start this time. I would disagree with you. I don't think it is accurate or adequate to call Jesus a peasant. I certainly don't think he was illiterate. I agree that he was a manual worker. *Tektōn* has various possible meanings. I would be very surprised if he was a highly impoverished one or that his family was, considering there was a boomtown being built right over the back hill from where he lived called Sepphoris. So I am not convinced by the illiterate-peasant model of Jesus. I think he was deeply steeped in the Scriptures. I think he could read the Hebrew text. I don't think our modern class system helps us very much in analyzing this. There wasn't an equivalent of a middle class in antiquity. There was basically the überwealthy, the 2 to 5 percent, and then there was everyone else. There was gradient scale all the way down to day labor and poverty.

I don't think we are really helped by the analysis getting at Jesus' social location. I am not like a prosperity preacher who teaches Jesus was wealthy. Foxes have holes, and birds have nests, and Jesus has nowhere to lay his head, he says while on the road. But at the same time, I don't think the category of peasant helps us at all. And I don't think it is historically accurate.

Crossan: We would disagree on that. I don't choose "peasant" to make any other point than that is what I think Jesus was. I found it horrifying that some people thought I was saying he was stupid. I thought we had learned that in Vietnam; those peasants weren't stupid. Let me take the Greek word *tektōn* (Mark 6:3), usually translated as "carpenter." When Mark uses it for Jesus' social location, I am very impressed by the fact that Matt. 13:35 changes Mark—and I think *changes* is the right word—to say that it is his father who is a *tektōn* but Luke 4:22 omits that term completely, for either father or son. When Matthew and Luke see something in Mark that embarrasses them—for example, when James and John want first places in the kingdom (Mark 10:35-37)—Matt. 20:20-21 says that it was their mother who requested it for them, and Luke leaves out the whole incident. Similarly, here, I think they are embarrassed by Mark calling Jesus a *tektōn*. A modern translation of *tektōn* that will give us some of its ancient connotation would be a laborer. I think *carpenter* doesn't help.

In one sense, I say that not to prove anything. I don't think that makes him stupid or any term like that. I think it is just the accurate word. In terms of how Jesus knows the Romans, I repeat that it is vitally important that at the time Jesus was born, around the death of Herod the Great, two Roman legions come south from Antioch in Syria to help a third Roman legion that got itself in trouble in Jerusalem. That's three Roman legions coming into the Jewish homeland. When they came, they came not just defensively but to teach rebels an imperial lesson: we won't come back for a couple of generations, and won't have to. They came in 4 BCE, 66 CE, and 132 CE. Count the generations. There was a Roman legion in Jesus' backyard about the time he was born. Now, we know what happens to villages when the legions come through. They live off the land. Any male who is not hidden securely will be killed, any female raped, any child enslaved. Now, I hope—and there is some evidence—that many people in Galilee had hiding places.

I cannot imagine that, throughout the life of Jesus, the day the Romans came was not a major topic of maybe story, legend, and everything else in his village. And I do admit completely my biases in that, because that is the way the Irish handled it when the Dragoons came. I could be wrong, but I think it is a valid opinion. It was the biggest thing in their life. How could he not know all about the Romans? And how could he not wonder where God was that day?

Witherington: Just a footnote to that: I would say that the lexicographical evidence about *tektōn* ranges from a worker in stone to a carpenter. It's somebody who has a skilled trade. So I think the evidence is pretty clear about that; we're not talking about a day laborer. There's different language to be used for that, whether we're talking about Hebrew or Aramaic or Greek. And that's not what Jesus is called, and so I think we're talking about something else. We're talking about either a carpenter or stoneworker.

Q: If Jesus was not only a man but also divine as he claims to be in the Gospels, how would that affect your matrix of the message of Jesus, which seems to paint Jesus as no more than a prophet who is reacting against his culture and circumstances which he cannot predict?

Crossan: That would not be my image. Jesus lives in a world where, whether we like it or not, it was possible for some human beings who had done some major, extraordinary, or transcendental service for the human race—and thereby manifested the character of divinity—to be considered divine. I repeat: certain human beings could be considered divine. A divine title was not given unless you had done something extraordinary for the human race or the local human race that was making the statement. Therefore, Caesar Augustus, having brought peace after twenty years of savage civil war, was considered divine. He was, of course, a human being. And the Romans were never imprudent enough to call a council at Nicaea to figure out how he could be both human and divine at the same time. They would have said, "We will not submit Roman imperial theology to Greek philosophy. We will explain it to the Greeks, if they have trouble understanding imperial divinity, with the legions."

I have no problem whatsoever with saying Jesus was absolutely human and the claim that he was divine is first-century language saying this person has done something of extraordinary or transcendental importance for the human race and thereby manifested the very character of divinity itself. And when the language then is precisely point-counterpoint with the language of Roman imperial theology, they are saying that the extraordinary thing this person (Christ) has done is the opposite of what that person (Caesar) has done. That's the language of the first century, whether we like or not. We might not use that language; they did. That was their language to make the claim that this is an incarnation of something extraordinary and therefore revelatory of divinity itself.

Q: Both of you made statements along the lines of "the world belongs to God," but the Genesis account is the world was stolen from God, almost like a kind of act of violence on the part of Adam and Eve—and Satan. It is interesting that the Jews chafed under the Roman Empire. The Messiah was supposed to overthrow the tyrannical powers of this world and establish a kingdom of peace and justice and righteousness. And Jesus obviously had the power. He told Peter he had twelve legions of angels at his disposal; that's a lot of killing power. I don't know if I agree with both of you on this, I don't know if you have a proper perspective on God's violence. Physical death is an act of violence; everybody in the room is under the violence of God, the curse of death. The kingdom itself in Revelation is ushered in through an act of violence. The Battle of Armageddon is a violent overthrow of Satan and the Antichrist. You have to resist an evil kingdom with violence. Christ does. I think there is something missing here. Obviously there is a kingdom of justice and peace, yet Peter was on to something, but it wasn't that.

Witherington: First of all, there is no Battle of Armageddon in the book of Revelation. Jesus simply says, "You are toast," fire falls from heaven, it's over. Secondly, there is nobody worthy to open up a can of you-know-what on the world in the book of Revelation but Jesus. The book of Revelation is the most antimilitaristic book in the whole New Testament, because only the Lamb is worthy to judge the world. And furthermore, the three sets of seven judgments that come down in the book of Revelation are not intended to be punitive or final. They are intended to be disciplinary so that repentance will come. That is why there is a gap between the sixth and seventh one, for God to hear the prayers. So if you look at the book of Revelation carefully, it does say "'Vengeance is mine,' saith the Lord." "You keep your hands off the guns and the throttle, thank you very much, human beings." It's a book that says that God is sovereign, and justice is in God's hands, and in the end, God will resolve these matters. That's what the book of Revelation says.

Crossan: And we would disagree on this one. Because what I see through the entire Bible, the entire Bible, is two streams of tradition: a stream in which God is violent and the final solution of divine violence is that God will destroy the evildoers; and also a stream of a nonviolent God of distributive justice. They are both there through the entire Bible.

The criterion for the Bible for me is the historical Jesus, also known, theologically, as the incarnation of God. Which God do I see in Jesus? I can't find the violent God in Jesus. I see Christianity working zealously to get a violent God back into Jesus. But I don't find such a God revealed in Jesus. Pilate got that one right. The violent God is not in Jesus. So as far as I am concerned, Jesus is the norm for the Christian Bible. That is why God so loved the world he didn't send us a book; he sent us a person. We are not the people of the book; we are the people of the person. "What would Jesus do?" (WWJD) is the question, not "What does the Bible say?" (WDBS). So I would insist that Jesus is the norm of the Bible, including the violent God of Revelation.

And I find that God has a monopoly on violence in Revelation. I agree with you that we are not supposed to be violent. I think the *Left Behind* novels are wrong to think that God is violent and have humans join in God's final apocalyptic violence. I find the idea of a violent God far more terrifying, because then we humans have a mandate for violence. Why not?

Witherington: So we are in agreement that the *Left Behind* series should be left behind? *[Audience laughter]*

Crossan: Yes. But they could have never gotten divine violence out of the Sermon on the Mount, but they could out of the book of Revelation.

Witherington: This is why I've been writing novels to replace them.

Crossan: Good luck!

Q: Dr. Crossan, I have a question for you. Would you say that Jesus dying on the cross was a result of the success of his message or the failure of his message? What is your view of the cross? What did Jesus actually accomplish on the cross, in your opinion?

Crossan: Is it a result of his message? Yes, yes. Everything I see Jesus doing his last week in Jerusalem is trying *not* to get himself killed. He leaves the city every night and goes to Bethany. That makes sense. The crowd is on his side, as Mark says, day after day after day. The crowd is on his side. So he is not trying to get himself killed—which, by the way, was very easy to do in the first century. You didn't have to work very hard to get yourself killed. Just knock on Pilate's door and call him a name or something.

What the cross did was show that a life of nonviolence, even when confronted with the ultimate violence of execution, is possible. It's possible to live a life of nonviolence, even unto death, even death on a cross. And what the resurrection means for me is that Jesus was executed by Rome, vindicated by God, and therefore God and Rome are on a collision course again.

Witherington: For me, I think Mark 10:45 has it absolutely right: Jesus says, "I didn't come to be served but to serve and give my life as a ransom for the many." We see this also in the Pastoral Epistles, almost the same identical kind of saying. It seems to me that Jesus died not just because of his message or who he claimed to be; there was a purpose in his death that he intended.

Now, there is plenty of evidence from earlier Maccabean literature that martyriological deaths could be used positively when you gave your life for somebody. In some of the literature, it is even said to atone for sin. So it was not like this idea was foreign to early Judaism. It existed before the time of Jesus. I certainly think Jesus saw himself in that way. I think he exegeted himself out of something like Isaiah 53, as well as Daniel 7. The problem, the human dilemma, was a sin problem that had both spiritual and social dimensions to it, and he believed he was giving his life to deal with that problem.

Q: What limitations do you both see on historiographical conventions putting on historical reconstruction with the Gospels being Greco-Roman biography or Luke-Acts being historical monograph? How much can we discern between Jesus' own social location and say of Matthew, Mark, Luke, John's audience(s), etc.?

Crossan: I actually think a huge amount. My method is, first, to bracket as best I can everything in the gospel texts and try to write my thickest description of Antipas's Galilee and what Antipas wanted to do there in the 20s. My point is not to take material out of the gospel at the start. What is the thickest description of the Galilean 20s that can be reconstructed with the help of archeology, anthropology, sociology, or history, or anything I can find? It's as if I were making a film about Antipas.

Then, secondly, I want to see what really fits in there from those initially bracketed gospel texts. And, of course, the thing that comes out again and again is the kingdom. It's in the Lord's Prayer. So immediately that puts me back with this: Antipas is busy building the kingdom of Rome in Galilee, and Jesus is building an alternative kingdom of God in that same Galilee. So I think I now have, just by history alone, some idea of what Antipas and Jesus are about.

That is just about all you can do. I think there is more than enough data there. You can add layers onto that if you want to get into an argument about whether Jesus is illiterate or whether Jesus can read the Scriptures. Those actually are not going to change Jesus much for me. I am not convinced Jesus was literate. But I am convinced that sometimes an ability to *read* the Scriptures may confuse you about the simplicity of its major challenge: who owns the world? You may get so involved in exegesis or something that you miss the obvious meaning of the Scriptures. So I think the data that we have gives us a good glimpse of what Jesus was like and why a Roman governor would decide to execute him (because he was a revolutionary) but not round up his followers (because he was nonviolent). I think we can make sense out of that.

Witherington: I would just say that written history, at its very best, is only a tiny subset of what actually happened. And if we are looking at the difference between Jesus in his historical milieu and the gospel writers writing—I would say between 38 CE up to the end of the first century, later than the death of Jesus—then of course the social context, the social provenance are different. I happen to think that the Gospel of Matthew was written to Jewish Christians, possibly in Antioch or even in Capernaum. So that may be the closest social matrix written to a people of a particular audience that is close to Jesus'. But even so, time has moved on. Matthew is probably writing after the destruction of the temple in Jerusalem. So yes, we have to distinguish the social context in which the gospels were written from the social context of Jesus, and they are certainly different.

What is interesting to me about that is that even if Mark's Gospel was written in Rome largely for Gentile Christians, if we take that view for a moment, nonetheless, he still faithfully reports all sorts of Jewish disagreements and arguments about corban, and about Sabbath, about plucking grain, and about clean and unclean—arguments that may have not been relevant to the daily life of Gentile Christians in Rome in particular. So what that says to me is that these people cared about history. They wanted to know who the historical Jesus actually was, and they wanted to be faithful to this Jesus tradition that had been passed down to them. And thankfully, we then have evidence that will help us not only understand something about Matthew, Mark, Luke, and John but also about Jesus himself. Thank you very much.

Concluding Comments and Final Q&A

Crossan: Just to talk about something that we touched on a couple of times, and that's about presuppositions when you handle miracles. Objections tell me that I just don't believe in miracles, or I don't believe in the supernatural. Actually, I don't believe in the supernatural because to believe in the supernatural, you have to believe in the natural. And as soon as you believe in the natural, you've already lost to the post-Enlightenment experience. I don't believe in a world in which it is all natural but periodically there are divine interventions that we call the supernatural. That's not the way I accept it. The major issue for me is this: It's not that I live in a post-Enlightenment world, though I certainly do, and I do hope for a divine consistency that will keep the aerodynamics of Continental the same tomorrow as when I flew here

Wednesday. I really do. And we have to admit that. I trust physics to a certain extent, and I trust divine consistency even more.

But my point is this: I'm reading in a pre-Enlightenment world, where I do understand that everyone in this world takes it for granted that wonderful things—let me use that term instead of miraculous things—wonderful things can happen. They really do. So in that world, no one can really say to the other, "This is unique!" And nobody can say back, "This is impossible!" For example, if in this world, it shows on the coins—the silver denarii minted by Augustus for his adopted father—that Julius Caesar has ascended into heaven, I take it for granted that most people accepted that. I have no idea whether people took it literally or metaphorically, and neither does anyone else. We know that they took it functionally, they took it pragmatically, and they took seriously—and it would have been very unwise to suggest to Augustus, "You do know this is just a metaphor." I wouldn't advise that at all. When Paul said that Jesus has ascended into heaven (and I know the difference about his body, and I am not getting into that here), in a pre-Enlightenment world, nobody can say, "Paul, that's not possible!" They can't say that. They might say, "I don't believe your story, Paul." But they cannot say it's impossible. And neither really can Paul say it is unique. And they don't. What they really say is, "If Julius Caesar is up in heaven, what's he doing for us?" And the answer is, "He is taking very good care of the Roman Empire and his adopted son down here, Augustus, and that's why things are going so well." OK, if I accept that, the polite pre-Enlightenment answer about the miracles, the resurrection, and everything about Jesus is, to quote Amy-Jill, "So what?" It's not a polite pre-Enlightenment answer to tell Paul, "I just don't believe your story." To do so would be tacky. You might say, "OK, so what?" Which means, "What's Jesus going to do for me?"

So in the pre-Enlightenment world, as I look at these miracles, I have to do with integrity one of two things. I can either say I accept them all. I accept the Roman ones, I accept the Jewish ones, I accept the Christian ones, I accept them all. And then I can ask, "So what did they mean?" I can take them all literally. Or I can take them all metaphorically. But it seems to me to lack historical integrity, to say of the Roman data, "We just don't believe that. It's mythical," but when we come to the Christian data to say, "That's fact." I think that lacks historical credibility. You either take the miraculous conception of Caesar Augustus literally, and then you take Jesus' literally. If you take this metaphorically, then you take that metaphorically. And either way, they are in confrontation with one another. Metaphors can fight one another just as well as facts.

So what I am trying to do is understand a pre-Enlightenment world that takes wonderful or miraculous things as possible and understand them. And the proof of this is that when I read Justin Martyr in the middle of the second century, he never argues that this stuff, the pagan stories, couldn't happen. He might argue that it's just the devil at work, but that's still happening. So he can write that when we Christians say that Jesus is ascended into heaven, we say nothing different than what you claim for your emperors. Now, of course, he is going to claim we *do* say something different, because our Jesus is worth more than all your emperors rolled up into a ball, which will get him killed eventually. And when Celsus argues back against that, he cannot say and does not say, "Your stuff is impossible." He just says, "Your Jesus has never done anything worthwhile for the human race." So our arguments for impossibility and uniqueness are post-Enlightenment arguments and equally invalid on both sides. If you want to understand the way I approach, if you want to, what I ask for is either take all of these miracles literally and recognize they are still adversarial, or take them all metaphorically and they're still adversarial. But we shouldn't spend our time arguing that their stuff didn't happen and our stuff did. I think that lacks historically integrity.

Witherington: Now is the time for summing up . . .

Crossan: Yes, it is.

Witherington: The question it raises for me is, why does Plutarch say, "Nowadays, people don't really believe that the gods are gods?"

Crossan: I take it for granted that very, very intelligent and sophisticated philosophers may not have believed a lot of this stuff. But I would still say that you would not tell Caesar Augustus, "You are divine, your imperial highness, but that's just a metaphor." I would not advise that, and Livy doesn't do it.

Witherington: OK. What we have tried to do in this time that we've had together since yesterday may seem to some of you like an exercise in futility, like arguing over the number of angels on the head of a pin. But I would like to suggest to you that it's not that at all. First of all, the importance of this is that we are having a discourse and a dialogue, not a debate. We are having a conversation among people who disagree on various things. So this is not an exercise in futility; it's an exercise in fertility, in cross-fertilization, an attempt to mutually understand even when we have to agree to disagree. So there is great importance in all of this.

Secondly, in an age that is, in my view, increasingly postmodern and gnostic, the very fact that you have people taking with deadly earnest the concept of the historical Jesus and what he said and what he did is refreshing and not very much like what is out there in our culture. But it matters greatly for Christianity and for Judaism, because Judaism and Christianity, and for that matter Islam, are historical religions, religions for whom history matters. It's not just a substratum that matters, but the very essence of what is being claimed about some of these religions is indeed historical. So why we are having this discussion about what the historical Jesus said, what he meant, and what his message was—you need to understand that theology is not something over here, and history over here. What we have in the gospels, when we study Jesus, is theological history if you want to put it that way, or historical theology if you want to put it that way. But either way, they are intermeshed one with another. It's important for all of us to help each other to be enlightened about what the real significance of Jesus is and not simply presume that we know. Why is this important? In a Jesus-haunted culture that is biblically illiterate, anything can pass for knowledge of the historical Jesus. And that is a very dangerous place for our culture to be.

I want to give one illustration, and then I will quit. A long time ago, in 1969, I was riding in the mountains in North Carolina on the Blue Ridge Parkway with a friend in my father's old 1955 Chevrolet. Now, if you know anything about the Blue Ridge Parkway, you know there are no gas stations, there are no signs, there is a forty-five-mile-per-hour speed limit, it's like the Natchez Trace. And my clutch blew out, and as the Bible says, my countenance fell. *(Crossan chuckles.)* And we had to have the car pushed off the Blue Ridge Parkway, down an exit ramp, and to a Texaco station. It was 1969, Neil Armstrong had walked on the moon, all kinds of things seemed to be possible. So my friend and I, my high school friend Doug Harris, decided to hitchhike back to Highpoint, and we were immediately picked up by a really ancient-of-days kind of couple driving a 1948 Plymouth. They were both dressed in black, and they were deadly earnest, but they told us to get in the back of the car. We did.

The first thing that happened after we only got two miles down the road was that my friend Doug, who is a lawyer now, said, "So what did you think about Neil Armstrong's landing on the moon?" And the driver said, "That's all fake. That's a Hollywood stunt on TV. Never happened." Doug, not recognizing invincible ignorance when he saw it *(Crossan chuckling)*, wanted to argue. He said, "What are you talking about? Of course he landed on the moon. Didn't you see those fabulous pictures of the world twirling in space, the beautiful round orb?" And then the man got really angry and said, "The world ain't round either." Doug kept pressing the matter. I kept saying *(whispers)*, "Shut up, Doug! We need this ride." Doug said, "What makes you think the world's not round?" "It says in the book of Revelations," says the man (beware of anyone who begins a sentence, "It says in the Book of Revelations"—that's not the name of that book), "It says in the book of Revelations that the angels will stand at the four corners of the earth. Can't be round if it has four corners, now, can it, Mister?" Doug wasn't finished. "What do you mean it's not round and doesn't revolve?" The man said, "'Course it doesn't revolve. You ever walked out at night into your front yard and found yourself standing upside down? I think not."

Now, what was this man's problem with the book of Revelation? It wasn't that he took it seriously. It was that he took figurative language, theological language, as if it were cosmological language describing the shape of the earth. The metaphor meant that the angels would come from all points of the compass to gather the elect. That's what it meant. But he assumed it was teaching him cosmology and he needed to hold on to that for dear life. He was a flatlander. Yes, in 1969, back in the dawn of time when the earth was still cooling, there were still flatlanders in North Carolina.

Now here is my point: The truth of the matter is that faith should be seeking understanding—*fides quaerens intellectum*. History, real history, is not a threat to real faith. Real history will help us understand our faith. And if our posture toward the study of the message of Jesus, which we have looked at during this time, becomes faith seeking understanding, then we will want to hear as many bright minds as we can and tease our own minds into active thought, so that together we will better understand the message of Jesus. Thank you very much.

Q&A

Q: I have a singular curiosity I've tried to ask in three different ways, and I am also using the language of *matrix* because it seems to be the smart thing to do, not because I am directing the question at anybody. Are matrix and messiah mutually exclusive? Are the message of Jesus and man Jesus defined by the matrix, or is the matrix the context by which we best understand his message? Could any mere man with the right characteristics intersecting the same matrix at the same time generate the same impact as Jesus did on the world? And does that imply that if we wait long enough, we should expect something similar to happen again?

Crossan: I am too old to remember five questions. Let me be clear on the reason I use the word *matrix*: it is to insist on the interaction of background-foreground, context-text. I also like it because it comes from the root *mater*, the word for mother. That's a bonus. It's not a major reason, but it's a major bonus.

When I put that thing up in the video, I put up four points. The crosshairs of the matrix for me are the tradition, which is the context in which you grow up and everyone tells you this is the way that it is, and vision, which is the simply the paradigm shift, as one person or group swerves the tradition. But there are also and always time and place. Time and place are not negotiable in the matrix. You can't say, "Well, couldn't somebody else have said what Jesus said?" or, "Didn't Amos almost say exactly the same thing as Jesus said?" That's why my window of opportunity was there as well. And you only know a window of opportunity, sometimes, when you hear the sound of it closing.

Precisely in the Roman Empire, and precisely in the lull in the Jewish homeland between two great insurrections, there was a window of opportunity. That does not explain Jesus as if a window of opportunity could create you. It doesn't. But you can understand why in that window of opportunity, something happened. Really fast, think of Jesus in the year 20 CE. Go back about fifty years. That's about 30 bc. Herod is taking over his kingdom; I'd give Jesus ten minutes. Fifty years later, 70 CE, the Roman revenge is in full play; I'd give Jesus five minutes. Time and place could not be taken out.

It's like saying you could write a Mozart symphony. Yeah, but now you'd be copying, not creating. Basically, the matrix is destiny. You can call it providence. I have no problem with that. But in this time span, something can happen. And this applies to Paul just as well. In this time span, something happens. But without the time span, it would not happen.

Q: Dr. Crossan, thank you so very much for your time. In light of your view of Jesus being nonviolent, I would be interested in hearing your thoughts on his cleansing of the temple. He fashioned a whip and drove them out. Please, this is not a challenge. I want to know what you think.

Crossan: A lot of speakers have touched on this. First of all, it really isn't a cleansing. What is important for me is that it is a symbolic destruction of the temple for the reason that Jesus quotes, namely Jeremiah 7. Jeremiah is told by God that if people use the temple, that is worship, as a refuge from justice—it's a constant refrain of the prophets—God will destroy the temple. But you can't say that, and Jeremiah is almost put to death for it (Jeremiah 26). I understand what Jesus does as a symbolic destruction of the temple following and quoting Jeremiah 7. The whip that you mentioned is only in John, and it is only in John because it's only in John that the animals are driven out.

It's not a cleansing of the temple. There is nothing I can see that needs cleansing in the outer courts of the temple, but turning over the money changers closes down the fiscal basis of the temple. It's a demonstration. And if you think that is a twentieth-century word put back into the first, I can't do anything about it. There were demonstrations. Pharisees and their students went up and took the golden eagle off the temple, and it cost them their lives as martyrs. That's a demonstration. They didn't storm the temple with swords. The demonstration cost them their lives. And that's what Jesus was doing. That was a demonstration. Demonstrations are on the dangerous cusp where they are not just talking and they are not just violence, but they are very dangerous. Demonstrations always are very dangerous. They can turn violent with or without your control. So I don't find anything violent in my sense in there.

Witherington: I would agree with Dom about that. There seems to be a difference between the use of force and violence. If I have to, which I do, over in the apartments push hard on my door to get it open because it sticks because of the humidity, that's a use of force. But I don't think I did any violence to the door. I could use the movie disclaimer. No animals were harmed in the production of this cleansing of the temple.

What I do think about that scene, which is very interesting, is that it appears to have been a recent practice to sell animals and do the money changing in the Court of the Gentiles. This was a new activity sponsored, I suppose, by Caiaphas and Ananias during the time of Jesus. Jesus is not taking umbrage with something that has been going on forever and ever. He may be taking umbrage to something that was a fairly recent practice. And he thought it was not appropriate in that particular venue, so I think I basically agree with Dom about that.

Crossan: Let me insist on Jeremiah 7, because that is quoted there, about "the den of thieves." A den of thieves is not where thieves do their thieving. There is no anti-Semitism or anti-Judaism here; there's no hint that somehow the money changers are thieving. That's not the meaning of Jeremiah's quote.

The meaning of the Jeremiah quote is that you do your thieving out there, and you get back to your safe house. It's part of the standard prophetic warning: do not use worship as a refuge from justice.

Witherington: Right.

Q: My question has to do with something you brought up, Dr. Crossan. But I'd appreciate if both of you addressed it. You had mentioned something about miracles recently, that if you believed in miracles, you'd have to be open to believing in all Greco-Roman miracles and birth stories if you also believed in the New Testament miracles. I disagree with that. I think there is a methodology that we could use that would help us to get a better understanding of when to accept a miracle. I don't have to be vulnerable just because I believe in miracles that anything anyone ever claims would have to be a miracle. I think that there are two things in my research that have been helpful. First of all, is the miracle significantly different from other classifications of miracles that I wouldn't accept? And second of all, is it not what I would expect? For example, take the virginal conception: the virginal conception is different from, say, the miracle story of Augustus's birth with Apollo and his mother being impregnated through that. For example, what we find in Matthew involves a spirit, it is nonphysical, and it's with a virgin. Those three aspects are not found in the ancient literature, at least in my research. Second, it is a very Jewish story. It's not a story that Jews have particularly been interested in, because the closest thing . . .

Stewart: Do you have a question?

Q (continued): Yes. In other words, *1 Enoch* is all about Genesis 6 and angels coming in, and that's the explanation for evil in the world in *1 Enoch*. It's not a Jewish story that they would be attracted to, so what methodology should you use for determining the veracity of a miracle?

Crossan: What I understand that Matthew and Luke, with possibly others before them, meant by a virginal conception is this. In the Greco-Roman tradition of a human being predestined for greatness (you are quite right), there was intercourse between a god and a human being. And in the traditional Jewish story about the predestined child of extraordinary future, there was intercourse, but between aged and infertile parents—that, by the way, would be a greater miracle than virginal conception, because it would be certain—if two ninety-year-olds produce a child, that's checkable—that is a miracle. Virginal conceptions are very dangerous. You have to take somebody's word for it. I think what Christianity tried to do was, by using the virginal conception, to say this child is extraordinary against *both* the Greco-Roman matrix *and* the Jewish matrix of his own time. It's a claim for a unique type of conception. I think you are quite right.

Does that make it therefore anything more than a claim about the extraordinary future of Jesus or, to retroject it, of his extraordinary past? I don't think you get a methodology to say this one really happened because it is different from all the others. I don't think that gets you there.

Witherington: As to critical discernment in regard to miracles, I do think there are criteria by which you can evaluate miracles ancient or modern, and they should be applied. On this one, I don't agree with Dom that just because we accept that there are miracles in the gospels, ergo we must accept that these other stories are also miracles. Now, what we can say is that there are claims about miracles in both of these sources, and that they both have to be evaluated critically to see whether we think the claims are valid or not. So that's one thing.

I am not even going to begin to say that there were no miracles that happened outside the ministry of Jesus, because, of course, even in the book of Acts, we hear of others doing miracles, and it wouldn't surprise me if there weren't miracles outside of the biblical tradition as well. So they all have to be critically evaluated.

In regard to the virginal conception, in particular, I don't think this can be called an example of prophecy historicized. Because, frankly, I don't think that Isa. 7:14 predicts—or was understood to predict in early Judaism—exactly what happened in the life of Mary. Now, what seems to be the case is that something unexpected and unusual happened in the life of Mary and Jesus' family, and then the early Christians said, "It has to be in the Old Testament somewhere; we need to find a text that helps us understand this." So what happened was that the history in the life of Mary forced a reevaluation of a prophecy like Isa. 7:14. It's not that the story was created to fit a preexisting notion of a virginal conception, because the Hebrew of Isa. 7:14 does not need to read that way at all. It's just a young woman of marriageable age conceives and gives birth to a child that is going to be a king. That's a whole different ball game. That's what I would want to say about that.

But the crucial thing is critical analysis of stories and whether there are criteria to apply to whether this could be a genuine miracle or not—whether it is in or outside the biblical tradition.

Stewart: Unfortunately, our time is up. Thank you to all of you who came to hear our speakers discuss the message of Jesus. Thanks especially to all of our speakers for presenting stimulating papers. Thanks especially to Dom and Ben for their warm spirit and enlightening dialogue. God bless you all.

2

The Place of Jewish Scripture in Jesus' Teaching

Craig A. Evans

The focus of Jesus' teaching was not on himself but on the rule of God (i.e., the "kingdom of God") and on the redemption of Israel, a redemption with profound implications for all of humanity. This proclamation was based on the earlier proclamation of God's rule that we see in the prophet Isaiah, especially in chapters 40, 52, and 61. Accordingly, we must assess the place of Jewish Scripture in Jesus' teaching if we are to answer the question, What did Jesus really teach?

I begin where most of our participants will probably begin: with Jesus' proclamation of the rule of God and the scriptural roots of this proclamation. I shall then inquire into how Jesus understood and applied the Jewish Scriptures. Did he understand and apply the Scriptures pretty much the way his contemporaries did? Was his understanding and application so similar to that of the church that followed him that we really cannot distinguish his use of the Scriptures from the church's use? Finally, I shall inquire into the larger and more controversial question of Jesus' relationship with the Judaism of his day, including the major tenets of Jewish faith and practice.

JESUS' PROCLAMATION OF THE RULE OF GOD

The fundamental element of Jesus' teaching was his proclamation of the reign (or kingdom) of God (Mark 1:14-15), by which he meant the powerful presence of God.[1] This proclamation reflected the vocabulary and imagery of the scroll of Isaiah, especially as it was emerging in the Aramaic-speaking synagogue. Passages such as Isa. 40:9 ("herald of good news . . . say to the cities of Judah, 'Behold your God!'" [RSV]) and 52:7 ("who brings good news . . .

who publishes salvation, who says to Zion, 'Your God reigns!'"), which in the Aramaic are paraphrased, "The kingdom of your God is revealed," provide the scriptural backdrop to Jesus' proclamation, while Isa. 61:1-2 ("The Spirit of the Lord God is upon me, because the Lord has anointed me to bring good news") identifies proclamation of the good news of God's reign as the specific task of the Lord's anointed one (or messiah). These prophetic passages provided the matrix out of which Jesus formulated the essence of his proclamation.

Appealing to these very passages, Jesus reassures an imprisoned and discouraged John the Baptist that he is indeed the "one who is to come," for "the blind receive their sight and the lame walk, lepers are cleansed and the deaf hear, and the dead are raised up, and the poor have good news preached to them" (Matt. 11:5 = Luke 7:22). The messianic and eschatological significance of the collocation of these words and phrases from Isaiah has been clarified by one of the scrolls from Qumran (viz., 4Q521), which appeals to these prophecies in the context of the appearance of God's messiah, "whom heaven and earth will obey."

Like other Jewish teachers of his day, Jesus is called "rabbi" or teacher (Mark 4:38; 5:35; 9:17; 10:17; 12:14, 19). He teaches as opportunities afford themselves, seated in the presence of his disciples and crowds, whether in the outdoors or in someone's home (Matt. 5:1; Mark 9:35; 12:41; Luke 5:3). Other times, he teaches in more formal settings, such as in the synagogue (Mark 1:21; 6:2; Luke 4:20). Although not a professional scholar, Jesus appealed to and interpreted Scripture in an ad hoc, experiential fashion, often reflecting the wording and interpretation of the Aramaic paraphrase (e.g., Isa. 6:9-10 in Mark 4:12; Hos. 6:2 in Mark 8:31; Zech. 14:20-21 in Mark 11:16; Jer. 7:11 in Mark 11:17; Isa. 5:1-7 in Mark 12:1-9; Ps. 118:22 in Mark 12:10-11).[2]

As Jesus understood it, the arrival of the reign of God entailed an escalation in the war between God and Satan. We are told that Satan has fallen from heaven (Luke 10:18), that his allies are now being trodden upon by Jesus' followers (Luke 10:19-20), and that Satan himself has been bound by the

---

1. For helpful studies that provide good coverage of the Old Testament backdrop to Jesus' preaching of the kingdom, see George R. Beasley-Murray, *Jesus and the Kingdom of God* (Grand Rapids: Eerdmans, 1986); M. Reiser, *Jesus and Judgment: The Eschatological Proclamation in Its Jewish Context* (Minneapolis: Fortress Press, 1997).

2. On Jesus and the Aramaic tradition, see Bruce Chilton, "Regnum Dei Deus est," in *The Historical Jesus in Recent Research*, ed. J. D. G. Dunn and S. McKnight, 115–22, Sources for Biblical and Theological Study 10 (Winona Lake, IN: Eisenbrauns, 2005); idem, "Targum, Jesus, and the Gospels," in *The Historical Jesus in Context*, ed. A.-J. Levine, D. C. Allison Jr., and J. D. Crossan, 238–55, Princeton Readings in Religion (Princeton: Princeton University Press, 2006).

"stronger" Jesus (Mark 3:27; cf. 1:7), who is now liberating those held captive by unclean spirits (Mark 3:27; Luke 13:16).

It is for this reason that Jesus saw his ministry of exorcism as tangible evidence of the reality of the presence of God's reign (Luke 11:20; "But if it is by the finger of God that I cast out demons, then the kingdom of God has come upon you") and that his contemporaries, who did not separate Jesus' verbal teaching from his acts of power, referred to his exorcisms as "teaching" (Mark 1:22, 27).[3]

The corollary of the proclamation of the reign of God was the hope for the redemption and restoration of Israel. We find this in the call throughout Israel to repent (Mark 1:15; 6:12; Matt. 11:21 = Luke 10:13), in the appointment of the Twelve and their commission to proclaim the kingdom and to engage in exorcism (Mark 3:14; 6:7), and in the promise that when the kingdom comes in its fullness, the Twelve will rule over the twelve tribes of Israel (Matt. 19:28; Luke 22:28-30).

Not only does Jesus proclaim the reign of God, he proclaims the compassion and goodness of God. Jesus teaches that God is ready and eager to receive repentant sinners (Luke 15:11-32), that he is a God who answers prayer (Matt. 6:5-13; Luke 18:1-7), rewards faithfulness (Matt. 24:45 = Luke 12:42), and expects his people to be, as he is, compassionate (Luke 6:36; 10:37) and forgiving (Matt. 6:12-15; 18:21-22). Above all, God is a personal God who knows humanity's needs, even minute details (Matt. 6:25-34; 10:30 = Luke 12:7). Therefore, people are to have faith in God (Mark 2:5; 4:40; 5:34, 36; 9:24; 10:52; 11:22, 24; Luke 7:50).

Jesus is also a teacher of wisdom and ethics, all of which must be understood in light of the coming judgment. Like Dame Wisdom herself, Jesus urges his hearers to come to him and to take upon themselves his yoke (Matt. 11:28-30; cf. Sir. 51:23-27; *m. Ber.* 2:2), even claiming that someone greater than Solomon is present (Matt. 12:42 = Luke 11:31). Jesus urges humility, warning that those who exalt themselves will be humbled, while those who humble themselves will be exalted (Mark 9:35; Luke 14:11). Jesus expects his followers to help the poor (Mark 10:21; Luke 14:13) and not assume that the sick and downtrodden are worse sinners than anyone else (Mark 2:17; Luke 13:1-5; 16:19-31; John 9:1-3).

Jesus' eschatological teachings crystallized after entering Jerusalem. He warned of a coming fearful judgment, if God's message and messenger were not received. The temple has become fruitless, its purpose left unfulfilled (Mark

---

3. Graham H. Twelftree, *Jesus the Exorcist: A Contribution to the Study of the Historical Jesus*, WUNT 2.54 (Tübingen: Mohr [Siebeck], 1993).

11:11-23). The ruling priests, God's stewards over his temple and people, will lose their stewardship because of theft and murder (Mark 11:17; 12:1-12). Indeed, the days will come when Jerusalem will be besieged, her inhabitants will be dashed to the ground, and not a stone of the city will be left upon another (Luke 19:41-44). Even the beautiful temple complex will be completely demolished (Mark 13:1-2). These terrible events will be preceded by signs, but the final events will unfold so swiftly that few will be prepared and many will perish (Mark 13:3-37). Accordingly, Jesus warns his disciples to be alert and faithful (Mark 13:9, 23, 33, 35, 37).

How Did Jesus Understand and Apply the Scriptures of Israel?

Half a century ago, the great British New Testament scholar C. H. Dodd investigated the function of the Old Testament in the theology of the early Christian community. At the end of his study, he remarked, "This is a piece of genuinely creative thinking. Who was responsible for it? . . . Whose was the originating mind here?" Dodd believed that the creative approach to the Old Testament found in the gospels and elsewhere in the writings of the New Testament originated with Jesus himself.[4] In a study published two decades later, R. T. France agreed with Dodd, adding, "The source of the distinctive Christian use of the Old Testament was not the creative thinking of the primitive community, but that of its founder."[5]

In my opinion, the conclusions reached by Dodd and France are fully justified. Here I would like to explore one aspect of Jesus' creative use of Scripture. This aspect appears to be a deliberately subversive interpretation of Scripture. We may see this in Jesus' remarkable subversions of passages and themes from Daniel and Zechariah, as well as in cases involving legal materials. Because this was not a tendency in the early church, where proof-texting emphasized correspondence and agreement, not dissonance, we may have here an important point of entry into Jesus' understanding of Scripture and of his own mission.[6]

However, before I go any further, I should say something a bit more general about Jesus' interest in Scripture. Recently, it is been argued that Jesus himself had little interest in Scripture and rarely, if ever, quoted or referred to it. It has been argued that Scripture was of interest to early Christians but not to Jesus. Therefore, when we encounter passages in the Gospels where Jesus

---

4. C. H. Dodd, *According to the Scriptures: The Sub-Structure of New Testament Theology* (London: Nisbet, 1952), 109–10.

5. R. T. France, *Jesus and the Old Testament* (London: Tyndale, 1971), 226.

quotes or alludes to Scripture, we should think it is the early church that is speaking, not Jesus.

This view is very strange. Jesus was nothing, if not a teacher. A teacher of what? Everything that Jesus taught, from the rule of God to the Golden Rule, is rooted in Scripture. His disciples—"learners"—learned and passed on his teaching. Is it really plausible to think that Jesus' original teaching made little or no reference to Scripture and that this is what his disciples had to add to it? No, this really makes little sense. A far better and far simpler explanation is that the reason certain passages of Scripture became important to the early church, understood in a certain way, is that this is what Jesus the teacher taught and his disciples the learners learned and passed on to other believers. The creative genius behind early Christian thought is Jesus himself, not several anonymous figures.

According to the Synoptic Gospels, Jesus quotes or alludes to twenty-three of the thirty-six books of the Hebrew Bible (counting the books of Samuel, Kings, and Chronicles as three books, not six).[7] Jesus alludes to or quotes all five books of Moses, the three Major Prophets (Isaiah, Jeremiah, and Ezekiel), eight of the twelve Minor Prophets,[8] and five of the Writings.[9] In other words, Jesus quotes or alludes to *all* of the books of the Law, *most* of the Prophets, and *some* of the Writings.

According to the Synoptic Gospels, Jesus quotes or alludes to Deuteronomy some fifteen or sixteen times, Isaiah some forty times, and the Psalms some thirteen times. These appear to be his favorite books, though

---

6. I am invoking here a form of the criterion of dissimilarity. This criterion functions helpfully when used with caution and usually with positive application. The problem is in its negative application, by which whatever the gospels say Jesus said or did that is not dissimilar to Christian belief or Jewish thought must be rejected. We should assume that Jesus in fact did and said many things that other Jewish teachers said and did and that many things he taught his followers accepted without revision. The misuse of the criterion of dissimilarity has been subjected to trenchant criticism in recent years. For example, see Morna D. Hooker, "On Using the Wrong Tool," *Theology* 75 (1972): 570–81; Tom Holmén, "Doubts about Double Dissimilarity: Restructuring the Main Criterion of Jesus-of-History Research," in *Authenticating the Words of Jesus*, ed. C. A. Evans and B. Chilton, 47–80, NTTS 28/1 (Leiden: Brill, 1998).

7. See the helpful tabulation in France, *Jesus and the Old Testament*, 259–63. For a more recent investigation, see Bruce Chilton and Craig A. Evans, "Jesus and Israel's Scriptures," in *Studying the Historical Jesus: Evaluations of the State of Current Research*, ed. B. D. Chilton and C. A. Evans, 281–335, NTTS 19 (Leiden: Brill, 1994).

8. The Prophets quoted or alluded to by Jesus include Hosea, Joel, Amos, Jonah, Micah, Zephaniah, Zechariah, and Malachi. Omitted are Obadiah, Nahum, Habakkuk, and Haggai.

9. The Writings quoted or alluded to by Jesus include Psalms, Proverbs, Job, Daniel, and Chronicles. Omitted are Song of Solomon, Ruth, Lamentations, Ecclesiastes, Esther, Ezra, and Nehemiah.

Daniel and Zechariah seem to have been favorites also. Superficially, then, the "canon" of Jesus is pretty much what it was for most religiously observant Jews of his time,[10] including—and especially—the producers of the scrolls at Qumran.[11] Moreover, there is evidence that villages and synagogues in the time of Jesus did in fact possess biblical scrolls.[12]

The data that have been surveyed are more easily explained in reference to a literate Jesus, a Jesus who could read Scripture, could paraphrase and interpret it in Aramaic (his native tongue), and could do so in a manner that indicated his familiarity with current interpretive tendencies in both popular circles (as in the synagogues) and professional circles (as seen in debates with scribes, ruling priests, and elders). Moreover, the movement that Jesus founded produced a legacy of literature, including four gospels, a narrative of the early church (the book of Acts), and a number of letters. This movement also collected older works, such as the writings we now recognize as the books of the Old Testament, the Apocrypha, and other related writings. The sudden emergence of a prolific literary tradition from an illiterate founder, who had little or no interest in Scripture, is not impossible, but it is less difficult to explain if Jesus was in fact literate and frequently appealed to Scripture.[13] How he appealed to it is our next concern.

More than twenty years ago, the late Bishop John Robinson asked if Jesus had a distinctive use of Scripture. Robinson concluded that he did, and he described it as a "challenging use" of Scripture.[14] This use of Scripture often

---

10. See Craig A. Evans, "The Scriptures of Jesus and His Earliest Followers," in *The Canon Debate*, ed. L. M. McDonald and J. A. Sanders, 185–95 (Peabody: Hendrickson, 2002).

11. In the nonbiblical scrolls of Qumran and the region of the Dead Sea, the book of Deuteronomy is quoted some twenty-two times, Isaiah some thirty-five times, and the Psalter some thirty-one times. See James C. VanderKam, "Authoritative Literature in the Dead Sea Scrolls," *Dead Sea Discoveries* 5 (1998): 382–402; idem, "Question of Canon Viewed through the Dead Sea Scrolls," in McDonald and Sanders, *The Canon Debate*, 91–109.

12. See 1 Macc. 1:56-57; Josephus, *War* 2.229 (in reference to Antiochus IV's efforts to find and destroy Torah scrolls); Josephus, *Life* 134 (in reference to scrolls in Galilee, during the early stages of the revolt against Rome).

13. For arguments in support of a literate Jesus, see my essay, "Jewish Scripture and the Literacy of Jesus," in *From Biblical Criticism to Biblical Faith*, ed. W. H. Brackney and C. A. Evans, 41–54 (Macon, GA: Mercer University Press, 2007). See also Paul Foster, "Educating Jesus: The Search for a Plausible Context," *Journal for the Study of the Historical Jesus* 4 (2006): 7–33.

14. John A. T. Robinson, "Did Jesus Have a Distinctive Use of Scripture?," in *Twelve More New Testament Studies* (London: SCM, 1984), 35–43; originally appeared in Robert F. Berkey and Sarah A. Edwards, eds., *Christological Perspectives: Essays in Honor of Harvey K. McArthur* (New York: Pilgrim, 1982), 49–57.

appears with a challenging question: "Have you never read what David did?" (Mark 2:25); or "Have you not read this scripture?" (Mark 12:10); or "Have you not read in the book of Moses?" (Mark 12:26). Other examples are introduced with *how* (πῶς): "How is it written of the Son of Man?" (Mark 9:12); or "How can the scribes say?" (Mark 12:35). Very intriguing is the series of counterquestions we find in Luke 10, where the legal authority asks what he must do to be saved. Jesus asks him in turn, "What is written in the law? How do you read?" (Luke 10:26). In essence, Jesus has asked this man to think about his hermeneutics. What is in Scripture, and how does he interpret it? Robinson concludes his essay by calling attention to Jesus' distinctive use of *amen*.

Let's consider three examples. In the first, we shall see Jesus making a remarkable claim of authority over the Sabbath. In the second example, we shall see Jesus challenging a significant teaching in the book of Daniel, the book from which Jesus derived his self-applied epithet "Son of Man" and from which important dimensions of his person and mission are clarified. In the third example, we shall see Jesus alluding to and subverting an important element relating to the Son of Man.

REVELATION

In a tradition preserved in Q (Matt. 11:25-27 = Luke 10:21-22), Jesus thanks God for special revelation. The Matthean version reads as follows: "I thank you, Father, Lord of heaven and earth, because you have hidden these things from the eyes of the wise and discerning and revealed them to babes" (ἐξομολογοῦμαί σοι, πάτερ, κύριε τοῦ οὐρανοῦ
καὶ τῆς γῆς, ὅτι ἔκρυψας ταῦ-
τα ἀπὸ σοφῶν καὶ συνετῶν καὶ ἀπεκάλυψας αὐτὰ νηπίοις; Matt. 11:25). In favor of authenticity is reference to Jesus' followers as "babes," suggesting naïveté. Indeed, the implication is that the disciples are not "wise and discerning" (cf. Wis. 12:24; 15:14, where "babes" occurs with "fools"). This is hardly a saying generated by the early church.[15]

It is probable that Jesus' prayer of thanksgiving alludes to Dan. 2:19-23, in which Daniel thanks God for making known his mysteries and giving wisdom and discernment to the wise.[16] The most relevant passage reads as follows:

> Daniel said: "Blessed be the name of God for ever and ever, to whom belong wisdom and majesty. He changes times and seasons;

---

15. See the comments in Ulrich Luz, *Matthew 8–20*, Hermeneia (Minneapolis: Fortress Press, 2001), 157–58, 161–64; Craig A. Evans, *Matthew*, New Cambridge Bible Commentary (Cambridge: Cambridge University Press, 2012), 245–46.

he removes kings and sets up kings; he gives to the wise wisdom [σοφοῖς σοφίαν] and to those with discernment [καὶ σύνεσιν] understanding; he reveals [ἀνακαλύπτων] deep and mysterious things; he knows what is in the darkness, and the light dwells with him. To you, O God of my fathers, I give thanks [ἐξομολογοῦμαι][17] and praise, for you have given me wisdom and intelligence [σοφίαν καὶ φρόνησιν], and have now made known to me what we asked of you, for you have made known to us the king's matter." (Dan. 2:20-23)

Two observations suggest that Jesus' prayer does indeed allude to Daniel 2: (1) the concentration of common vocabulary, and (2) the subversive relationship between Jesus' prayer and Daniel's prayer. By "subversive relationship," I mean that Jesus thanks God for not revealing his mysteries to the "wise and discerning," by which is probably meant the educated and professional, that is, the professional wise man, such as Daniel and his colleagues.[18] No, God has not revealed his deepest truths to such as these; he has revealed his truth to the followers of Jesus, who in another context are described as unlettered and untrained (Acts 4:13). Jesus' followers are mere "babes" in expertise in religion, but thanks to God, who reveals his truth to the innocent, they now have a deeper understanding of the divine will than do the professionals.

AUTHORITY

Criticized for permitting his disciples to pluck grain on the Sabbath, Jesus asserts his authority over the Sabbath (Mark 2:23-28). His reply is as follows: "The Sabbath was made for man, not man for the Sabbath; so the son of man is lord even of the Sabbath" (vv. 27–28). Jesus' self-reference as "Son of Man" almost certainly derives from Dan. 7:13-14, where the figure, who is "like a Son of Man," receives from God royal authority. Invested with this divine authority,

---

16. W. Grimm, "Selige Augenzeugen, Luk. 10,23f: Alttestamentlicher Hintergrund und ursprünglicher Sinn," *TZ* 26 (1970): 172–83; idem, "Der Dank für die empfangene Offenbarung bei Jesus und Josephus," *BZ* 17 (1973): 249–56; idem, *Jesus und das Danielbuch*, Band I, *Jesu Einspruch gegen das Offenbarungssystem Daniels (Mt 11,25–27; Lk 17,20–21)*, ANTJ 6.1 (Frankfurt am Main: Peter Lang, 1984), 1–69.

17. The verb "give thanks" renders the Aramaic ידא, whose cognate ידה was chosen by Franz Delitzsch in his Hebrew translation of ἐξομολογοῦμαι in Matt. 11:25. ידה, of course, is the verb that regularly appears in 1QH, the Hodayot, or Thanksgiving Hymns.

18. Luz, *Matthew 8–20*, 163: "Especially noticeable is the contrast with Dan 2:20-23."

Jesus as Son of Man may pronounce sins forgiven (as in Mark 2:1-12) and even assert lordly authority over the Sabbath itself.

This is an amazing statement, which I believe authentically derives from Jesus.[19] It flies in the face of the high regard in which Jews in late antiquity, including early Christians, held the Sabbath. The sacredness of the Sabbath reaches back to creation itself, as seen in the following selection of texts:

> And on the seventh day God finished his work, which he had done, and he rested on the seventh day from all his work, which he had done. So God blessed the seventh day and sanctified it, because on it God rested from all his work that he had done in creation. (Gen. 2:2-3)
>
> But the seventh day is a Sabbath to the Lord your God; in it you shall not do any work, you, or your son, or your daughter, your manservant, or your maidservant, or your cattle, or the sojourner who is within your gates; for in six days the Lord made heaven and earth, the sea, and all that is in them, and rested the seventh day; therefore the Lord blessed the Sabbath day and hallowed it. (Exod. 20:10-11)
>
> Blessed is the man who does this, and the son of man who holds it fast, who keeps the Sabbath, not profaning it, and keeps his hand from doing any evil. (Isa. 56:2)

In the face of traditions such as these, Jesus' claim to have the authority to make pronouncements concerning what is allowed and not allowed on the Sabbath is extraordinary. But even more than this, Jesus says that as "Son of Man," he is the "lord of the Sabbath." On what basis can Jesus or anyone else possess this kind of authority? The answer lies in the interesting epithet "Son of Man," which in my opinion—despite some loud and influential voices to the contrary[20]—derives from the vision of Daniel 7, a vision that in his own way Jesus experienced and applied to himself. Accordingly, as "Son of Man," he "has authority *on earth* to forgive sins" (Mark 2:10). The curious prepositional phrase "on earth" is not otiose, but stands in contrast to the *heavenly* setting, in which the Danielic son of man received his authority.[21] Possessing this authority, Jesus

---

19. For discussion of linguistic and cultural details, see Maurice Casey, *Aramaic Sources of Mark's Gospel*, SNTSMS 102 (Cambridge: Cambridge University Press, 1998), 138–92, esp. 148–51. Casey rightly argues for a *Sitz im Leben Jesu*. I follow Casey on most points.

the Son of Man may now forgive sins and make Sabbath pronouncements. Jesus has in effect subverted a major teaching of Scripture, but has done so through his dynamic appropriation of other Scripture.

Service and Mission

We have just seen how appeal to the authority of the son of man figure in Daniel 7 provided the rationale for claiming authority over the Sabbath itself. In the present example, we see Jesus subverting Daniel 7, almost in effect denying the authority of the son of man. In a saying of uncertain context but probable authenticity, Jesus says to his disciples, "The Son of Man has come not to be served, but to serve (ὁ υἱὸς τοῦ ἀνθρώπου οὐκ ἦλθεν διακονηθῆναι ἀλλὰ διακονῆσαι) and give his life a ransom for many" (Mark 10:45). We have here an unmistakable allusion to Dan. 7:13-14:

> I saw in the night visions, and behold, with the clouds of heaven there came one like a son of man [υἱὸς ἀνθρώπου ἤρχετο], and he came to the Ancient of Days and was presented before him. And to him was given dominion and glory and kingdom, *that all peoples, nations, and languages should serve him* [πάντα τὰ ἔθνη τῆς γῆς κατὰ γένη καὶ πᾶσα δόξα αὐτῷ λατρεύουσα / יפלחון]; his dominion is an everlasting dominion, which shall not pass away, and his kingdom one that shall not be destroyed. (emphasis added)

The saying in Mark 10:45, which I believe does derive from Jesus, though it was probably uttered in a different context (perhaps in the context of the Last Supper), is quite remarkable.[22] It seemingly contradicts Dan. 7:14, in which it

---

20. For examples, see G. H. Boobyer, "Mark II.10a and the Interpretation of the Healing of the Paralytic," *HTR* 47 (1954): 115–20; C. P. Ceroke, "Is Mark 2:10 a Saying of Jesus?" *CBQ* 22 (1960): 369–90; L. S. Hay, "The Son of Man in Mark 2:10 and 2:28," *JBL* 89 (1970): 69–75; Karl Kertelge, "Die Vollmacht des Menschensohnes zur Sündenvergebung (Mk 2, 18)," in *Orientierung an Jesus: Zur Theologie der Synoptiker*, ed. P. Hoffmann, N. Brox, and W. Pesch, 205–13, J. Schmid Festschrift (Freiburg: Herder, 1973), 208–11; Norman Perrin, *A Modern Pilgrimage in New Testament Christology* (Philadelphia: Fortress Press, 1974), 88–89.

21. The epithet Son of Man is not a title, nor is it messianic. It means human (as opposed to beast or angel). But its consistent articular usage on the lips of Jesus, throughout the Gospels, is in reference to a specific human figure—the one described in Daniel 7. Jesus understood himself as this figure, who from God, *in heaven*, received authority and now, *on earth*, exercises that authority.

22. For discussion of linguistic and cultural issues, see Casey, *Aramaic Sources*, 193–218.

is emphatically stated that "all peoples, nations, and languages should serve" the son of man figure described in verse 13. No, Jesus says, the Son of Man has not come to be served, but to serve.

Many critics, of course, have interpreted Mark 10:45 as a community formulation, which gave expression to the post-Easter understanding of the saving significance of Jesus' death. This line of interpretation is plausible and may well be correct. But I have my doubts. Elsewhere I have argued for its setting in the *Sitz im Leben Jesu* ("setting in life").[23] Here I only wish to point out that Jesus' tendency to subvert Scripture provides a context for understanding the ransom saying as yet one more instance of this tendency. Contrary to popular beliefs, in which the Lord's anointed was expected to crush Israel's enemies (as seen, for example, in 4Q285, in which the armies of the Kittim will be slaughtered and the king of the Kittim, that is, the Roman Emperor, will be slain by the Branch of David, that is, the Messiah), Jesus states that the Son of Man will give his life in exchange for the lives of others.

The events of Passion Week may well have colored the form of the saying that we have in Mark 10:45, but the subversion of Dan. 7:13-14 in all probability derives from Jesus. The ransom idea, which may well reflect Isaiah 53, is what encouraged the subversion.

There are other examples in which Jesus challenges the thinking of his contemporaries, including the thinking of his own disciples. Without question, some of this teaching created tension. Therefore, we must ask, in light of Jesus' use of Israel's Scriptures, what was his relationship with the Judaism of his day?

WHAT WAS JESUS' RELATIONSHIP WITH THE JUDAISM OF HIS DAY?

It has been fashionable down through the centuries to view Jesus as opposed to Judaism in various ways. Christian theologians have assumed that Jesus criticized the religion of his people for being legalistic (or "Pharisaic"), for being caught up with externals, and for having little or no place for grace, mercy, and love. Jesus' action in the temple, which has been traditionally referred to as the

---

23. Craig A. Evans, *Mark 8:27–16:20*, WBC 34B (Nashville: Thomas Nelson, 2001), 114, 119–25. See also C. K. Barrett, "The Background of Mark 10:45," in *New Testament Essays: Studies in Memory of Thomas Walter Manson 1893–1958*, A. J. B. Higgins, 1–18 (Manchester: Manchester University Press, 1959); Werner Grimm, *Weil ich dich liebe: Die Verkündigung Jesu und Deuterojesaja*, ANTJ 1 (Bern and Frankfurt am Main: Lang, 1976), 231–77; Morna D. Hooker, *The Son of Man in Mark: A Study of the Background of the Term 'Son of Man' and Its Use in St Mark's Gospel* (London: SPCK, 1967), 140–47; Peter Stuhlmacher, "Vicariously Giving His Life for Many, Mark 10:45 (Matt. 20:28)," in *Reconciliation, Law, and Righteousness* (Philadelphia: Fortress Press, 1986), 16–29.

"cleansing of the temple" (Mark 11:15-18 and parallels), was directed, we have been frequently told, against the system of sacrifice. Religion is supposed to be a matter of the heart, not rituals. Jesus understood this, but his Jewish peers did not. So goes this understanding. It is deeply flawed.

THE TENETS OF THE JEWISH FAITH

Several scholars, both Jewish and Christian, have rightly complained against this caricature. Perhaps the most influential challenge in recent years has come from E. P. Sanders.[24] He rightly argues that there is no evidence that would suggest that Jesus opposed Judaism or criticized it as a religion of externals and rituals. Instead, there is substantial evidence that *Jesus accepted all of the major tenets of the Jewish faith*. These tenets include the unity and sovereignty of God, the value and sanctity of the temple of Jerusalem, the authority of the Jewish Scriptures, the election of the people of Israel, and the hope of Israel's redemption.

Jesus, moreover, observed many of the practices associated with Jewish piety of his day: alms, prayer, and fasting (Matt. 6:1-18). Jesus fasted in the wilderness during his period of temptation (Mark 1:12-13); he prayed and taught his disciples to pray (Matt. 6:7-15; Luke 11:1-13; 22:39-46); he and his disciples gave alms, and he taught others to do likewise (Luke 11:41; 12:33; John 13:29). Jesus presupposed the validity of the temple, the sacrifices, and Israel's holy days (Matt 5:23-24; Mark 14:14). He read and quoted from the Jewish Scriptures and clearly regarded them as authoritative (Luke 4:16-22; 10:25-28; Mark 10:19; 12:24-34). Apparently, he attended synagogue services regularly (Luke 4:16); his style and interpretation of Scripture reflect at many points the style and interpretation that emerged within the synagogue.[25]

Predicting that Jerusalem faced disaster, Jesus wept over Israel's ancient city (Luke 19:41-44). Jesus loved his people and longed for their salvation. His original disciples—all of them Jewish—embraced the same hope.

THE TORAH

Jesus accepted the authority of Torah (i.e., the law of Moses); he did not reject it, as has sometimes been asserted. What Jesus opposed were certain interpretations and applications of the law. In the so-called antitheses of the Sermon on the Mount (i.e., "You have heard it said . . . , but I say to you"; cf.

---

24. E. P. Sanders, *Jesus and Judaism* (London: SCM; Philadelphia: Fortress Press, 1985). For an earlier and broader criticism of Christian misinterpretation of first-century Judaism, see Sanders, *Paul and Palestinian Judaism* (London: SCM; Philadelphia: Fortress Press, 1977).

25. On Jesus and the synagogue, see Bruce Chilton, *A Galilean Rabbi and His Bible: Jesus' Use of the Interpreted Scripture of His Time*, GNS 8 (Wilmington: Glazier, 1984).

Matt. 5:21-48), Jesus does not contradict the commands of Moses; he challenges conventional interpretations and applications of those laws. The antithetical "but I say to you" does not oppose the commandments themselves. For example, Jesus agrees that killing is wrong but adds that hatred is wrong, too. He agrees that adultery is wrong but adds that pre-divorce lust (which often led to divorce and remarriage) also is sin. He agrees that swearing falsely is wrong but speaks against the practice of oath taking in his time. Jesus does not oppose restitution ("an eye for an eye"), but he does oppose using this command as pretext for revenge. He agrees that people should love their own people but adds that they should love other people as well, even enemies.

Jesus may very well have believed that his own authority, which derived from God's Spirit, with which he had been anointed (Mark 1:10; Luke 4:18), equaled that of Torah. But his authority did not undermine the authority of Torah; it explained it and applied it in new ways conditioned by his strong sense of the dawning of the kingdom (rule) of God and the changes it would bring.

Jesus' innovative interpretation is consistent with parallel innovations expressed by Israel's classical prophets. As did theirs, Jesus' interpretation challenged conventional interpretations and applications of Israel's sacred tradition. For example, in Isaiah 28, the prophet declares that the "Lord will rise up as on Mount Perazim, and he will be angry as in the Valley of Gibeon" (Isa. 28:21a). Here Isaiah has alluded to stories of David's victory over the Philistines (cf. 2 Sam. 5:17-21; 5:22-25 = 1 Chron. 14:13-16), stories that no doubt Isaiah's contemporary opponents interpreted as guaranteeing victory in the face of a foreign threat. But Isaiah found in this sacred story no guarantee of Israel's victory in his day. On the contrary, the Lord will do a "strange deed" and an "alien work" (Isa. 28:21), by which the prophet means God will give the victory to Israel's enemies. Isaiah says this because he rightly perceived that God was God of all people. God was not Israel's private deity.

Jesus also interpreted Israel's sacred story in this manner. In his Nazareth sermon (Luke 4:16-30), Jesus read Isa. 61:1-2, a passage understood to promise blessing for Israel and judgment for Israel's enemies, and then appealed to the examples of Elijah and Elisha (Luke 4:25-27). From these examples, where these mighty figures of old ministered to Gentiles (1 Kings 17:1-16; 2 Kings 5:1-14), Jesus declared that his "anointed" task was to bless the marginalized and the suspect, not only the righteous of Israel. This kind of interpretation may have been daring—and surely would have been opposed by many teachers—but it presupposed the authority of Israel's Scriptures; it did not attack this authority. Jesus' respect for Jewish Scripture places him squarely within first-century Judaism.

Sinners

One of the most surprising elements in Jesus' thought was his teaching that "sinners" and outsiders (Samaritans and Gentiles) would be included among the righteous.[26] Jesus frequently associated with "sinners" and tax collectors and was criticized for doing so (Mark 2:15-16). Gentiles, like the centurion of Capernaum (Matt. 8:5-13 = Luke 7:1-10) or the woman of Syro-Phoenicia (Mark 7:24-30), can possess more faith than Israelites themselves. Indeed, even a Samaritan can fulfill the Great Commandments of love of God and of neighbor (as in the parable of the Good Samaritan; Luke 10:25-37). None of this should be taken in an anti-Jewish sense. What it points to is a remarkable openness to non-Israelites, a thinking that in the time of Jesus was quite rare.

Concluding Remarks

Jesus taught many things, with a focus primarily on the rule of God. But everything he taught was rooted in, or at least presupposed, the Scriptures of Israel. His approach to Scripture may have been unusual in some respects, but it always exhibited respect for Scripture. There is also little doubt that Jesus' experience of God at work in him informed his understanding of Scripture.

It is this experience of God that lies behind Jesus' understanding of himself as the Son of Man figure in Daniel 7. I know that many scholars have argued that it was the early church that interpreted Jesus in the light of Daniel 7 and that Jesus' self-application of the idiom *Son of Man* was no more than a manner of speaking. But the dominical tradition is too deeply influenced by Daniel 7 for this argument to be convincing. After all, Daniel 7 and the Son of Man figure hardly come into play in the Christology of the early church. No, it was Jesus himself who interpreted his person and mission in the light of this important passage of Scripture, just as he interpreted his message—that of the rule of God—in the light of other important passages of Scripture. To understand what the historical Jesus really taught, we must understand well the place of Scripture in what he taught.

Perhaps the most original element of all is seen in the words of institution, where Jesus, faced with the grim reality of his approaching death, spoke of his death as in some sense bringing about the promised new covenant (Mark 14:22-25; 1 Cor. 11:23-26).[27] We have in Jewish thought the idea that through

---

26. Sanders, *Jesus and Judaism*, 174–211, 384–92.

the death or suffering of the righteous, divine judgment upon Israel is ended or averted (as in 1 Macc. 6:44; 2 Macc. 7:33, 37-38; 4 Macc. 1:11; 17:21-22; 18:3-4), but the idea that through the shedding of his blood (and here we have an allusion to the language of Exod. 24:8), Jesus himself brings about the prophesied new covenant (Jer. 31:31) is truly remarkable. This teaching, in combination with the resurrection, is what gave rise to the distinctive essence of the Christian movement.

27. Evans, *Mark 8:27–16:20*, 385–96.

3

Standard and Poor
The Economic Index of the Parables

Amy-Jill Levine, Myrick C. Shinall Jr.

Biblical scholarship, like the Bible itself, does not exist apart from its historical context, and the context of twenty-first-century United States of America provides biblical scholars new lenses through which to interpret the ancient narratives. For example, during the second Bush administration, as the number of biblical scholars dissatisfied with American policies increased, so did the bibliography that saw in the first century's *Pax Romana* disturbing connections to the twenty-first century's *Pax Americana*. In this construction, with its intertwined agenda of colonialism, militarism, jingoism/ethnocentrism, and patriarchalism, Jesus and Paul—and the (usually liberal) Christian today—appear as standing against the "empire."[1]

Given current fiscal concerns, exegetical attention is tilting from empire to economics, with Jesus and Paul helping their followers to negotiate questions of unemployment, low wages, employer-employee relations, taxes, and especially government support to the poor.[2] Granted, neither Paul nor Jesus escaped the economic contexts of their time: they are men of the first century, a time of advanced agrarian systems functioning under a militarily enforced state, and not

---

1. For a helpful summary, see John Dart, "Jesus and Paul versus the Empire," *Christian Century* (Feb. 8, 2005): 20–24. John Dominic Crossan comments in the prologue to his *God and Empire: Jesus against Rome, Then and Now* (New York: HarperCollins, 2007): "I have been hearing recently two rather insistent claims from across the spectrum of our religio-political life. The first one claims that America is now—and may always have been—an empire. . . . The second and subsidiary claim is that America is Nova Roma, the New Roman Empire, Rome on the Potomac" (2). See also Richard Horsley, *Jesus and Empire: The Kingdom of God and the New World Disorder* (Minneapolis: Fortress Press, 2003).

2. See, e.g., Ben Witherington III, *Jesus and Money: A Guide for Times of Financial Crisis* (Grand Rapids: Brazos, 2010).

of the democratic systems of modern (if not "late") global capitalism. However, their followers, especially those who foreground questions of society rather than soteriology, nevertheless typically understand them to represent the values of the left wing of the American political system.

This paper looks to the parable of the Laborers in the Vineyard (Matt. 20:1-16)—which could be called the parable of the Conscientious Householder (titles do make a difference)—to examine how a text of the first century might instruct readers two millennia later. It does so with explicit awareness that contemporary concerns affect the exegetical enterprise; it also takes seriously the ways the Bible has been used to justify inequity as well as to promote reform. The concerns are not simply hypothetical or merely academic; how one understands the Bible does have political and economic implications for present practice. If Christianity is reduced to confession, and if the confession does not cash out (after all, "faith without works is dead"), then we find its claims to be no more meaningful than the belief in Santa Claus and the Easter Bunny. If those who function as clergy read only what already supports their presuppositions, then they are betraying their congregations and, by extension, their tradition.

Theology vs. History

The conventional view, which crosses the liberal Christian academic spectrum, claims that Jesus promoted a "religious and economic egalitarianism that negated alike and at once the hierarchical and patronal normalcies of Jewish religion and Roman power."[3] Otherwise put, he promoted "a radical reordering of all relationships into a greater egalitarianism under the one Householder, God (see 20.1, 11)."[4] Thus, Jesus is an economic visionary, the first "egalitarian" (quite a miracle, given that the idea of egalitarianism is primarily understood to be a product of the Enlightenment), unique in his social context.

The devil is, of course, in the details, and the details do not point to an egalitarian system. Politically, the movement is not egalitarian: Jesus is not taking votes about whether to go to Galilee or speak against the temple. Jesus is not the first among equals. Religiously, he does not appear to be egalitarian either: he speaks on his own authority, he is not interested in consensus, and his followers view him as their master (hence titles such as κύριος and ἐπιστάτα).

---

3. John Dominic Crossan, *The Historical Jesus: The Life of a Mediterranean Jewish Peasant* (San Francisco: HarperCollins, 1991), 421–22.

4. Michael H. Crosby, *House of Disciples: Church, Economics, and Justice in Matthew* (Maryknoll, NY: Orbis, 1988), 110.

Economically, the idea of an egalitarian system finds purchase with the oft-quoted but seldom seriously considered statement "It is easier for a camel to go through the eye of a needle than for a rich person to enter the kingdom of heaven" (Matt. 19:24//Mark 10:25//Luke 18:25). However, that comment no more defines behavior among Jesus' followers than the injunction that they should pluck out the offending eye or lop off the offending foot. Imperatives such as "Sell your possessions and give alms" (Luke 12:33) must have been case-specific, since Jesus apparently did not think everyone needed to divest. Among Jesus' followers, some had substantial resources, some had little, and some gave up what they had and relied on the patronage of others.

Jesus' immediate followers are neither (mostly) the rich and famous (Nicodemus may be the exception) nor the degraded and destitute; they include men and women with some financial independence, such as tax collectors and boat owners. Further, the late 20s and early 30s in Galilee witnessed relative prosperity—no famines, no major wars, no direct Roman occupation, no reported uprisings. The gospel tradition consistently depicts Jesus in the company of people above the subsistence levels, as his multiple invitations to banquets testify. Among his supplicants are a "synagogue ruler" and a centurion. The former was likely a patron, that is, someone with the funds to construct and maintain the building or at least arrange for the place for the locals to assemble. Inscriptions more or less contemporaneous with Matthew's Gospel suggest that the ἀρχισυνάγωγος had substantial funds (see Mark 5:22 on Jairus; Matthew makes this figure, Jairus, simply a "leader"; 9:18).[5] The latter, the centurion, was likely a pensioned officer, since no Roman troops were stationed in the Galilee during Antipas's tenure. Under Augustus, centurions were paid between 3,750 and 15,000 denarii per annum. Rabbinic sources regard them as wealthy.[6] Jesus' supporters also include Joanna the wife of Herod's steward and other women of independent income (Luke 8:1-3), the householder Martha (Luke 10:38-42), and the council members Joseph of Arimathea (Matt. 27:57 notes that he was "wealthy") and Nicodemus (John 3:1).

---

5. Bernadette Brooten has collected a number of inscriptions according women the feminine version of this title. For example, a second-century Greek inscription from Smyrna reads, "Rufina, a Jew, head of the synagogue, built this tomb for her freed slaves and the slaves raised in her house" (215). Rufina, who may be a widow (in any case, she is not identified as anyone's wife or daughter), is not among the impoverished. See Bernadette J. Brooten, "Female Leadership in the Ancient Synagogue," in (eds.), *From Dura to Sepphoris: Studies in Jewish Art and Society in Late Antiquity*, ed. Lee I. Levine and Zeev Weiss, 215–23, JRASup 40 (Portsmouth, RI: JRA, 2000).

6. Details in David Gowler, "Text, Culture, and Ideology in Luke 7.1-10: A Dialogic Reading," in *Fabrics of Discourse: Essays in Honor of Vernon K. Robbins*, ed. David Gowler et al., 89–125 (Harrisburg, PA: Trinity Press International, 2003).

Jesus' general message seems to have extolled less the "holy poverty" of Francis of Assisi, who "conformed himself to the poor in all things,"[7] and more the holy stewardship of Tony Campolo: "There is nothing wrong with making a million dollars. I wish you all would make a million dollars. There is nothing wrong with making it, but there is something wrong with keeping it."[8] Both models intend to promote friendship with the poor, although Campolo's might better provide those in need with economic support. In order for some of Jesus' followers—those who have "left everything and followed" (Mark 10:28 and parallels)—to receive support, householders with homes and food must provide it. The system involves reciprocity, and so economic patronage, ideally stripped of its social privileges.

The "Jesus as economic visionary" argument also frequently invokes a false view of Jewish mores. In this construct, all Jews believed—as if there is some monolithic Jewish view—that poverty is an indication of sin and thus of punishment, with a similar analogy between wealth and righteousness. Concerning the parable of the Laborers in the Vineyard, one scholar comments, "To distribute accrued blessing (profits) to down-and-outs, making them equal to their fellows, could be viewed as folly at best and sacrilege at worst," since "prosperity and property are signs of blessing within the tradition of Israel, and thence also in Jewish tradition."[9] Sacrilege?

Surely not all Jews equated wealth with righteousness, as if the dominant ethos in the first century was a Semitic version of the prosperity gospel. While parts of Deuteronomy and the Wisdom literature do suggest that the person who behaves in a righteous manner will reap righteous rewards and the sinner will be punished, these views are also countered both by other texts and by personal and national experience. The widows, orphans, and strangers who find themselves in the care of the divine are not wealthy, but they are not regarded as "sinners" responsible for their plight. Nor is there any major view that suggests poverty is caused by sin. Rather, the prophetic and apocalyptic traditions fiercely criticize the rich, and much of Wisdom, from Job to Ecclesiastes, questions the easy Deuteronomic view. The poor, which means

---

7. See, e.g., Kenneth Baxter Wolf, *The Poverty of Riches: St. Francis of Assisi Reconsidered* (New York: Oxford University Press, 2003), 20, citation from *The Life of St. Francis*.

8. Jim White and Robert Dilday, "Campolo Asks Baptists, 'Which Jesus Should We Preach?'" *New Baptist Covenant Celebration*, n.d. http://www.newbaptistcelebration.org/index.php?option=com_content&task=view&id=94&Itemid=1.

9. V. George Shillington, "Saving Life and Keeping Sabbath (Matt 20.1b-15)," in *Jesus and His Parables: Interpreting the Parables of Jesus Today*, ed. V. George Shillington (Edinburgh: T&T Clark, 1997), 97.

just about everyone, well knew the tradition's critique of the wealthy, its warnings that possessions can be a snare, and its insistence on caring for the have-nots.[10] The Scriptures of Israel offer a complex view of wealth and poverty, and it is foolish (if not worse) to construe the "Jewish view" as a combination of select verses in Deuteronomy and Proverbs read through Ayn Rand, or Christian apologetic.

Parables that begin "There was a rich man who . . ." end badly for the rich man: the rich man who ignored Lazarus epitomizes the problem. This was no surprise to Jesus' Jewish audience. Even the famous "parable of the prodigal son" [11] shows that wealth cannot buy *shalom bayit*, peace in the household.[12] All this Jews knew. But what we know—whether in ancient Galilee or present-day America—is not necessarily what we practice. Jesus speaks to some who do not recognize their responsibility to people with less.

Landowners, Laborers, and a New Form of Unionizing (Matt. 20:1-16)

Our parable begins, "The kingdom of heaven is like a householder (οἰκοδεσπότης) who went out early in the morning to hire workers for his vineyard." Contracting with a set of workers for the "usual daily wage," he sends them into the vineyard. He subsequently hires more workers at nine o'clock, noon, three o'clock, and finally five o'clock in the afternoon. When evening arrives, he orders his manager to pay the workers, beginning with the last hired, and to them, the manager gives the "usual daily wage." The first hired, believing that since they worked much longer hours, they will receive comparably more pay, are distressed to find they received only the amount of the original contract. They grumble. The householder strikes back: "Take what is yours and get out." The parable concludes with the floating saying "So the last will be first, and the first will be last."

For generations interpreters viewed the householder as a symbol for G-d, a figure of "extraordinary forgiveness and grace."[13] His generosity mirrors that of the divine. In turn, the first-hired workers are those stereotypically

---

10. See, e.g., Isa. 3:15-24; cf. 10:1-3; Jer. 5:27-28; Ezek. 7:19; Amos 2:6; 4:1-12; 6:4; Mic. 6:10-12; and elsewhere. The point is taken up in apocalyptic literature. See *1 Enoch* 91-92; 97-98 *passim*; 106-107.

11. For connections between the two parables, see Rudolf Hoppe, "Gleichnis und Situation: Zu den Gleichnissen von guten Vater (Lk 15.11-32) und gütigen Hausherrn (Mt 20.1-15)," *BZ* 28 (1984): 1–21.

12. See William Brosend, *Conversing with Scripture: The Parables* (Harrisburg, NY: Morehouse, 2006), 48: "The man's money only seemed to create the conditions for his misery."

recalcitrant, grumbling Jews (or Jewish followers of Jesus) who rejected the equal entry of gentiles into the church and so the kingdom. They are the ones who sought to be judged by "works," and in particular the demanding burden of the law, which is how their claim to have "borne the burden of the day and the scorching heat" (Matt. 20:12) was understood. The last hired, who get their payment simply for showing up, are of course the gentiles, who enter by grace. Neat and tidy, the parable proclaimed a message of ecclesial inclusivity, Jewish xenophobia, and Jesus' generosity. Nothing could be more obvious.

Today, this consensus reading is breaking down. It provides no challenge and so defeats the purpose of parables. (Whatever parables are supposed to do, confirming stereotypes and encouraging complacency are not part of the job description.) Klyne Snodgrass appropriately finds Matt. 20:1-6 "one of the three most difficult parables."[14]

However, the alternatives to the consensus wind up reinscribing the same ideals of Jesus the economic visionary and the Jews as the grumbling capitalists; the alternatives simply get to the conclusion by different means. In some circles today, the landowner cannot be a symbol for the divine. He is, rather, the exploitative (Hellenistic) capitalist. In turn, the workers are from families thrown off their land by the expansionist policies of the exploitative elite.[15] They are ignored by the landowners, who took their land. They are the degraded, the expendables, and it is on their behalf that Jesus speaks.

We must not dismiss the concerns of day laborers, then or now. However, we do well to query this contextualization of exploitation. If we begin with the presupposition that all landowners are exploitative and all laborers victims, we have already skewed the reading. Even areas with good economic indicators have day laborers, and 100 percent employment really would be the kingdom of God. The parable shows no indication of economic stress, and neither in general does Antipas's Galilee. Archaeological studies not only of Sepphoris and Tiberias but also of Cana and Capernaum, Gamla and Yodefat, as well as cites in the Decapolis and Caesarea Maritima, show flourishing communities,

---

13. So Klyne R. Snodgrass's summary of Arland Hultgren's reading, and many others. See Snodgrass's *Stories with Intent: A Comprehensive Guide to the Parables of Jesus* (Grand Rapids: Eerdmans, 2008), 362.

14. Ibid.

15. The parable "may well be exploring a pervasive conflict present in first-century Roman-occupied Jewish Palestine ["Palestine" is not a term the Gospel uses, although it was used by Rome to erase Jewish presence in the land, and Galilee was not "occupied" at the time of Jesus] . . . . This chronic aristocratic expropriation had forced many land-owning peasants into the marginal under-class of day laborers." Richard Q. Ford, *The Parables of Jesus: Recovering the Act of Listening* (Minneapolis: Fortress Press, 1997), 115, following William R. Herzog II, *Parables as Subversive Speech, Jesus as Pedagogue of the Oppressed* (Louisville: Westminster/John Knox, 1994), 79–97.

both urban and rural. The two cities Antipas built, Sepphoris and Tiberias, lack the massive scale that would have drained the countryside of resources. Nor do those cities, or any others, provide direct information about the status of laborers, other than that construction creates jobs.[16]

Nor does the parable suggest that Jews would have viewed these workers as expendable or degraded, let alone impure or sinful. Jewish culture in general highly values labor, including manual labor.[17] Nor again are all workers disenfranchised landowners. Some are prodigal sons; others freed slaves; still others the children of the working poor, who live in every country.

The householder goes out at six o'clock in the morning to contract with them, and William Herzog proposes that "no elite would perform such a chore" as going out to the marketplace to hire laborers.[18] While perhaps a seminary professor would not head to the market to find graders for his or her large Bible classes, Jewish landowners seek labor in this way, as we see from Jewish examples. For example, *m. Baba Metziah* 7.1 states, "He who hires workers and tells them to begin early and finish late cannot force them to it if beginning early and finishing late does not conform to the custom of the place. Where the custom is that they be fed, he is obligated to feed them; where it is that they be served dessert, he must serve them dessert. Everything goes according to the custom of the place." We cannot facilely claim this Mishnah as the background to the parable, but it does illustrate a similar model of Jewish business practice.

We might linger on this mishnaic statement, in part because it sets up a possible parameter for the parable and also in part because Emmanuel Levinas did, and he has become one of the current go-to Jews for Christian theologians.[19] Glossing this mishnah, Levinas writes:

---

16. For more on the economic situation and its apologetic interpreters, see my "De-Judaizing Jesus: Theological Need and Exegetical Execution," in a volume commemorating the Aaron Aronov Lecture Series in the Department of Religious Studies at the University of Alabama, ed. Steven Ramey (forthcoming), as well as the earlier version of the article, "Theory, Apologetic, History: Reviewing Jesus' Jewish Context," *Australian Bible Review* 55 (2007): 57–78.

17. David Fiensy, "Leaders of Mass Movements and the Leader of the Jesus Movement," *Journal for the Study of the New Testament* 21, no. 74 (1999): 3–27, 22, cites rabbinic sources that "extoll both manual labor (*n. Ab.* 1.10; *ARN B* XXI, 23a) and teaching one's son a craft (*m. Qid.* 4.14; *t. Qid.* 1.1 1; *b. Qid.* 29a)." Witherington, *Jesus and Money*, 46, misreads Sir. 38:25-34 as showing "disdain towards those who worked with their hands"; comments such as "without them no city can be inhabited" and "they maintain the fabric of the world" are hardly disdaining. For Sirach, however, Torah study is more important.

18. Herzog, *Parables as Subversive Speech*, 84.

Our text teaches that not everything can be bought and not everything can be sold. The freedom to negotiate has limits which impose themselves in the name of freedom itself. It matters little that the limits formulated here are not the same as those demanded by modern trade unions. What matters is the principle of limits imposed on freedom for the greater glory of freedom. It is the spirit in which the limits are set: they concern the material conditions of life, sleep and food. Sublime materialism! . . . For the nature of the limits imposed is fixed by custom and evolves with custom. But custom is already a resistance against the arbitrary and against violence. Its notion of a general principle is tribal and somewhat childish, but it is a notion of a general principle, the root of the universal and the Law. Sublime materialism, concerned with dessert.[20]

Had the householder followed the customs of the time, which is the meaning of the phrase "usual daily wage" (δηναρίου τὴν ἡμέραν, literally, "denarius of the day"; Matt. 20:2), he is therefore constrained. The Roman silver denarius would supply a family three to six days of food;[21] it was a fair but not exorbitant payment. The householder cannot offer less than the going rate. He is not "free" to do what he wants. Perhaps this direct hiring placed landowner and worker in a partnership relationship and thus mitigated the relationship of wealthy to underclass. Matthew 20:2 states that the landowner and the workers "agreed" upon the payment. The agreement is precisely that: the Greek is συμφωνήσας, whence "symphony" (cf. Matt. 18:19, "If two of you agree on earth about anything you ask, it will be done for you by my Father in heaven").

Herzog next proposes, "Vineyards were most likely owned by elites because they produced a crop that can be converted into a luxury item (wine), monetized, and exported."[22] The point is correct in that all crops can be converted into monetized commodities. However, wine was also a staple of poorer classes. Had wine been so associated with exploitative monetization, then one wonders why Jesus made wine the feature of his fellowship meals, analogized his blood to it, and mass-produced it at Cana. Nor is the overused

---

19. Following a long line of Jewish philosophers who have found more recognition in Christian seminaries than in the synagogue; predecessors include Franz Rosenzweig, Martin Buber, and even Abraham Joshua Heschel.

20. Emmanuel Levinas, "Judaism and Revolution," *Nine Talmudic Readings*, trans. Annette Aronowicz (Bloomington: Indiana University Press, 1994), 97.

21. Douglas Oakman, "The Buying Power of Two Denarii," *Forum* 3 (1987): 33–38.

22. Herzog, *Parables as Subversive Speech*, 85.

term *elites* helpful, since it is necessarily relative, dependent on several factors (e.g., economics, honor, and family).

When we view the parable as about exploited marginals and degradables, the householder can only be the enemy. He is not the constrained contractor; he is certainly not the representative of the divine. Readers so inclined find, in the landowner's insistence that the last hired be the first paid and that the same amount be paid to those who worked only a small amount and those who "have borne the burden of the day" (Matt. 20:12), the abusive capitalist who sows discontent among the laborers and so prevents them from unionizing. The parable then reveals to the workers their own manipulation: "Once the οἰκοδεσπότης becomes a member of an oppressing elite class, his actions and words are open to scrutiny."[23] This is Jesus as Paolo Friere or, more recently, Michael Moore.

But this it not what Jesus' hearers would have heard.[24] First, they might well have already known about what we today call unions. According to the Tosefta, *Bava Metzia* 11:24-26, "The wool workers and the dyers are permitted to say, 'we will all be partners in any business that comes to the city.' The bakers are permitted to establish work shifts amongst themselves. Donkey drivers are permitted to say, 'we will provide another donkey for anyone whose donkey dies' . . . The shipmasters are permitted to say, 'we will provide another ship for anyone whose ship is destroyed.'" In other words, the Tosefta recognizes the guild (voluntary association, collegia) structure. Perhaps such understanding existed in Jesus' time as well. Had the workers in the parable taken a cue from the local bakers, they could have set up a system to work for all. They choose not to do that. They are interested in receiving their own payment, not in whether or not the other workers have enough food.

Further, instead of seeing the owner as a union breaker, that original audience would likely have seen him in the role of G-d. To be sure, not all kings or vineyard owners need to be related to the divine. But some are.[25] Jesus' Jewish auditors knew God as the vineyard owner and Israel as the vineyard in Isa. 5:7a and Jer. 12:10. If Jesus told a story about a vineyard and an owner, the cultural repertoire of his audience presumed the association of Israel with the vineyard and the owner with God.[26]

---

23. Ibid, 96–97.

24. Less charitable is Klyne R. Snodgrass: "The view that the parable confronts exploitation of workers and that the owner is a negative figure has no basis." *Stories with Intent*, 372.

25. Arland J. Hultgren, *The Parables of Jesus: A Commentary* (Grand Rapids: Eerdmans, 2000), states that the owner is "surely a metaphor for God" (36).

Although our vineyard owner is first called an οἰκοδεσπότης (a "householder"; 20:1),[27] verse 8 calls him the "lord of the vineyard" (ὁ κύριος τοῦ ἀμπελῶνος) and so secures the identification between householder and divine. For this verse, the NRSV translates κύριος not as "lord" but as "owner" and so masks the theological implication.[28]

However, the householder need not refer *only* to God, for what God does is often what those who claim to follow God should also do. We can see in this householder a description of how ordinary householders do act, or even should act. Matthew makes the case with other uses of the term οἰκοδεσπότης, such as 13:52 (the analogy of the οἰκοδεσπότης to the scribe "trained for the kingdom of heaven") and 24:43 (the οἰκοδεσπότῃ who is prepared for the thief in the night). Thus, auditors would have been prepared to identify this householder both with God and with their own position, as scribes trained for the kingdom of heaven and as prudent stewards who are prepared for eschatological judgment.

Things become a tad strange in the next verses. The owner goes out again at nine o'clock, and he finds "others standing idle" (ἀργούς, literally "without work") in the marketplace." He tells them, "You also go into the vineyard, and I will give you whatever is right" (δίκαιον). Some have suggested that the owner takes "advantage of an unemployed workforce, to meet his harvesting needs by offering them work without a wage agreement."[29] This suggestion misreads both ancient and contemporary economics. Were the landowner untrustworthy, he would have no future workers. He is also constrained by local custom, as the aforementioned *Bava Metzia* 7.1 indicates.

Nor need we see him as a "cheapskate" in that he "keeps trying to have as *few* workers to pay as possible."[30] Were his interest in saving money, his generous payment at the end of the parable would become inexplicable. Were

---

26. See Shillington, "Saving Life and Keeping Sabbath," 87–101, for a listing of commentators who take the theological reading and/or who approve of the owner.

27. Hultgren, *Parables of Jesus*: "The landowner who goes out to hire laborers is surely a metaphor for God. . . . To make him God is 'not to allegorize'; to 'fail to do so or to refuse to do so' is to tear the parables from their symbolic universe" (36).

28. Matthew speaks of householders in 10:25; 13:27, 52; 20:1, 11; 21:33; and 24:43, and may think of the church in household terms. See Michael H. Crosby, *House of Disciples: Church, Economics, and Justice in Matthew* (Maryknoll, NY: Orbis, 1988). While the church/household analogy is more a Matthean than a historical-Jesus issue, Matthew's view is a logical continuation of Jesus' teaching.

29. Herzog, *Parables as Subversive Speech*, 86; see Hultgren, *Parables of Jesus*, 40, who says that this reading is "to ruin a good story."

30. So John Dominic Crossan, *The Power of Parable: How Fiction by Jesus Became Fiction about Jesus* (San Francisco: HarperOne, 2012), 97.

he known as a cheapskate, again, his reputation would have worked against him, and his honor would have been compromised.

Rather than dismiss our householder as an ancient Gordon Gekko, we might take him at his word: "right" is δίκαιον, with the connotations of just, fair, and proper. The parable repeats the term, also on the householder's lips, in verse 13: οὐκ ἀδικῶ σε ("I am not unjust to you"), an echo masked by the NRSV's "I am doing you no wrong." Beneath this term is the Hebrew root צדקה, which connotes both charity and righteousness. Again, the language suggests that the householder is, if not God, at least a moral exemplar.

At noon, three o'clock, and five o'clock, the householder returns to the marketplace. Commentators, having noted these various trips, move either to historical speculation that does not help us understand the parable or, worse, to allegory that usually depends upon a negative stereotype of Judaism. That the householder was able to find workers each time need not indicate a "situation of high unemployment";[31] we do not know the numbers of people involved; we do not know if he found those who had been waiting since six in the morning, people who had already worked another job, sons and daughters who had to spend the morning taking care of aged parents, or people from the neighboring villages who could not find employment there.

Nor need we necessarily conclude, as some do, that the last hired were the old and infirm, or worse, that they were the ancient equivalents of "the undesirables—the boozers, the goof-offs, the careless. . . . In our racist society, they could also be minorities."[32] Narratively, the owner's querying of why those left are not working suggests that they should have been hired.

Increasingly common, and more frequently hitting the anti-Jewish register, is the view that the parable "probably served to defend [Jesus'] association with those conventionally branded 'tax collectors and sinners' (cf. 9.10-13)."[33] One scholar summarizes, "Whether one thinks of Gentiles or other excluded classes, recognizing the exaltation of the socially, ethnically, or morally excluded fits Jesus' emphasis elsewhere."[34] Such views have a long legacy. John Wesley claims the "primary scope" of the parable is "to show, That many of the Jews would be rejected, and many of the Gentiles accepted."[35] Other scholars find in the parable a lesson of legalism versus grace, and speak of

---

31. Herzog, *Parables as Subversive Speech*, 86; Luise Schottroff, "Human Solidarity and the Goodness of God: The Parable of the Workers in the Vineyard," in *God of the Lowly*, ed. Willy Schottroff and Wolfgang Stegemann, 129–47 (Maryknoll, NY: Orbis, 1984), 133.

32. David Buttrick, *Speaking Parables: A Homiletic Guide* (Louisville: Westminster John Knox, 2000), 114.

the Pharisees' "impenetrable legalistic understanding of" life in the kingdom as "ground in the effort to secure their own security."[36]

The parable need not lead in these directions either; unhired laborers are not neatly analogous to tax collectors in Rome's employ or those who break community trust. Nor does the parable suggest "outcasts" or gentiles in the market: the workers are all part of the same labor pool, and the first hired, as far as we can tell, willingly worked alongside those who started at nine, three, and even five o'clock. Nor is reference to "excluded" classes helpful, since Judaism does not have a caste system: all are welcome to worship the God of Israel, who cares for all; all are welcome to affiliate with the Jewish community. Nor is there an "elevation" of any class in the parable, since all the workers are paid equally. Nor are the first workers "rejected" for their grumbling; they receive the denarius just as the last hired do. Further, the parable makes no qualitative distinction in terms of those hired early and those hired late in the day.

Byrne claims that the "parable addresses the resentment felt by those who had spent long years in faithful observance to Torah at the welcome and acceptance Jesus gave to those who appeared to come so late to any sense of conversion."[37] We might here query what religious group teaches that there is a point in one's life beyond which sincere repentance or affiliation is not desirable. Once Torah observance gets dragged into the parable, insinuations of

---

33. Brendan Byrne, *Lifting the Burden: Reading Matthew's Gospel in the Church Today* (Collegeville, MN: Liturgical, 2004), 152–53. The view of those hired after the first group as "marginals," "outcasts," "sinners," or other generally undefined but certainly negative terms is common. See also Daniel Harrington, *Matthew*, Sacra Pagina (Collegeville, MN: Liturgical, 1991), 284, on the parable's defending "Jesus' special concern" for the "tax collectors and sinners" who were "marginal in Jewish society"; Craig L. Blomberg, *Matthew*, vol. 22 of *The New American Commentary: An Exegetical and Theological Exposition of Holy Scripture* (Nashville: Broadman, 1992), 305: "In its original historical setting, the latecomers to the kingdom were the 'tax collectors and sinners.'"

34. Craig S. Keener, *A Commentary on the Gospel of Matthew* (Grand Rapids: Eerdmans, 1999), 481.

35. Matthew Henry (1662–1714), in his *Concise Commentary on the Bible* (available at Christian Classics Ethereal Library, http://www.ccel.org/ccel/henry/mhcc), taught, "The direct object of this parable seems to be, to show that though the Jews were first called into the vineyard, at length the gospel should be preached to the Gentiles, and they should be admitted to equal privileges and advantages with the Jews" (http://www.ccel.org/ccel/henry/mhcc.xxxii.xx.html). Bernard Brandon Scott proposes that, in the Matthean context, the "latecomers are the disciples, and those first hired are the Pharisees. Furthermore, the lord of the parable is Jesus as judge." *Hear Then the Parable: A Commentary on the Parables of Jesus* (Minneapolis: Fortress Press, 1989), 285. Matthew, however, does not depict Jesus as calling the Pharisees at all, let alone first.

36. See Dan O. Via, *The Parables: Their Literary and Existential Dimension* (Philadelphia: Fortress Press, 1967), 154–55.

37. Byrne, *Lifting the Burden*, 153.

Jewish "elitism" are not far behind, as if the culture had no tradition of God's always welcome hand extended to the sinner. When Jewish culture becomes the negative foil to Jesus or the church, we might reread both the parable and our own stereotypes.

So if the shock of the parable, at least to this point, is not that the allegorized latecomers, such as gentiles or sinners, are invited, where's the surprise? And why haven't commentators found it? When commentators insist that something cannot be practical, perhaps, like Hamlet's mother, they protest too much. Common are claims such as "The parable surely does not make an economic prescription"[38] and "[The] parable is not a lesson is corporate economics or an example of how employers, even Christian ones, are to treat their employees."[39] The practical readings of union busting may not be what Jesus' followers heard, but they do suggest, correctly, that the parable may tell us something about labor and employment practices.

The householder continues to go to the market,[40] but the parable makes no mention of the *need* for more labor.[41] He may have thought that the others would be hired; when they are not, he brings them in himself.

And now we begin to see the challenge. Maybe it has to do with practical economics after all. It is easier to condemn legalistic Pharisees or ethnocentric Jews than to think that the wallets of well-off churchgoers are involved. The parable opens up the view that the householder—that is, the well-off disciple—should continue to go to the market, should continue to invite others in.

At payment time, the owner has the laborers paid, "beginning with the last and then going to the first" (20:8). Then 20:10-12 states, "[The first] thought they would receive more; but each of them also received one denarius. And when they received it, they grumbled against the householder, saying, 'These last worked only one hour, and you have made them equal to us who have borne the burden of the day and the scorching heat.'" According to David Buttrick, the owner is both "unjust and arrogant."[42] William Loader says, "The scene is now not only one of exploitation but also of arbitrariness and

---

38. Hultgren, *Parables of Jesus*, 35. See also W. D. Davies and D. C. Allison Jr., *Matthew*, International Critical Commentary (Edinburgh: T&T Clark, 1996), 3:69 and n. 20.

39. Thomas G. Long, *Matthew*, Westminster Bible Companion (Louisville: Westminster John Knox, 1997). See also Blomberg, *Matthew*, 303: "The story scarcely models good management-labor practices."

40. Here we find a connection to Jesus, who continues to call, and to the king who invites "everyone you find" to the banquet (Matt. 22:9).

41. Suggested by Long, *Matthew*, 225.

42. Buttrick, *Speaking Parables*, 114.

injustice."[43] Rather, these views seem at best arbitrary. The owner gives what had been generously contracted to all.[44] Buttrick, Loader, et al. are reading from the perspective of the first-hired laborers.

The parable could be understood as setting up readers to see from this perspective. Readers may choose to identify with the first hired: they worked harder than those hired later; they put in the time; they are like us; they are not lazy. A feminist reading might advocate even more strongly for the first-hired. Their story finds a contemporary analogy in the woman who settles for a set wage in doing factory work, only to find that men hired after she began her job received the same amount of money for doing less work.

But the parable again presents a challenge. It does beguile readers to identify with, and sympathize with, the first hired. There is no necessity of plot for the latecomers to receive their denarii first. Had the first hired been paid first, and then the latecomers paid the same amount, the first-hired would still have complained. By reversing the expected order, the landowner builds an expectation that the first-hired workers will receive more: "Now when the first came, they thought they would receive more" (19:10). Readers are induced into making the same assumption and therefore to place themselves in the perspective of the first hired. Then the parable rejects their perspective. The landowner and the parable have set up the workers. It may not be nice, but it is effective. It is also a good lesson to those who would begrudge fellow workers a living wage. The question is why this perspective, so carefully cultivated and harvested, is rejected.

The complaint of the first hired is not rejected because the first called are Jews and the last as sinners, gentiles, outcasts, publicans, or whoever. The parable resists the reading of the workers as allegorical representations of Jews and gentiles, or saints and sinners. The number of times the householder goes to the market precludes such dualistic readings; so does the parable's refusal to differentiate among the workers in terms of descriptions or qualifications.

A rabbinic parable with the same plot line—the worker who toils fewer hours gets paid the same, or more, than those who put in a whole day—does not move into the sinners/gentiles/outcasts mode to explain the discrepancy.

---

43. William Loader, "First Thoughts on Passages from Matthew in the Lectionary," Bill Loader's Home Page, n.d., http://wwwstaff.murdoch.edu.au/~loader/MtPentecost14.htm.

44. Brad H. Young is correct that "the laborers should have been happy about the good fortune of their coworkers who, because of the generosity of the landowner, would not have enough provision for their families," but he is perhaps romantic in his claim that "In my opinion, often the poor are genuinely happy for an unexpected blessing that someone else in their station in life receives." See his *The Parables: Jewish Tradition and Christian Interpretation* (Grand Rapids: Baker Academic, 1998), 78.

Nor does it see injustice. Snodgrass adduces, from the Jerusalem Talmud, Rabbi Zeira's eulogy for Rabbi Bun bar Hiyya in *Berakot* 2.7:

> To what [story] may [the life of] R. Bun bar Hiyya be compared? [To this story.] A king hired many workers. One worker excelled in his work. What did the king do? He took him and walked with him back and forth [through the rows of crops and did not let him finish his day's work.] Toward evening, when all the workers came to be paid, he gave him a full day's wages along with [the rest of] them. The workers complained and said, "We toiled all day, and this one toiled only two hours, and he gave him a full day's wages!" The king said to them, "This one worked [and accomplished] more in two hours than you did in a whole day." So R. Bun toiled in the study of Torah for twenty-eight years, [and he learned] more than an aged student could learn in a hundred years.[45]

A similar story appears in several other rabbinic sources, including *Ecclesiastes Rabbah* 5.17 and *Midrash Tanhuma Ki Tissa* 110.

The midrash also shows that, for the rabbis, what God wants is not necessarily what "we" think is appropriate: in its version of the laborers in the vineyard, the king is the one who prevents the excellent worker from putting in his time. Moreover, regardless of the amount of time spent in the field, everyone gets the same wage. For the rabbinic parable, the workers did not consider what the king wanted; they were judging him according to their own standards. They had a sense of what was fair; the king had a sense of what was right, or important, or valuable. The same structure holds for the Matthean parable. The workers seek what they perceive to be "fair"; the householder teaches them a lesson by showing them what is "right." The comparison helps us see that the focus is not finally on the worker, but on the assessment of the householder, the owner, the lord of the vineyard.

The comparison may also help us in determining the import of the conclusion of the parable: "So the last will be first, and the first will be last" (19:16). The meaning is not obvious, since at the end of the parable, there are no firsts or lasts; everyone is paid the same amount. The parable teaches a lesson about creating equality among the workers, not about inverting a hierarchy. The juxtaposition of the logion to the parable suggests that the first will have to wait and to watch the last receive what God determines is right; they will have to resist the temptation to grumble about the "unfairness" when God (or

---

45. Snodgrass, *Stories with Intent*, 365.

an employer) gives them the same reward as the last. Herein lies part of the challenge of the parable.

If we take the householder as the protagonist, whether as a cipher for the divine or as a model for the wealthy in the congregation, then we can develop this challenge. For example, Matthew's language suggests that, ironically, the first hired recognize a connection between the householder and the last hired. The first hired accuse the householder, "These last worked (ἐποίησαν) one hour, and you have made (ἐποίησας) them equal to us" (20:12). The translation misses the pun: the owner and the workers have both been "working."[46]

Next, continuing the ironic use of language, Matt. 20:13 reads, "But he replied to one of them, 'Friend (ἑταῖρε), I am doing you no wrong; did you not agree with me for the denarius?'" Matthew uses "friend" three times, each time ironically. Along with 20:13, the term appears in the Parable of the Wedding Banquet wherein the king asks, "Friend, how did you get in here without a wedding robe?" (22:12). At Gethsemane, Jesus says to Judas, "Friend (ἑταῖρε), do what you are here to do" (26:50).[47] If we did not realize the ironic use of the term in 20:13, the next two uses confirm this point. The first hired are analogized to the man tossed out of the wedding banquet and to Judas Iscariot. The connection is complementary, not complimentary.

One could read the householder as disingenuous at best. Richard Ford suggests, "The landowner's assertion that he collaborated in setting the wage . . . represents either self-deception or else a deliberate insult. Given a market flooded with impoverished, unemployed workers, the owner knows full well that none of these laborers can bargain with him."[48] There is no complaint about the initial wage; the complaint is about the last hired receiving it. The dishonor that would come from paying starvation wages also provides a disincentive. Rabbinic regulations, although not necessarily applicable to the time of Jesus, and not necessarily descriptive as opposed to prescriptive, provide a third counter to this negative view.

This householder is no evil tyrant or elitist exploiter; it is the laborers—who do not want the last hired to have a living wage; who like Judas betray their companions out of their own greed—who are in the wrong. In 20:14-15, the householder states, "Take what is yours and go; I wish to give to this last as I give to you. Am I not allowed to do what I wish with what is mine? Or is your

---

46. Pheme Perkins notes the repetition of the Greek in her *Hearing the Parables of Jesus* (New York: Paulist, 1981), 140.

47. Whether original or not, the term precludes the parable from serving as an indication of the gap between elite and marginal, rich and expendable.

48. Ford, *Parables of Jesus*, 117, again following Herzog.

eye evil because I am good?" That is, "Are you casting an evil eye on me? Do you want to curse me?"

If the landowner were just a landowner and we were inclined to see the parable as bringing to our awareness his exploitation of his workers and the unfairness of the system, we could disagree: "No, you should not be allowed. You have cheated us." But that would be an unfair report. No one was cheated. Nor will these disgruntled employees have any credible complaint outside of their immediate situation. William Brosend suggests that the next time the owner heads to the market, no one will respond to the six a.m. call.[49] Yet a wage is a wage, the wage here offered is a fair one, and to refuse to work might lead to starvation. Given the patron-client system and honor-shame cultural codes (both overdone in New Testament scholarship, but why not use them when they work?), the first hired will not gripe in public; there is nothing against the owner of which they have to complain. The only thing they can do is to testify to his generosity. To complain about his compensating the last hired at the same amount would be ungenerous on their part, and it might even add to the owner's positive reputation. Since there is no guarantee that he will continue to return to the labor pool, the suggestion that workers might wait until five o'clock in the afternoon in order to get a good wage for less work is not compelling.

Hence, the householder is both analogous to God and a model for the follower of Jesus. The divine connection is reinforced by the echo of Matt. 19:17, "There is only one who is good" (ὁ ἀγαθός), in the householder's comment "because I am good" (ὅτι ἐγὼ ἀγαθός εἰμι; 20:15). This association is no Mary Daly-esque view that all householders should be seen as divine; it is instead a warning to the owners that they should act as God does, rather than as "some rich guy" (e.g., Luke 12:16; 16:1; 16:19, 22).

One could insist at this point that the analogy between divine figures in parables and real-life people does break down. At times, especially in Matthew's Gospel, the violence of the divine figure should not be imitated. Vengeance is the Lord's (Deut. 32:35; cf. Rom. 12:19), and Matthew's parables describe the (divine?) king who will "put those wretches to a miserable death" (21:41) and "send his troops, destroy those murderers, and burn their city" (22:7). Matthew is not commending such actions as something Jesus' followers should repeat.

Hultgren states that the parable's "outcome is untypical of ordinary life, and that is what makes it so memorable."[50] The outcome may be memorable, but it is not atypical. According to Josephus (*Antiquities* 20.220), when the Jerusalem

---

49. Brosend, *Conversing with Scripture*, 64.
50. Hultgren, *Parables of Jesus*, 35. See also Davies and Allison, *Matthew*, 3:69 and n. 20.

Temple was completed and the eighteen-thousand-plus workmen were in want, "if any one of them did but labor for a single hour, he received his pay."[51] What commentators have insisted is "not a lesson in corporate economics" or have denied to be a "model of good management-labor practices" may well be both. Maybe the concern is to work within the localized system and provide, if resources allow, a living wage for all. Maybe, indeed, support for labor in the private sector is a good thing.

A connection of our parable to 1 Sam. 30:21-25 also is possible. David insists that "the share of the one who goes down into the battle shall be the same as the share of the one who stays by the baggage; they shall share alike" (v. 24), and the Deuteronomic historian glosses, "From that day forward he made it a statute and an ordinance for Israel; it continues to the present day" (v. 25).[52]

Dismissing the parable's practical implication is to make the parable safe, and so to lose its challenge. Jesus "encouraged landowners" to enact the graciousness of God by "speaking of a vineyard owner who generously assisted some impoverished day laborers."[53] The owner is the role model for the rich: continue to call others to the field; pay equally and generously.

And if the landowner pays everyone a living wage, and if the workers can be content with what is right, rather than what they perceive to be fair, then a soteriological message can also be adduced. The soteriological view of equal pay for unequal work is also known in Jewish contexts. *Semachot de Rabbi Chiyah* 3.2 asks:

> How do the righteous come into the world; through love, because they uphold the world through their good deeds. How do they depart? Also through love. R. Simeon b. Eliezer told a parable. To what may the matter be compared? To a king who hired two workers. The first worked all day and received one denarius. The second worked only one hour and yet he also received one denarius. Which one was the more beloved? Not the one who worked one hour and received a denarius! Thus Moses our teacher served Israel

---

51. Keener, *Commentary on the Gospel of Matthew*, 483, cites *Testament of Job* 12.3-4 as well as later rabbinic sources indicating that "Jewish hearers would consider it pious to give wages even to those not expecting it."

52. See also Philo, *Life of Moses* 1.313, and brief discussion in Davies and Allison, *Matthew*, 3:71.

53. Brian J. Capper, "Jesus, Virtuoso Religion, and the Community of Goods," in *Engaging Economics: New Testament Scenarios and Early Christian Reception*, ed. Bruce W. Longenecker and Kelly D. Liebengood, 60–80 (Grand Rapids: Eerdmans, 2009), 66.

one hundred and twenty years and Samuel only fifty two. Nevertheless, both are equal before the omnipresent.

Midrash Psalms reads, "Solomon said to the holy one, blessed be he: 'Master of the Universe: When a king hires good laborers who perform their work well and he pays them their wage, what praise does he merit? When does he merit praise? When he hires lazy laborers and still pays them their full wage.'"[54]

Ratings—or Conclusions: Four Points

In scriptural study and stock market speculation, both profit and prophecy are in play. We seek a valuable outcome; we do our best to interpret the signs. We realize what may yield much today—an allegorical reading or a start-up company—may be bankrupt tomorrow; a reading or a product that offered much to one generation can even prove toxic for the next. With our parable, we find profit for all the workers as well as for the owner, and perhaps for ourselves as well. And we also find prophecy: we are forced to think of the poor in our own midst and of those who have the resources to help them; we are forced to think about the good of all, not just the personal profit-margin; we are placed into the real world of labor relations and employment practices, and we are encouraged to ask about the "good news." In this parable, much good news can be found.

1. The householder not only fulfilled his contract with those he first hired, he also paid a full wage to those who might not have expected it. With these two moves, he proved himself sufficiently clever as to foreclose, in the honor-shame and patron-client system, any harm to himself. The only point that the workers could make about him was that he was generous to others. And in making that point, the workers learned their own economic lesson: the point is not that those who have "get more" but that those who have not "get enough." One does the work—in the labor force; in the kingdom—not for more reward, but for the benefit of all. The next day, perhaps, the first will be last, and those who grumble in the evening about bonuses will be desperate in the morning for any job at all.

2. While we can see the laborers as "among the poor for whom the kingdom of God would bring change,"[55] the parable does not promote

---

54. Or again, Antigonus of Socho: "Do not be like workers who serve their master for the sake of receiving a reward." *M. Avot* 1.3, reading *avadim* (slaves) as "workers." See also Hultgren, *Parables of Jesus*, 34–35, with other rabbinic parables with comparable images and themes. We do not adduce these parables as "background" to Matthew; rather, they attest to a general trope or thematic.

egalitarianism; instead, it encourages householders to support laborers, all of them. More than just aiding those at the doorstep, those who have should seek out those who need. If the householder can afford it, he should continue to put others on the payroll, pay them a living wage (even if they cannot put in a full day's work), and so allow them to feed their families while keeping their dignity intact. For those workers who are hired first, the parable reminds them that their fellow workers are also the "neighbors" they are to love. Their lack of generosity *in the economic sphere* condemns them. The point is practical, it is edgy, and it is a greater challenge to the church than the entirely unsurprising idea that God's concern is *that* we enter, not *when*.

3. Jesus is neither Marxist nor capitalist. Rather, he is both idealist and pragmatist. His focus is not only on "good news to the poor"; it is also on "responsibility to the rich." Jesus follows Deut. 15:11, "Since there will never cease to be some in need on the earth, I therefore command you, 'Open your hand to the poor and needy neighbor in your land.'" Moreover, the rich who fail to open their hand will be dishonored in the present and will face eschatological punishment.

4. Jesus is not an individualist, and his address presumes a corporate (that is the word) personality. Just as God "makes his sun rise on the evil and on the good, and sends rain on the righteous and on the unrighteous" (Matt. 5:45), so the righteousness of one person or group benefits not only that group, but others as well. Each group needs the other: the workers need the money; the owner needs the labor. But the corporate point is even stronger.

The prodigal son benefits from the work of the elder brother; the sinful Roman tax collector benefits from the righteousness of the Pharisee; in Christian tradition, sinful humanity benefits from the righteousness and sacrifice of Jesus. And in this parable, the last hired benefit from the labor of the first hired: the heavy lifting has already been done; the bulk of the crop has been collected. Thus, not only do owner and laborer need each other, but the work of some benefits the lives of others. In the end, all have enough to eat; the workers recognize their responsibility to each other; the rich recognize their responsibility to those who are less well off—a responsibility that includes not simply giving a handout, but hiring "workers" who can thus preserve their dignity. They, too, "went into the vineyard" (20:7).

If we take away the complacent anti-Judaism that sometimes marks parable interpretation, we can keep Jesus in his own social context. If we refocus the

---

55. Loader, "First Thoughts." Loader also observes that "the rawness of being at other people's whim is humiliating, being an expendable resource to be exploited."

parable from "who gets into heaven" and toward "who gets a day's wage," we can find a message that challenges rather than prompts complacency. If we look at economics, at the pressing reality that people need jobs and others have excess funds, we find what should be a compelling story that should challenge any hearer. And in that story, we learn what it means to act as God acts, with generosity to all. That is what parables are supposed to do.

4

Everything in Parables
On Jesus' Style

Stephen J. Patterson

> *We are concerned . . . not so much with what the early Christians said as how they said it.*
>
> –AMOS WILDER, *THE LANGUAGE OF THE GOSPEL*

In the fourth chapter of the Gospel of Mark, just following the parable of the Sower, Jesus is heard to utter these words to his close followers: "To you has been given the mystery of the Kingdom of God, but for those outside everything is in parables" (ἐν παραβολαῖς; Mark 4:11 [author's translation]). Now, Jesus has just spoken what we would all call a parable, but we should remember that the use of παραβολη here is not coterminous with our word *parable*, meaning these short narrative fictions that populate the Jesus tradition. Rather, the language of mystery and insider-outsider status suggests something more generic to the term, like figure or riddle or *mashal*. Jesus speaks in riddles.

The saying, I assume, is not historical. Rather, it is one of several passages in which the author of the Gospel of Mark gives expression to that most enigmatic of Marcan motifs, the Marcan "messianic secret." But there is also a faint air of historicity about it. For here is something true and perhaps a little troubling about the Jesus tradition: when one considers the many parables, aphorisms, and prophetic sayings in the Jesus tradition, it bears marking that Jesus' words can often be somewhat enigmatic. Perhaps that word is too strong; others have used of both parable and aphorism the more delicate term *polyvalent*.[1] Jesus said things that could be interpreted in more than one way.

Why did Jesus speak in this way? Mark's Jesus says that it was to prevent outsiders from understanding what he was really talking about, "lest they turn again and be forgiven" (Mark 4:12b). Mark would not be the first, nor the last, to assert that Jesus was a teacher of mysteries intended only for insiders. Paul spoke of a "secret and hidden wisdom of God" (1 Cor. 2:7); the *Gospel of Thomas* is a collection of "secret sayings, which the living Jesus spoke" (*Thomas*, prologue); and the Fourth Evangelist, like Mark, draws on Isa. 6:9-10 to explain why Jesus' public audience did not embrace him: "He has blinded their eyes and hardened their heart, lest they should see with their eyes and perceive with their heart, and turn for me to heal them" (John 12:40). But I am skeptical of the idea that Jesus spoke in parables in order deliberately to confound people. It just does not make very much sense for a teacher to try to confound, rather than to enlighten his followers. So why *did* Jesus speak in this way? In this paper, I would like to open up this question for our common consideration: why is so much of the Jesus tradition polyvalent?

First, however, we need to make a sampling of the phenomenon so that we all know more or less what we are talking about. Let us consider first a well-known parable of Jesus, the Prodigal Son (or better, the Prodigal and His Brother): Luke 15:11-32. Recall how the story builds to its dramatic conclusion: elder son and father face-to-face in the fields, father entreating son to come in to the celebration, son resisting—with good reason. But how will it end? Will he go in, embrace his brother, and join in the celebration, or will he stay out and preserve his dignity? Exactly half of the performance of this story in Luke explores his predicament, yet we never hear how this older son resolves his dilemma. Many scholars think this is typical of Jesus' parables. In spite of the fact that gospel writers often resolve them into a moral or lesson to be learned, originally they were all like the Prodigal Son—open-ended.[2]

Yet, even when parables are given endings or are otherwise performed in such a way as to give them a definite meaning, the phenomenon of polyvalence can still be observed. Perhaps the parable of the Great Feast will illustrate what I mean. In the Gospel of Luke, we find it in the narrative context of a dinner (14:1), where it is used as one of several pieces of advice on dining (14:1-24),

---

1. The term has been used most recently by Jacobus Liebenberg, *The Language of the Kingdom and Jesus: Parable, Aphorism, and Metaphor in the Sayings Material Common to the Synoptic Tradition and the Gospel of Thomas*, BZNW 102 (Berlin: de Gruyter, 2001), but its coinage goes back to the conversation about parables that took place in the SBL Parables Seminar in the 1970s, especially in the work of Robert W. Funk, Amos Wilder, and John Dominic Crossan (see note 2).

making in particular the very Lukan point that when you feast, you should invite "the poor, the maimed, the lame and the blind," not simply your rich so-called friends—who probably won't come anyway! (14:13//14:21b). So is that what it means? In Matthew, recall, it is really quite different—so different that many even doubt that it could have come from the source Matthew shared with Luke. In Matthew, the parable appears as an elaborate allegory (22:1-14), structured very similarly to the parable of the Wicked Tenants, which immediately precedes it (21:33-46), so that both similarly illuminate the history (and future) of salvation, including oblique comments on the Jewish War and the destruction of the second temple (22:7), as well as a more local dispute presumably unfolding within the Matthean community itself over who is fit for the kingdom (22:11-14). So is that its meaning? There is yet a third version of this parable in the *Gospel of Thomas* (logion 64). It is almost identical in structure to Luke's version, but for the ending: "Businessmen and merchants shall not enter the places of my Father." With this mere flick of the wrist, the spotlight is thrown onto those who snub the host, and the parable now condemns those various worldly attachments that would prevent one from embracing the feast and all it represents. Three versions, three very distinct meanings. This, too, is the phenomenon of polyvalence.

In his recent monograph, Jacobus Liebenberg takes a closer look at the phenomenon of polyvalence, extending his investigation into the aphorisms of Jesus.[3] This is, of course, a natural trajectory to follow, as aphorisms often have that same thought-provoking quality we associate with parables. But there is another thing to say about the phenomenon of polyvalency that is better seen with the aphorisms. Let us take, for example, the first beatitude: "Blessed are the poor, for theirs is the kingdom of God" (Luke 6:20b//Matt. 5:3 [=Q]; *Gos. Thom.* 54). This is a very short utterance; there is little to work with. Try as you might, you can't change it very much. Yet when seen in context in three different sources, it shows a remarkably broad range of meaning. In Luke 6:20, where poverty stands alongside hunger, depression, and persecution, it is clear that the kingdom belongs to those who are materially poor, that

---

2. One may recall C. H. Dodd's delightful formulation: "leaving the mind in sufficient doubt about its precise application to tease it into active thought." C. H. Dodd, *The Parables of the Kingdom* (New York: Charles Scribner's Sons, 1961; orig. 1935), 5. This view of parables is in the modern era associated especially with Robert Funk and John Dominic Crossan. See, e.g., Funk, *Language, Hermeneutic, and the Word of God: The Problem of Language in the New Testament and Contemporary Theology* (New York: Harper & Row, 1966); Crossan, *The Dark Interval: Towards a Theology of Story* (Sonoma: Polebridge, 1988; orig. 1975).

3. Liebenberg, *The Language of the Kingdom and Jesus*.

is, distressed by circumstance. In Matt. 5:3-12, however, where the list of the blessed includes the merciful, the peacemaker, and those who hunger and thirst for justice, the first beatitude now grants the kingdom to someone who possesses the virtue of being "poor in spirit." Whatever this obscure term means, the context tells us that it is some quality one could embrace as a matter of choice. The reformulation of the saying alone would not tell us this; meaning is conveyed by context. The necessity of context is made even clearer perhaps by the third example of this saying, *Gospel of Thomas* 54. In a list like the *Gospel of Thomas*, how shall we decide what an isolated saying means? Are the poor to be understood as Jesus' disciples,[4] ascetics,[5] or anyone who reads the gospel?[6] In the bare bones of the list, the polyvalence of the saying is underscored.

In addition to parables and aphorisms, I have recently begun to see the same kind of polyvalence in a third, more numerous class of sayings that populate the Jesus tradition: prophetic sayings.[7] This may at first seem unlikely, for the prophets of Israel, while indulging in symbol, metaphor, farce, and other oblique forms of speech, generally do convey their critique with a certain force and clarity. Yet, when one looks closely at the many prophetic sayings attributed to Jesus, there is often a certain lack of clarity and consequently the potential for polyvalence.

Let us take, for example, the prophetic saying in Luke 12:49: "I have come to cast fire upon the earth, and would that it were already kindled." The casting of incendiary bombs using catapults or archers would have been a well-known horror to anyone living in lands conquered by Rome. But how shall we understand this talk of incendiaries—or incendiary talk, if you will—on the lips of Jesus? When heard in the context of Luke 12, it clearly has the ring of apocalyptic threat and judgment. All through chapter 12 (extending to 13:9), the coming judgment hangs like a cloud on the horizon: "Fear the one who, after he has killed, has the power to cast into Gehenna" (12:5b); "Fool! This night your soul is required of you" (12:20a); "You also must be ready, for the Son of Man is coming at an unexpected hour" (12:40); "Unless you repent, you will all likewise perish" (13:3, 5). In this context, "I have come to cast fire upon the earth" is clearly to be understood apocalyptically. Judgment will come like

---

4. Thus, R. M. Grant and D. N. Freedman, *The Secret Sayings of Jesus* (Garden City, NY: Doubleday; London: Collins, 1960), 159.

5. So, Karen King, "Kingdom in the Gospel of Thomas," *Forum* 3 (1987): 69–71.

6. Richard Valantasis, *The Gospel of Thomas*, New Testament Readings (London: Routledge, 1997), 131–32.

7. See Stephen J. Patterson, "Apocalypticism or Prophecy and the Problem of Polyvalence: Lessons from the Gospel of Thomas," *Journal of Biblical Literature* 130 (2011): 795–817.

a firebomb hurled over your walls. The bombs are ready; they need only to be lit. But consider the same saying in the *Gospel of Thomas* 10, without Luke's rhetorical context: "I have cast fire upon the world, and look, I am guarding it until it is ablaze." Here the bomb has already been thrown. But to what does the metaphor refer? Thomas is a collection of sayings, *logoi*. Is the bomb, then, his incendiary speech, his words, or his ideas? The text does not direct us further than our own reflection. In any event, Luke's meaning is not the only possible one.

Thomas helps us to see this with several of the sayings that have been assembled into this Lukan discourse. Luke, for example, follows Q in using the "thief in the night" as a metaphor for the returning Son of Man (Luke 12:39-40). In Thomas, it is used quite differently: the thief is the world, against which one must always remain vigilant (*Gos. Thom.* 21:5-7). The saying about "reading the face of the sky" is not about failing to heed the signs of judgment (as in Luke 12:54-56), but people's inability to recognize God's messenger in their midst (*Thomas* 91), a common sapiential motif. Polyvalence reigns in this handful of sayings.

These illustrations from the *Gospel of Thomas* will no doubt have some thinking of James Dunn's alternate explanation for what we are seeing here: it is not an example of gnomic polyvalence, but the result of a Thomas redactor systematically removing the apocalypticism from the more original synoptic tradition.[8] I believe that theory to be mistaken for a number of reasons. Nonetheless, it might be helpful to look at one further example where this is clearly not the case.

In Mark 13:31, Jesus is heard to utter the following prophetic logion: "Heaven and earth will pass away, but my words will not pass away." The context is, of course, the Marcan apocalypse, so the apocalyptic meaning of "heaven and earth will pass away" is relatively straightforward. When Matthew and Luke incorporate this material from Mark, they simply repeat the saying verbatim, and it has, more or less, the same meaning.[9] But the prophetic utterance "heaven and earth will pass away" occurs elsewhere in the tradition as well. In Q, the phrase occurs in a saying found now in both Matthew and Luke:

> For truly I say to you, until heaven and earth pass away, not one iota, not one dot will pass from the Law, until everything comes to pass. (Matt. 5:18)

---

8. James D. G. Dunn, *Unity and Diversity in the New Testament: An Inquiry into the Character of Earliest Christianity*, 3rd ed. (London: SCM, 2006), 310.

9. See Matt. 24:35; Luke 21:33.

But, it is easier for heaven and earth to pass away, than for one dot of the Law to become void. (Luke 16:17)

In its Matthean context (Matt. 5:17-20), it makes the point that the law is still valid. Jesus did not come to abolish the law (5:17), and anyone who relaxes even the least commandment is to be reprimanded (5:19). The point is not to back off from a Pharisaic effort at Torah observance, but to exceed the Pharisees in righteousness (5:20). But in Luke, the context is very different. It also involves a dispute with Pharisees (16:14-15). But here, the argument is enjoined first with Luke's version of the Q saying: "The Law and the Prophets were until John, but since then the Kingdom of God is proclaimed as good news and everyone is forced into it" (Luke 16:16; cf. Matt. 11:12-13). Here we should understand Luke to be saying that the Pharisees' priorities lie in the past epoch, the time of the law and the prophets, which lasted until the career of John the Baptist; now is the time of the kingdom of God. The final phrase ("and everyone is forced into it") should be understood very straightforwardly as an observation that things aren't going very smoothly: people have to be dragged kicking and screaming into this new era—to wit, the opponents, Pharisees, whose scoffing is the occasion for this chreia. Then comes our prophetic saying: "But, it is easier for heaven and earth to pass away, than for one dot of the Law to become void" (Luke 16:17). Now, given the immediate rhetorical context of this saying in Luke, we must read it ironically, something like "Hell will freeze over before you Pharisees will let up even a little on the law." Luke does not use it as a prophetic saying, but as a complaint, a lament full of exasperation. "Heaven and earth will pass away" has become here something like a cliché meaning an unreasonably long time.

Finally, the original prophetic saying appears again in the *Gospel of Thomas*. In fact, it occurs twice—a doublet—once in logion 11 and again in logion 111. I will cite only the second as more relevant for our purposes here: "Jesus said: 'The heavens and the earth will roll up before you, and whoever is living from the living one will not see death.' Does not Jesus say: 'Whoever has found himself, of him the world is not worthy'?" (*Gos. Thom.* 111). Here is yet a third use of the saying. Now it is neither Jesus' words, nor the law, nor the Pharisees' devotion to the law that will outlast the span of heaven and earth, but the true believer, the enlightened follower who "lives from the Living One" and is grounded in the experience of self-discovery. Note, however, that this third valence is achieved not by stripping away the eschatology of the saying, but by embracing it. Notice how this *Thomas* version seems to invoke something of Isa. 34:4: "and the heavens will roll up like a scroll." This gives the *Thomas* version of the saying more, not less, of an eschatological valence. The result is a tiny aphoristic apocalypse, in which those who "live from the Living One" will survive the impending cosmic collapse. Heaven and earth may roll up and disappear, but the elect will not.

In all, there are seven occurrences of this prophetic utterance in the extant gospels, and no less than four distinct applications. This is polyvalence.

Amos Wilder taught us that language matters. The act of communication comprises not just content, but a style and a form. The epigraph I offered up at the beginning of this paper comes from his classic *The Language of the Gospel: Early Christian Rhetoric*.[10] In that work, Wilder was, of course, concerned with the forms of early Christian *literature*. His questions were crystalline, basic: "What modes of discourse are specially congenial to the gospel? What is the special role of oral against written discourse? What is the theological significance of particular rhetorical patterns used or neglected in the Early Church?"[11] These questions are important not only in the study of the early church and its literature, but also in the study of the historical Jesus, even if our access to the modes of discourse that might have characterized his speech is severely limited. From the hoary mists of oral tradition we can retrieve little. But it is important to retrieve what we can, especially those things that might be masked by the surviving written word.

One of those things is the polyvalence of the Jesus tradition. Polyvalence is a necessary casualty of the passage from the oral to the written word. Think of how the evangelist must use a parable—a parable Jesus would have told many times on many varied occasions. The evangelist cannot tell the parable many times, but must create a single occasion, a single context in which to present it, which necessitates the prior act of deciding what it means. Even before the written work of the evangelists, the polyvalence of a saying gives way to univalence as soon as it is locked into a chreia or even grouped with other sayings based on their perceived similarity. These are not necessarily betrayals of the Jesus tradition. Polyvalence, after all, is not an end in itself. Polyvalence is unstable. It must give way to resolution; it invites resolution into particular meanings. Each resolution makes its own claim to truth. But behind the resolution there is still the invitation, and this is also important for understanding who and what Jesus was. If we look only to the surviving written word, in which all meaning is resolved (this, of course, overstates the matter), in which polyvalence has given way to various efforts to say what the words mean, then we gain the impression that Jesus was a kind of answer man. Can

---

10. A. N. Wilder, *The Language of the Gospel: Early Christian Rhetoric* (New York: Harper & Row, 1964).

11. Ibid., 11.

this be the whole truth about a person who taught using parables, aphorisms, and prophetic utterances? No. Consider again Mark's parables theory. Before Mark tells us what the Sower means, he admits that the meaning is not obvious. Here is polyvalence peeking through the curtain Mark has drawn over the undisciplined possibilities of the parable. Does John, too, bear a hint of this reality in his misunderstanding motif? And even *Thomas*, which presupposes that there is a meaning ("Whoever discovers *the* interpretation of these words"; *Gos. Thom.* 1) behind each of its sayings that unlocks the key to life, begins with the invitation to seek and to find (*Gos. Thom.* 2). It is an invitation that managed to survive also in Matthew (7:7) and Luke (11:9), thanks to the source they shared, which like *Thomas*, also laid particular importance on the aphorisms and parables of Jesus.

If we follow this particular form of the invitation, to seek and to find, we discover a rich history in the wisdom traditions of Israel (Prov. 8:17; Sir. 4:11-12; Wis. 6:12). Here is just one of the later iterations of this sapiential theme:

Wisdom is radiant and unfading,
She is easily discerned by those who love her,
And found by those who seek her.
(Wis. 6:12)

What is striking here is the utter optimism that comes to expression in this saying. Wisdom is "easily" discerned by those who love her.

Remember that winsome tone of optimism as we turn to the theme in the Hellenistic philosophical tradition, where, from the pre-Socratics on, it expresses the invitation to discovery.[12] Early on, seeking and finding was advanced as an alternative to learning by revelation from oracles or the gods.[13] Later we find in it the watchword of later Stoics and Middle-Platonists, who sought to turn back the tide of skepticism from the later Academy. Epictetus would fall into this later category, but he extends the notion beyond the merely metaphysical, to the moral and social good: "When then neither kings, nor even the friends of kings are able to live as they would, what free souls are left? Seek and you will find. For nature has given you the resources to find the truth" (*Disc* 4.1.51).

---

12. For discussion, see Hans-Dieter Betz, *The Sermon on the Mount*, Hermeneia (Minneapolis: Fortress Press, 1995), 501–502.

13. The citation is as follows: H. Diels, *Die Fragmente der Vorsokratiker* (2. Aufl.; Berlin: Hermann, 1906), I:49 (Xenophanes, B, 18); see Betz, *Sermon*, 501.

Only a little less optimistic is Philo, who nonetheless stands firmly in this tradition. He embraces the method. So, commenting on Exod. 33:7, where Moses pitches the tent of meeting outside the camp, so that everyone who sought the Lord would go out to it, he declares, "Well-said. For if you, Mind (διάνοια), seek God, go out from yourself and seek diligently; but if you remain within the distractions of the body or the self-conceits of the mind (νοῦς), even though you may appear to be seeking, your search is not aimed at God."[14] But never mind, he goes on. For even so, seeking in itself has its own rewards, even if one does not ultimately find the truth one is looking for: "And yet, just seeking itself brings us good things, for trying to do something noble, even if one falls short of the goal, always brings rewards to the one who tries."[15]

I do not suppose that Jesus was a reader of someone like Epictetus, or Philo, or any of the various educated seekers of the ancient world in which we find this admonition, or a reader at all, in fact. But in this literature, we find a notion that seems to ring true for a person who used such polyvalent forms as parable and aphorism and prophetic utterance to convey what he wished to say. These forms invite reflection, seeking—what Kloppenborg has called a "hermeneutic of penetration and research."[16] And this in turn implies an assumption about those to whom Jesus would have addressed his words: he must have thought them up to it. He must have thought, like Epictetus or Philo, that people had a certain capacity to arrive at truth, if not *the* truth, at least *some* truth. The aphorism discloses nothing by itself. The parables—these brief little stories or images—they mean nothing on their own. They begin to *mean* only when they are spoken to another person, who then begins to think. And in that thought—perhaps in the form of discussion, banter, argument, or a simple feeling of dis-ease—revelation begins to take place.

The Christian tradition begins with an aphorist and storyteller. Some will argue that he was more, but he was surely no less. This means that there lies at the root of this tradition a certain optimism about human beings that assumes we are up to it. Revelation can be provoked from our own thoughts and experiences, called forth in story and by wry observation about the way we live and treat one another. Thus, Jesus' style is also content. He believed in the capacity of his fellow human beings to discover things. With the right prompt or provocation, something true would reveal itself in the human imagination.

---

14. Philo, *Leg. All.* 3.47.
15. Ibid., 3.48.
16. John Kloppenborg, *The Formation of Q: Trajectories in Ancient Wisdom Collections*, Studies in Antiquity and Christianity (Philadelphia: Fortress Press, 1987), 305.

The polyvalence of the Jesus tradition is important for the content it discloses about the preaching and assumptions of Jesus. We do not have Jesus' own voice. But in the multiple voicings of his stories and sayings that survive in the tradition, we can see that he may have said less than we are led to believe by any one of our extant sources. He did not always tell his audience what he meant, what inference to draw, what moral to learn. He left that work in their capable hands.

5

How Matthew Helped Jesus Fulfill Prophecy

Robert J. Miller

The belief that Jesus fulfilled prophecy has been a cornerstone of the notion that Christianity supersedes Judaism.[1] From the first century until now, Christians have correlated statements about Jesus with carefully chosen Old Testament prophecies to document their belief that God's plan for human salvation reached its fulfillment in Jesus. That interpretive practice is evident in much of the New Testament, but it is Matthew's Gospel that carries it out most thoroughly and most explicitly. The way Matthew matches prophecies to the story of Jesus creates the strong impression that anyone who believes in the Scriptures of Israel must see that Jesus is the promised Messiah. Matthew thus uses prophecy as a proof that Israel's history had all along been preparing for the coming of Jesus.

Since Matthew's proof-from-prophecy theme has been foundational to Christianity's conviction that it is superior to Judaism, and since that conviction has had such pernicious consequences historically, Christian scholars and all who are committed to the honest examination of Christian origins have an ethical obligation to examine Matthew's claims critically and to assess their value for Christian theology. This essay is offered as a step in that direction. First, we will examine how Matthew handled prophecy—or, more precisely, how he manipulated it—as he integrated the words of the prophets into his narrative. Second, we will investigate how the proof-from-prophecy theme works in Matthew's Gospel. Third, we will assess whether the belief that Jesus fulfilled prophecy is helpful or harmful to contemporary Christian faith.

---

1. This essay is an excerpted and revised version of "Did Jesus Fulfill Prophecy?," in my *Born Divine: The Births of Jesus and Other Sons of God* (Santa Rosa, CA: Polebridge, 2003).

How Matthew Uses Prophecy

There are sixteen scenes in the Gospel of Matthew in which the narrator (or Jesus himself) interrupts the action in order to quote a prophecy and point out that it was fulfilled in that scene. Nearly half of those scenes occur early in the story, before Jesus becomes a public figure—five of them in the infancy narrative alone. This gospel thus starts with a flurry of fulfillment, creating a strong impression that Israel's sacred history has been building up to Jesus.

In the limited length of this essay, it is not possible to examine every prophecy fulfillment scene in Matthew nor to inquire into every technique Matthew uses in integrating quoted prophecies into his narrative. For our present purposes, it will suffice to briefly analyze a few examples of two of the ways in which Matthew handles prophetic passages: first, tailoring his stories so that they can fulfill prophecy, and second, rewording prophecies so that they match the stories that fulfill them.

Tailoring Stories to Fulfill Prophecy

The large number of prophecy fulfillment scenes in Matthew is an obvious indication that the author considers prophecy to be a vital part of his story of Jesus. In a few scenes, Matthew goes so far as to treat prophecies as source material for his narrative, using details in the prophecies to shape the scenes in order to spotlight how the actions in the scenes fulfill the prophecies with extraordinary precision. There are three scenes in which it is fairly easy to track how Matthew tailors the stories to fit the prophecies.

Matt. 4:15-16

In recounting the start of Jesus' public career, Matthew follows Mark's outline: Matt. 4:12 = Mark 1:14, and Matt. 4:17 = Mark 1:15. Between Mark 1:14 and 1:15, Matthew inserts a detailed geographical elaboration of Jesus' movements in Galilee (Matt. 4:13), followed by Matthew's fulfillment formula (Matt. 4:14) and his quotation of Isa. 9:1-2 (Matt. 4:15-16). The prophet cited, Isaiah, mentions Galilee along with the old Israelite tribal names Zebulun and Naphtali and locates them on the way to the sea and across the Jordan River (Isa. 9:1). In Matt. 4:13, Matthew uses the geographical markers from Isa. 9:1 to fill out the description of Jesus' movements that he found in Mark. Matthew knows from Mark that Jesus had a house in Capernaum, a town on the coast of the Sea of Galilee. (Mark refers to "his house" there in Mark 2:1 and 2:15.) So Matthew reports that Jesus moved from Nazareth to Capernaum, which allows

Matthew to work the word *sea* from the Isaiah verse into 4:13. He also describes Capernaum (somewhat inexactly) as "in the territory of Zebulun and Naphtali." He cannot work Isaiah's "across the Jordan" into 4:13, because Jesus does not cross that river in traveling from Nazareth to Capernaum. All of Galilee is on the west side of the Jordan, and Capernaum is several miles around the lakeshore from the point where that river enters the Sea of Galilee. To be geographically precise, Nazareth is in Zebulun, and Capernaum in Naphtali. Strictly speaking, then, Matthew describes Jesus leaving Zebulun to move to Naphtali. But this is to pick nits: Matthew is focused on the phrase *pagan Galilee*. For Matthew, that is what brings out the religious point of this prophecy about geography. By portraying Jesus as fulfilling this prophecy, Matthew shows that he was sent for both Jews and gentiles.

MATT. 21:4-5

In the scene depicted in Matt. 21:1-9, Jesus rides into Jerusalem to the cheers of a crowd. Matthew follows Mark 11:1-10 closely, except for two features.

First, Matthew interrupts the narrative to announce the fulfillment of a prophecy (21:4), which he then quotes (21:5). Verse 21:5 begins with a phrase from Isa. 62:11 and then selectively quotes Zech. 9:9. Mark's scenario, in which Jesus rides a donkey into Jerusalem while a crowd cheers for the "coming kingdom," apparently reminded Matthew of Zechariah's prophecy. Zechariah 9:9 seems to mention two animals, a "donkey" and a "colt, the foal of a donkey." In the Hebrew text of Zech. 9:9, it is clear that these are two descriptions of the same beast. Parallel phrasing like this (scholars call it "synonymous parallelism") is quite common in Hebrew poetry. But in the Septuagint version of Zechariah, the Greek work for *and* appears: "a pack animal *and* a young colt." Matthew's "quotation" of Zech. 9:9 blends elements from the original Hebrew with the Greek version: the gentle king is "mounted on a donkey and on a colt, the foal of a pack animal" (Matt. 21:5).

Second, Matthew takes the Septuagint wording of this prophecy quite literally, as if it describes a king riding two animals. Accordingly, Matthew rewrites Mark's story so that now the disciples bring a donkey *and* a colt to Jesus, and sure enough, he sits on both of them (21:7). For consistency, Matthew also goes back earlier in the scene and adds a second animal to the report of the disciples finding the donkey (Mark 11:2//Matt. 21:2). He also changes the two pronouns referring to the donkey in the next verse so that Mark's "it" becomes "them" (Mark 11:3//Matt. 21:3). By way of comparison, note that the Gospel of John also quotes Zech. 9:9 in connection with its much briefer version of this scene (John 12:12-15). John's version of the prophecy sensibly mentions only one animal.

MATT. 27:9

Mark 14:10-11 tells of Judas' approach to the high priests and his offer to betray Jesus, for which the priests promise to pay him. When Matthew rewrites this brief scene, he has Judas demand the money up front. Matthew also specifies the amount of money agreed on by Judas and the priests: thirty silver pieces (Matt. 26:14-15). Mark never mentions the amount, nor do Luke or John. From what source has Matthew obtained this inside information? Answer: the prophets.

Later in Matthew's story, Judas, overwhelmed by guilt, flings the money back at the priests and then commits suicide (Matt. 27:3-5). When the priests use the money to buy some land, Matthew informs us that this purchase fulfilled Jeremiah's prophecy about thirty pieces of silver (Matt. 27:6-10). The prophecy in question is actually from Zechariah, not Jeremiah. (See the next section for attempts to explain Matthew's mistake.) A close comparison of Zech. 11:12-13 and Matt. 27:3-10 (a scene unique to Matthew's Gospel) reveals where Matthew discovered that Judas had returned the money and had done so by throwing it into the temple.

WHAT THESE THREE EXAMPLES REVEAL ABOUT MATTHEW'S USE OF PROPHECY

In Matt. 4:14-16, to position Jesus as fulfiller of prophecy, Matthew chooses descriptive details from Isaiah and crafts them into elaborations on the reports and clues that he found in Mark. The reason why Jesus' movements match the words of prophecy so closely (though not exactly) is that Matthew has derived Jesus' itinerary from those very words.

In Matt. 21:4-5, Matthew creates a ludicrous scene: Jesus stunt-rides two animals into Jerusalem. The only possible purpose Matthew could have had in changing Mark's straightforward narrative into such a spectacle is to demonstrate that Jesus fulfilled prophecy to the letter. Obviously, Matthew's Jesus can fulfill this prophecy in this odd manner only because Matthew rigs the story with details cribbed from the "fulfilled" prophecy. This bizarre scene shows to what extremes Matthew can go in portraying Jesus as the fulfiller of prophecy.

With the thirty silver coins in Matt. 26:15 and 27:9, Matthew again inserts a detail from a prophecy into a story he borrowed from Mark. A chapter later, Matthew relies on the readers' memory of that detail to confirm that the prophecy was fulfilled to the letter.

Matthew's specification of thirty silver pieces and his report that Judas returned the money are small but lucid examples of how Matthew used the Old Testament as a *source* of information for the story of Jesus. It is not the case that Matthew knew a factually accurate account of the life of Jesus and then realized, from his knowledge of Scripture, that the life of Jesus fulfilled prophecy. Rather, the process worked in the opposite direction: Matthew started with the conviction that Jesus' life must have fulfilled Scripture, and then went back to study the Old Testament with the intention of finding out more about what had happened in Jesus' life. That is how he, alone out of the four evangelists, "knows," for example, that Jesus rode two animals into Jerusalem and that Judas was paid thirty silver pieces.

Retrofitted Prophecies

The three scenes analyzed in the previous section are passages in which Matthew has crafted his story so as to adjust it to prophecy. Those prophecies can be fulfilled only because Matthew adds details from them into his narrative. Another process used by New Testament authors to match prophecy to events works in the opposite direction, altering the prophecies so as to adjust them to the circumstances that fulfill them. I call that process "retrofitting." The term comes from engineering and names a process in which an already built object is added to or changed in some way so that it can perform a function for which it was not originally designed.

Applied to the New Testament, retrofitting is an apt analogy for the manner in which Old Testament passages which by themselves do not work well as predictions about Jesus are rewritten so they can be more easily correlated with beliefs or stories about Jesus. Sometimes that rewriting involves deleting parts of the Old Testament passage that would ruin the correlation with Jesus. Sometimes it involves changing key words in the passage or adding some new ones. Sometimes it involves stitching together parts of two or more different scriptures to produce a hybrid passage. The most elegant retrofits are the ones that require the least rewriting inasmuch as the connection between the Old Testament and Jesus is more convincing the closer the New Testament quotation of the passage is to its original. But the fact that New Testament writers felt the need to change the Old Testament verses at all shows two things:

1. The New Testament authors were well aware that the Old Testament in its own words often would not be seen as a prediction of Jesus. In other words,

they figured it was most unlikely that someone reading or hearing the Old Testament text in question would think that it foretold Jesus. The connection the New Testament author saw between the Old Testament and Jesus was seen *despite* the actual words of the original passage, which is why it needed to be retrofitted.

2. The textual retrofitting also shows that the "flow" of meaning in these cases is *from* Christian beliefs about Jesus *to* the Old Testament, not the other way around. As we will see over and over again, the Christian authors came to see the meanings in the Old Testament that they did because they already believed in Jesus. It is, emphatically, not the case that they come to believe in Jesus because of what they read in the Old Testament. If that had been the case, there would have been no need for the retrofits.

Let's survey four examples of retrofitting in Matthew.

THE PARTHENOS WILL CONCEIVE

> Look, the *parthenos*[2] will conceive and will have a son
> and they will name him Emmanuel.
> (Matt. 1:23, author's translation)

> Look, the *parthenos* will conceive and will have a son
> and you will name him Emmanuel.
> (Isa. 7:14 LXX, author's translation)

Matthew has made a slight but necessary alteration in the wording of Isa. 7:14: he has changed the form of the verb *to name* from second person singular to third person plural. In Isaiah (LXX), it is "you" who will name the child, whereas in Matthew, "they will name him Emmanuel." This grammatical adjustment is necessary because without it, the "you" in the prophecy would refer to Joseph and thus contradict the angel's command to him to name the boy Jesus (1:21). So who is the "they" who will call Jesus Emmanuel? According to the way Matthew lays out his sentence, the antecedent of "they" is the people whom Jesus will save from their sins. Matthew's grammatical design here is ingenious because it makes his Christian audience—not characters in the

---

2. This Greek word usually means "young woman" but can mean "virgin" in certain contexts. I am convinced that Matthew understands *parthenos* in its customary sense of "young woman" and that his gospel does not provide evidence for the belief in the virgin birth, a distinctive Lukan notion. See *Born Divine*, 195–206. I leave *parthenos* untranslated here because its translation does not affect our analysis of Matthew's retrofitting.

story—the ones who will refer to their savior by the name that means "God is with us."

BETHLEHEM, (NOT) THE LEAST

> You, Bethlehem of Ephrathah,
> who are the smallest of the clans of Judah.
> (Mic. 5:2, author's translation)
>
> You, Bethlehem, in the land of Judah,
> in no way are you least among the leaders of Judah.
> (Matt. 2:6, Scholars Version)

Matthew has altered the text of Micah's prophecy about Bethlehem in two ways. First, he replaces "Ephrathah" with "the land of Judah," probably to make the geographical reference more intelligible to his audience. That is not really retrofitting, but the second alteration is. He adds one Greek word (*mēpote*) that means "not at all" or "in no way" to the beginning of the second line, emphatically contradicting Micah's assertion that Bethlehem is "the smallest of the clans of Judah."

From Matthew's perspective, Jesus had changed the status of Bethlehem. Although it had been a small and unassuming town, it was now famous because it was the birthplace of the Messiah. Matthew's alteration here is interesting because it was unnecessary. The prophecy would work fine without Matthew's retrofit, but with the new wording, it works even better.

THE MESSENGER WHO WILL PREPARE THE WAY

In Matt. 11:10, Matthew found a quotation already retrofitted in Q: John the Baptizer "is the one about whom it is written, 'See I am sending my messenger before you, who will prepare your way before you.'" The quotation is based on God's declaration in Mal. 3:1 that he is sending his messenger who "will survey the way before *me*," which Q had tweaked to "will prepare *your* way before *you*." Q's retrofit was necessary because the "way" in Malachi is the way before God ("me"). Only by altering the wording as Q did could the prophecy be made to mean that John prepared the way before Jesus ("you").

Thirty Silver Coins

> And they took the thirty silver coins, the price put on a man's head (this is the price they put on him among the Israelites), and they donated it for the potter's field, as my Lord commanded me. (Matt. 27:9-10, Scholars Version)

> Yahweh said to me, "Throw it to the potter"—this handsome price at which I was valued by them. So I took the thirty silver coins and threw them to the potter in the house of Yahweh. (Zech. 11:13, author's translation)

We saw already how Matthew uses elements in this prophecy to craft the story of the events that fulfill it. Matthew also takes great liberties in the wording of the prophecy he presents. It is based on Zech. 11:13, from which Matthew quotes a few words and paraphrases some others, and to which he adds some of his own words. Strangely, Matthew attributes the oracle to Jeremiah, to whose prophecy it indirectly alludes, but from which Matthew has taken not a single phrase. Although the prophecy is based on Zech. 11:13, it is essentially Matthew's own construction, for the central action it describes and the deed that Matthew narrates as its fulfillment—the purchase of a field from a potter—are not found in Zechariah, nor anywhere else in the Old Testament.

Although Matthew has clearly worded the prophecy to match his story, in this example his extensive textual manipulation goes beyond retrofitting, since he has not only reworded Zechariah, but has freely composed parts of the prophecy himself. In this unusual case, it is fair to say that Matthew has created both the prophecy and the event that fulfills it.

Did the Prophets Know What They Were Talking About?

From our perspective, it is obvious that Matthew was reading Jesus *into* the prophecies he quoted. When we examine those prophecies in their own contexts, it is clear, for example, that Zechariah had no foreknowledge of Judas when he spoke about the thirty silver coins, and that Isaiah was not thinking about the birth of Jesus when he challenged King Ahaz with the news that "the young woman is pregnant and will have a son and will name him Immanuel" (Isa. 7:14, quoted in Matt. 1:23). The woman in question was someone Isaiah and Ahaz knew (note that she is "*the* young woman"), almost certainly one of Ahaz's wives. Respect for the Bible requires us to understand the prophets as speaking to their own times, with messages that they and their audiences understood in relation to their situations centuries before the time of Jesus.

Respect for the Bible also requires us to understand Matthew on his own terms. Matthew, like all Jews of his time, treated the words of the prophets as coded messages having significance beyond the prophets' own understanding. This view of prophecy was absorbed into Judaism during the Hellenistic period, having originated among the ancient Greeks, who believed that their prophets spoke under the influence of a "spirit of prophecy" that overrode the speaker's own rational capacities. As a result, sometimes neither the prophets nor their audiences could understand the true significance of their words, and thus the real meaning of some of those pagan prophecies could be discerned only after the predicted events had already occurred. First-century Jews applied these Greek beliefs about prophecy to the biblical prophets, and so came to believe that God had planted throughout their writings cryptic clues about his plans for the future.

Many Christians hold that same belief today. They think that prophets such as Isaiah and Ezekiel, as well as New Testament authors such as Paul, Peter, and John unwittingly wrote about events happening in our own time or about to happen in the near future. Today you can find books in the "End-Times Prophecy" sections of Christian bookstores that claim to understand the prophets better than the prophets understood themselves. Inevitably, these books explain that we are living in the last generation, a time of unparalleled evil from which only a few will be saved.

Rather than pursue this issue further, I ask only that you pause for a moment to consider three interrelated premises of that view of prophecy:

- The belief that all of history has been building up to our own lifetime
- The assumption that the prophets did not fully understand their own messages, but we do
- The outlook that we are among the "saved" and the rest of humanity is therefore "unsaved," awaiting its eternal damnation

What human needs are answered by such self-centered beliefs? What kind of God is worshipped by a religion that caters to these needs?

The Polemical Function of Proof-from-Prophecy

It is a deeply rooted Christian belief that Jesus fulfilled prophecy. In its most common version, this belief entails several conditions:

- The Old Testament contains a number of prophetic predictions about the coming Messiah.
- These prophecies were, in effect, waiting to be fulfilled.
- People would know the Messiah when he finally came, because he would fulfill these prophecies.

That is how most Christians throughout history have understood the concept of "Old Testament prophecy," and Matthew's Gospel has been instrumental in fostering this notion. His method of quoting numerous specific prophecies and pointing out exactly how they were fulfilled gives the cumulative impression that it should have been fairly clear to people who knew the Scriptures that Jesus was the long-awaited Messiah.

So effective has Matthew's Gospel been in this regard, that Christianity has long puzzled over why the Jews of Jesus' time "rejected" him. Matthew conveys the unmistakable impression that the Jewish leaders knew (or at least should have known) that Jesus was the Messiah, but that they opposed him because of their hypocrisy and hard-heartedness. At the very end of the Gospel, Matthew makes his accusation explicit: those authorities knew that Jesus had risen from the dead but conspired to deceive their own people about the truth of his resurrection:

> Some of the guards [at the tomb] returned to the city and reported to the ranking priests everything that had happened. They met with the elders and hatched a plan: they bribed the soldiers with an adequate amount of money and ordered them: "Tell everybody that his disciples came at night and stole his body while you were asleep. If the governor should hear about this, we will deal with him; don't worry." They took the money and did as they had been instructed. And this story has been passed around among the Jews until this very day. (Matt. 28:11-15, Scholars Version)

We should pause to examine this brief story because Matthew's attitude toward the Jewish leaders bears directly on his proof-from-prophecy theme. The first thing to be said about this scene is that there is not a shred of historical evidence for the conspiracy Matthew describes. The conspiracy Matthew imagines is utterly implausible, for it asks us to believe that soldiers would confess to the most serious sin soldiers on guard duty can commit: sleeping while on watch, an offense that came with an automatic death penalty in the Roman army. Besides being stupid, the excuse is also exceedingly lame: if the guards were asleep, how could they know that the disciples had stolen the body? Moreover, if the scenario had happened the way Matthew says it did, he could not have known about it: if the soldiers really "took the money and did as they had been instructed" (28:15), no one could have known about the alleged bribery and the lying. It isn't difficult to conclude that Matthew made this story up. It is fiction. Now, the Gospels contain many fictions that express truth—stories that while not historically true communicate truths that are more important than historical facts. (Jesus' parables and the stories that he multiplied bread and fish are good examples.) But the story about Jewish leaders who covered up Jesus' resurrection is not like those benign fictions. This story is a malicious lie. That Matthew told it to counteract the accusation that the disciples stole Jesus' body helps us understand the motivation for the lie, but does not excuse it.

Matthew's proof-from-prophecy argument is intertwined with his polemic against official Judaism. He asserts not only that his people are right to follow Jesus as the Jewish Messiah, but also that Jews who do not follow Jesus are unfaithful to Judaism. In its simplest form, Matthew's message to his people is:

1. "We" have a right to exist as a Jewish community, despite the fact that "they" say we don't; and
2. "We" are the only real Jews.

The debate between Matthew's people and the keepers of official Judaism at that time (i.e., the Pharisees) must have been fierce, to judge from the polemical rhetoric in Matthew's Gospel. See, for example, the way Matthew's Jesus rips into the Pharisees in chapter 23.

We don't expect cool logic in heated debates, which too often end up with each side even more convinced of its own rightness. And that is precisely the sort of framework in which Matthew's use of prophecy must be placed. Matthew's rhetoric was not designed to win over the Jewish opponents of his community. Nor was Matthew's manipulation of Scripture meant to persuade the open-minded, if in that situation there were any such people. It was intended to reinforce the belief of Matthew's own people that all of Jewish history had been building up to Jesus, and thus up to them.

Matthew's Context and Contemporary Faith

It seems most unlikely that Matthew's presentation would change the mind of anyone who was not already inclined to believe that Jesus was the Messiah. Perhaps some people neither knew what the prophets really said nor questioned whether Matthew's stories were literally true; those people might be convinced that Jesus had fulfilled prophecies. And while this may well have been the effect of Matthew's Gospel on a few, we need not conclude that Matthew's purpose was to trick the gullible. A more responsible line of inquiry into Matthew's purpose in correlating prophecies with stories about Jesus is to imagine the circumstances that would allow Matthew and his audience to honestly believe in his presentation of Jesus as the fulfillment of prophecy.

Scholars generally agree on what those circumstances were. We have to try to see things the way Matthew and his people did, regardless of whether we see things that way today. Matthew and his audience already believed that Jesus was the Messiah. They also believed that God must have been dropping hints about the long-awaited Messiah in the Scriptures, especially in the books of the prophets. So Matthew went back to the Scriptures and studied them carefully, looking for clues about Jesus the Messiah. For Matthew, the recognition of Jesus as the Messiah is the newly revealed key that unlocks the hidden meaning of prophecy. When Matthew found a prophetic statement that *could* be about Jesus, he tried to match it up with something he already knew—or believed—about Jesus' life. Furthermore, and this is crucial, whatever a prophet says about the Messiah, or the future Davidic king, or God's son, Matthew could take to be information about Jesus not previously recognized as such.

In Matthew's presentation of Jesus fulfilling prophecy, then, it was not the case that the meanings of the prophecies he fulfilled were evident *before* he fulfilled them. It was only later, after Jesus' death, that his followers were able retrospectively to link events in his life to specific prophecies. (Luke and John independently admit this and even explain why the disciples did not realize at the time that Jesus was fulfilling prophecies; see, for example, Luke 24:25-27 and John 2:13-22; 12:12-16.) That was not primarily because the prophecies involved were not well known, but rather because their meanings became clear to Jesus' followers only after they became convinced that he had fulfilled them. Only after his followers came to believe that Jesus was the promised Messiah did they draw the conclusion that he had fulfilled prophecy, for that is what the Messiah was supposed to do. Only after they believed that Jesus had fulfilled prophecies were they able to detect the specific prophecies that had reached their fulfillment in his life. And only after his followers had identified which prophecies he had fulfilled did their hidden meanings come to light.

The net result of all this is plain enough: The early Christian belief that Jesus fulfilled prophecy arose after and because of the belief that he was the promised Messiah. This important finding needs to be emphasized. The belief that Jesus was the Messiah was the basis for the belief that he was the fulfillment of prophecy. It was not that people noticed that Jesus had fulfilled a series of prophecies and so concluded that he must be the Messiah. The process worked the other way around. It was because Christians were convinced that Jesus was the Messiah that they went searching through the Scriptures to discover which prophecies he had fulfilled. The proclamation that Jesus fulfilled prophecy is a testimony to Christian faith, not a description of its origin.

With this in mind, we can easily see why Matthew's Jewish contemporaries were not persuaded by his "proof from prophecy." It had nothing to do with having hard hearts or closed minds, or being deceived by their leaders. All of that is Matthean caricature. It had to do with the fact that Matthew's presentation of prophecy makes sense only from the perspective of prior belief in Jesus. Outside of that perspective, Matthew's use of prophecy has no persuasive power and can even look like a deliberate distortion of the Scriptures aimed at deceiving those who are uninformed and easily impressed.

Matthew must have known that he was not going to change minds with his fulfillment-of-prophecy theme. He designed it to support the faith of his own Christian-Jewish community, not to convert outsiders. Matthew's message is that since the prophets confirm that Jesus is the Messiah, his followers are the true heirs of Israel and children of Abraham, despite what the vast majority of other Jews might say. This message would have offered encouragement to a tiny Jewish sect like Matthew's community at a time when the belief that Jesus was the Messiah could make you an outcast in Jewish society. Believing that Jesus was the fulfillment of prophecy helped to reassure his Jewish followers of the rightness of their cause, at a time when the prestige of Jewish authority made that cause seem religiously illegitimate.

But that time no longer exists. It has not existed for nineteen centuries. The viability of Christian belief is not even remotely threatened by Judaism. Today there is not the slightest possibility that Christians will stop following Jesus because Jews do not regard him as the Messiah. In the first century, perhaps it was necessary for followers of Jesus to believe that the Scriptures pointed to Christ, that Jews did not understand the true meaning of their Scriptures, and that therefore the Scriptures of Israel properly belonged only to Christians (who eventually made them into their own "Old Testament"). Christian history is stained with the ugly consequences of the anti-Judaism fostered by those beliefs. In view of the horrifying price that Christians have forced Jews to pay for keeping their covenant with God, isn't it time to stop insisting on Matthew's mistaken premise? Do not Christians now have the moral obligation to let go of the notion that if Jews truly understood their Scriptures, they would become Christians?

The belief that the prophets were pointing to Jesus, though perhaps helpful at the time Matthew wrote his Gospel, has long since outlived its usefulness. It is a belief that distorts the Scriptures and has had ugly consequences in history. Out of respect for Judaism and for the Bible, therefore, I propose that Christians have an intellectual and moral duty to abandon this obsolete, self-serving, and dangerous belief. What do you think?

Postscript: The Historical Jesus

Since this essay appears in a volume dealing both with the message of Jesus and the historical Jesus, I need at last to raise the question, What does the fulfillment of prophecy, as it plays out in the Gospel of Matthew, have to do with the historical Jesus? My answer, which should surprise no one who has read this far, is this: Nothing.

The clearest evidence for this verdict comes from the literary format in which the fulfillment of prophecy is presented in this gospel: not as comments attributed to Jesus, but as interruptions in the narrative, through which the author communicates directly with the audience. (There are two exceptions: in Matt. 11:10 and 26:31, it is Jesus who quotes a prophecy and announces its fulfillment. Both scenes are ones Matthew copied from his sources—the first from Q, the second from Mark.) Moreover, Matthew's presentation of Jesus as the fulfillment of prophecy involved significant manipulation of the evangelist's texts, tailoring his stories to match prophecies and rewriting prophecies to match his stories. All that textual bending and stretching occurred in the process of literary composition and can easily be imagined as the work of the learned scribe that Matthew's meticulous composition shows him to be. But in what plausible scenario can we imagine those textual manipulations on the pages Matthew composed as going back to the historical Jesus? Does anyone seriously want to argue that Jesus actually rode two donkeys into Jerusalem, for example, in order to fulfill prophecy, or that he misquoted scripture (as in Matt. 11:10, described earlier) so that he could point out the fulfillment of reworded prophecy?

Does all this prove that Jesus did not imagine himself to be fulfilling prophecy? No. To demonstrate that would require proving a negative—an impossible task. (It cannot be proven, for example, that Jesus did not speak Swedish.) What these considerations do indicate, however, is that Matthew's Gospel provides no evidence that Jesus saw himself as the fulfillment of prophecy. It's possible that Jesus did see himself that way, but in the critical study of the historical Jesus, saying "it's possible" is as close as one can get to saying nothing. (It's possible that Jesus spoke Swedish.) If one wants to advance the proposal that the historical Jesus claimed to be fulfilling prophecy, one is obliged to offer evidence and arguments. And for that project, the Gospel of Matthew will be no help at all.

6

Faith and the Historical Jesus
Does A Confessional Position and Respect for the Jesus Tradition Preclude Serious Historical Engagement?

Darrell L. Bock

Can the lion and the lamb lie together? For many people, no matter where they are on the spectrum, the idea of an Evangelical engaging in a historical-Jesus discussion is an oxymoron. For many critics, the Evangelical view of Scripture is said to skew Evangelicals' discussion of Jesus issues. For many Evangelicals, especially lay Evangelicals, the skepticism surrounding much of historical-Jesus work is to be shunned as a rejection of the Bible as the word of God. So can there be Evangelical approaches to the historical Jesus that can contribute to the lively discussion about the historical Jesus?

I believe the answer is yes. To get there, however, one must appreciate the nature of what historical-Jesus work seeks to achieve, as well as the limitations such a historically oriented study operates under when it seeks to cross thousands of years to do its work. In addition, there is a difference between what one might believe in part by faith and in part because of trajectories one might see in historical work and what one can make a strong case to show is likely rooted in the accounts tied to Jesus. These distinctions are important in this discussion. There are differences between what one can show, what one can think plausible and make a case for, and what one can't.

PRELIMINARY REMARKS ON THE VALUE, LIMITS, AND ROOTS OF HISTORICAL-JESUS STUDY

Historical-Jesus study has developed over time and has had many different emphases and shifts in method over that time.[1] The goal is to pursue what it can show to be most likely about Jesus through the variety of sources and objects (*realia*) we currently possess. It does so with a limitation of total available sources, as well as the boundaries of time that have impeded our ability to understand first-century culture. We have to try to reconstruct in its pluralistic complexity both Greco-Roman and Jewish elements. This gives the results of such study a very provisional nature. New finds could greatly change "established facts," just as the discovery of the Dead Sea Scrolls brought a new and significant impetus to the understanding of Jesus in a Jewish context. This development came long after Albert Schweitzer pleaded for us to understand Jesus in such a milieu almost a half century earlier, when he was sounding a death knell for what has come to be called the first quest. What he lacked, the scrolls helped to supply, giving fresh routes by which to appreciate Jesus and his world.

Historical-Jesus study began as a project of the Enlightenment to strip Jesus of the doctrinal layers said to be tied to him by the early church, so that only a historical Jesus should remain, stripped of any dogmatic or theological accretions. It was rooted in an intense skepticism about the Jesus tradition. The history of historical-Jesus study has shown the process is a little like trying to divide an atom or separate out cleanly a strand of DNA. It is a difficult exercise, that is, full of judgments. Some say there have been three quests, while others suggest that once the quest started down this road in the eighteenth century, it never let up.[2] Numerous Jesus portraits have resulted. Some say this diversity negates the exercise and shows its inability to cope with the data.[3] But recent historical-Jesus study has for the most part started in a Jewish context to understand Jesus, a starting place that makes sense in light of Jesus' roots and our still-accumulating knowledge of Second Temple Judaism.[4] It is a method committed to a kind of corroborative model, setting a high burden of proof. To

---

1. In the history of this pursuit, three approaches have dominated. The first sought to strip what was perceived as dogmatics from the portrait of Jesus using a worldview that ruled out certain possibilities a priori and working with what were argued to be differences between the accounts. It also introduced into the study genre categories as ways to make the case for separating out the dogmatics from the history. The second approach thought it could locate later additions of a more exclusively Hellenistic emphasis and remove them as anachronistic. It also was the period in which important criteria of authenticity were developed from a tradition-historical approach. The third approach, the one this essay will emphasize, tries to place Jesus in his Second Temple period setting. These three approaches are commonly called the three quests, with some simply referring to the third stage as the Jesus Research. The actual history is more complicated than this threefold division suggests, especially in claiming there was a no quest period, but I note these divisions because they are commonly used and do give some important distinctions in how historical-Jesus work has been pursued.

make it over this burden or to show plausibility for authenticity is significant, when it can be done.

This approach beats the other options of earlier quests. The first quest was flawed, arguing that dogmatics can have no place in studying Jesus (as if Jesus did not engage in theology). It also carried with it worldview issues about God's activity in the world that are still discussed as a part of historical Jesus method today. How does one treat a book that claims God is a major actor in events, when generally historical method moves in a direction where God is bracketed out of the discussion?[5]

The second quest struggled, arguing that Hellenistic layers could be discovered and surgically and cleanly removed from the gospel portraits about Jesus, only to have the Dead Sea Scrolls raise the possibility that some of those Hellenistic roots could also be quite Jewish.

The strength of the so-called third quest, if it really is a third quest or not, is its starting point in the very milieu in which Jesus lived and spoke. This has opened up fresh ways to appreciate what Jesus claimed and how he likely went

---

2. The status of the three-quest model is debated, being heavily dependent on a Germanic perspective. Nonetheless, the first quest ran from the late eighteenth century to the early twentieth century, while the second quest began in 1953 with Ernst Käsemann and runs to the present. In English, Ernst Käsemann, "The Problem of the Historical Jesus," *Essays on New Testament Themes* (London: SCM, 1964), 15–47. The third emerged in the 1960s and 1970s, with work by Joachim Jeremias and Martin Hengel setting the pace, and gained momentum in the late 1970s with work by Ben Meyer. Joachim Jeremias, *New Testament Theology* (London: SCM, 1971); idem, *The Eucharistic Words of Jesus*, rev. ed. (London: SCM, 1966); idem, *The Parables of Jesus*, rev. ed. (New York: Scribner's, 1963); Martin Hengel, *Judaism and Hellenism* (Philadelphia: Fortress Press, 1974; Ben Meyer, *The Aims of Jesus* (London: SCM, 1979). The third quest is still quite active, having a variety of representatives.

3. Most recently, such a position has been taken by Dale Allison, Richard Hays, and Beverly Roberts Gaventa in two works, but its roots go back to Martin Kahler. Luke Timothy Johnson has also contended for such an understanding. See Dale Allison, *The Historical Christ and the Theological Jesus* (Grand Rapids: Eerdmans, 2009); Beverly Gaventa Roberts and Richard Hays, eds., *Seeking the Identity of Jesus: A Pilgrimage* (Grand Rapids: Eerdmans, 2008); Luke Timothy Johnson, *The Real Jesus: The Misguided Quest for the Historical Jesus and the Truth of the Traditional Gospels* (San Francisco: HarperOne, 1997); Martin Kahler, *The So-Called Historical Jesus and the Historic, Biblical Christ*, trans. Carl Braaten (Philadelphia: Fortress Press, 1964; English ed. of 1896 German work from an 1892 lecture).

4. This starting point has been crisply defended recently by James Charlesworth in *The Historical Jesus: An Essential Guide* (Minneapolis: Abingdon, 2008).

5. Wrapped up in this question are huge historical-method and philosophical issues traced most effectively by Robert Webb in Darrell L. Bock and Robert Webb, *Key Issues in the Life of the Historical Jesus*, WUNT 247 (Tübingen: Mohr Siebeck, 2009), 9–93. Much of what I would say technically and in detail about method is found here. My preference is for the "Critical Theistic History" model in that chapter.

about it, at least during most of his public ministry.[6] There is great value in seeing what can be shown historically to be likely in understanding Jesus and his relationship to his Second Temple Jewish context.

One other factor in historical-Jesus study is that our portrait of Jesus is mediated to us in the sources. We have no autobiography of Jesus; rather, the Jesus of Scripture is a Jesus remembered by those who associated themselves with him or those who did walk with him.[7] Those same people are likely responsible for the roots of tradition we have about Jesus. On the other hand, we also have to negotiate the issues tied to the genre of the materials we have. Are the gospels best read as a form of *bios*?[8] How do Greco-Roman expectations in presenting historical claims parallel and differ from our own, and how much difference do those differences make?

That this kind of non-autobiographical portrait of someone can be accurate and/or valuable is easy to establish. We often think that the only testimony worth having about a person is his or her autobiography. However, this is mistaken. Granted, first-person material is nice to possess. To have it certainly helps in understanding an aspect of what drives a person. However, in the case of Jesus, all we have is what others have said about him and what others have reported that he said. To be in such a position does not mean that we have lost access to Jesus; it just makes things more difficult. On the positive side, just think of how history is enhanced when colleagues of a great figure write about their impressions of that figure. The story of Jesus is very much a story of his impact on others. Without that, his life and work matters little. So in this case, such multiple angles on a personality are of great significance in dealing with a leader's impact and motivations. This is what the gospels give us, at least in part, and such an impression can be as historical as the words of the individual.

I make this point about impact because a prominent university Jewish scholar once asked me how we can know anything about Jesus because he left us no writing of his own. (We were discussing my claim that Jesus is to be appreciated within a context of messiahship that can make sense in a Second Temple Jewish context.) He issued his challenge at an informal dinner with his

---

6. Some studies, such as those by Ben Meyer, are careful to distinguish what Jesus did publicly and what he taught his disciples privately, a key distinction to keep in view when discussing how Jesus went about disclosing his intentions.

7. The phrase "Jesus remembered" has been made most visible recently by James Dunn, *Jesus Remembered* (Grand Rapids: Eerdmans, 2003), where he reminds us of how important oral tradition is in the development of the Jesus materials we have.

8. So, of course, Richard Burridge, *What Are the Gospels? A Comparison with Greco-Roman Biography*, 2nd ed. (Grand Rapids: Eerdmans, 2004).

program's graduate students, who ironically numbered about twelve, in honor of my visit. I responded by saying, "Let us assume that you died and left no writing. Do you think I could ask your students about what you taught and how, so that I might get a multidimensional read on who you were and what you taught? Could I discover something of value about the historical professor?" I think the gospels give us this in significant ways.

One of the ways we can come to this conclusion is through careful historical study, using the rules historical-Jesus scholars use, while understanding that the bar is being raised to a level of significant demonstration. It is a method of corroboration, which makes sense when one is dealing with sources as complex as ours. The limits of time traversed, the task of trying to reconstruct culture, and the difficulty that method has with singular, uncorroborated testimony means the results in many particulars are likely to come up short of demonstration on the one hand. The method and its standards mean that a full portrait is lacking that might well emerge if singular attested testimony could be more easily integrated into the method.[9] In an approach where so much rests on some type of corroboration, much potential evidence has been lost or at least hangs in a kind of suspended animation by not meeting the historical researchers' standards that point in more comprehensive ways to demonstration than singular testimony does.

Thus, the results of historical-Jesus study, using the criteria of authenticity (multiple attestation, dissimilarity in one of its variety of forms, coherence, Aramaic substratum, embarrassment, cultural appropriateness, and/or historical plausibility), are likely to be varied and will only give us, at best, access to the gist of Jesus, relying as it does on sources whose origin and construction are complex. These criteria are not perfect by any means, but they give us a start for the conversation and are among the best tools we have for making assessments. Historical-Jesus studies can give us a start and can open doors for discussion between people of distinct approaches to Jesus. For these reasons, the discussion is worth having and pursuing, even if its results will always be limited in scope and varied in conclusions.

---

9. Singular testimony is one of the reasons the Gospel of John is so little used in such study. Well more than 80 percent of John's material is unique to his Gospel. Most scholars use it sparingly in such work, even though there is a growing sense that this material is also significant in what it contributes at key spots. It is to be remembered that just because singular testimony cannot be corroborated does not mean something did not happen. The problem is we cannot confirm this one way or the other, so in an approach that asks for corroboration, such material cannot be used directly. This is a nice reminder that failure to meet the criteria does not mean a failure to be historical. Those are two different things. In using the criteria, one can conclude this likely happened, this likely did not happen, or one cannot say.

The last concern to introduce, and a major one for this essay, is one of reader locatedness. Much of what I have said here represents a very brief but reflective summary of historical-Jesus study as it stands. I think most of us, no matter where we are on the spectrum, would recognize what I have outlined as the general path most historical-Jesus studies take. The core question I have been asked to pursue is whether someone with a confessional approach to the material can engage in such a conversation as I have just sketched. I have taken the time to work through this because historical-Jesus study is one way to engage the material we have and the problem of how to assess the mix of theology and history we have. Often, if one has such a confessional conviction and moves over into this area, one is accused of either engaging in historical positivism, being a maximalist, or being a theological apologist. Such reactions are not only an issue for Evangelical treatments. Some Jewish scholars and archaeologists face similar assessments for their work in Old Testament, as do Catholics and other scholars who teach in theological contexts and write in this area.

My response to such reactions and the skepticism about the work it assesses in this manner is that the value of such criticism depends on the details of the work in question. At one level, it is understandable that someone who sees severe problems with our sources or who has their own located position in terms of how God can or cannot act and what we can say about that historically would see a more positive assessment of sources or divine activity in such ways. Relative to where that critic is on the spectrum, those descriptions appear to be accurate. However, I'd like to submit that things are not so easy, which is why conversation is so important here.

For example, I find it hard to accept the description of being a maximalist when I concede when I walk into the historical-Jesus arena that there are significant portions of sources that are excluded from playing a key role because of the way singular attestation is to be assessed by the approach. I commend to everyone's attention how others are making more complex cases for using some of this material, much of which involves John.[10] Yet in my own work, I hardly ever appeal to John. Confessionally, he is seen as one of our most important witnesses, but in the historical-Jesus discussion, I am aware that the use of John

---

10. I think here of work by Paul Anderson, as well as works he has edited. In addition, there is the recent presentation by James Charlesworth on John at the Princeton-Prague Symposium, which to my knowledge is in preparation for publication soon. Paul Anderson, *The Christology of the Fourth Gospel: Its Unity and Disunity in Light of John 6* (Valley Forge: Trinity Press International, 1997) and two volumes, edited with Felix Just (vols. 1 and 2) and with Tom Thatcher (vol. 2 only) entitled *Jesus, John, and History*, published by SBL in 2007 and 2009.

in many cases is not persuasive to most, and so I do not often appeal to it in my own historical-Jesus work because I understand and accept for the historical-Jesus discussion that its use raises questions.

I would argue that historical positivism is one of those charges that are in the eye of the beholder. In other words, something looks positivist to anyone who sits on the more skeptical side of the spectrum than the person being assessed. We all have locatedness as we read. It is important to recall that there is a lot of judgment each of us makes, some of it fundamentally philosophical and worldview rooted versus purely historical, as we render an opinion about the authenticity of events.

As to the charge of being an apologist, this one I think often is true. However, the reason one makes a defense for something is that one believes such a case is worth defending and, hopefully, also brings forth reasons that can be shared for why such a conclusion deserves serious consideration. Unfortunately, in our academic and historical-Jesus circles, we often use the term *apologetics* as a way of dismissing a study by appealing to a motive that implies the case that is put forward is not "pure" history, whatever that really is. I suspect there are others of us sitting here, not Evangelical, who could well be described as apologists for one view or another, whether it be for biblical theology or narrative theology over historical work, feminism, historical skepticism, or colonialism. That description, as long as it locates, is OK, but we should be careful not to use it in ways that become dismissive of engaging in the details of one's position. Too often, even in our academic culture, we use labels dismissively, mirroring the kind of public discourse we often criticize when we see such tactics used in the public square.

Everything I have said up to here has spoken in the generalities of method and approach. In the end, the proof of contribution is in the pudding. Behind my remarks is a technical study of Jesus I carried out with several Evangelical colleagues. It was published in the Wissenschafliche Untersuchungen zum Neuen Testament series last year and is currently being released by Eerdmans in a paperback edition for reasons your pocketbook will appreciate.[11] This study of over eight hundred pages has a methodological essay and then presents twelve events that this team of eleven writers plus a few others contributed to in an annual weekend seminar format that spanned a decade. Each essay was discussed line by line by the group, as a whole day was given to each event. The book takes these twelve events and makes a case for the core authenticity of each while bringing together the whole to try to obtain a sketch about Jesus. It is

---

11. Darrell L. Bock and Robert L. Webb, *Key Events in the Life of the Historical Jesus* (Grand Rapids: Eerdmans, 2010).

both a micro study of units and a macro study attempting to build a synthesis. It is here that what I have been only able to say in outline form was applied to specific passages in detail. The position of this book was that, at the least, these twelve key events and what they tell us about Jesus are significant and need to be dealt with in understanding him. Whatever one might think of how Evangelicals see Jesus as a whole, our hope was that in presenting these twelve events, a case had been made for where to start such a discussion, having rooted these events in a historically credible defense of their core authenticity.

In the remainder of my essay, I am going to take one key, very small sliver of the argument for one key event as a sample of how I think Evangelicals can contribute to the larger discussion. I hope to show that when engaging in historical-Jesus study, one makes the case using standards and rules historical-Jesus scholars of all locations on the spectrum seek to apply. Doing so means what Evangelicals say and how they say it fits into the conversation that comes with debate about the historical Jesus.

This discussion about how Evangelicals engage such an important area of theological reflection is important for a couple of reasons. Obviously, it is helpful for how we engage each other within this subdiscipline of historical-Jesus studies. Secondly, the discussion is important in a context where as recently as the summer of 2010, very public complaints were made about the participation of Evangelicals in the Society of Biblical Literature (SBL). The argument was made that somehow their presence besmirches the organization. I actually think it speaks well of the SBL. Part of the value of SBL is that the entire spectrum of views can gather and engage each other, having conversations we normally might not have.

The Example Passage: Peter's Declaration at Caesarea Philippi

I select as an example the group's work on Peter's confession at Caesarea Philippi. Peter's declaration at Caesarea Philippi about Jesus being the Messiah is recognized by virtually all scholars as the turning point of the Jesus story in Mark, Matthew, and Luke. Yet as clear as Peter is, Jesus initially advises that this recognition be handled with silence. In scholarly circles, this hesitation is called "the messianic secret," an idea that has engendered no lack of debate in historical-Jesus discussion. Why the word to be silent after the declaration? Why keep the understanding in-house? This event is so crucial that much time shall be spent interacting with objections to it. Only a careful look at the first-century perspective on Messiah and Jesus' handling of it can help us to understand the caution Jesus initially had for this title.

THE RELEVANT CRITERIA

Beyond multiple attestations, this event meets the other criteria of Palestinian environment, of embarrassment, and of coherence. We proceed in this order.

MULTIPLE ATTESTATION

The central passage is Mark 8:27-30 = Matt. 16:13-20 = Luke 9:18-21. Though presented with some variation, Peter says Jesus is the Christ in every rendering in these gospels. This is the gist of the event we examine. *Messiah* means "anointed" in Hebrew. The Greek term is Christ. However, all kinds of figures can be anointed in the Jewish context, especially kings, prophets, and priests. Still, when Peter uses the term, the remark is placed in a final-deliverance context. Messiah is to be distinguished from a prophetic understanding of Jesus. The account makes this point through the contrast with the previous answer that the crowds understand Jesus to be some kind of a prophet.

A passage with a theme similar to this messianic declaration is John 6:66-69, where Peter declares the disciples will not leave Jesus because he is the "Holy One of God" (v. 69). This may point to multiple attestations for this idea. Jesus is specially commissioned by God and is distinct from a prophet.

Also important to the context of the synoptic event of Peter's declaration are Jesus' remarks after the declaration that he will suffer (Mark 8:31-33 = Matt. 16:21-23 = Luke 9:22).[12] John's Gospel does not have such an explicit prediction of suffering (John 3:14-15 is an allusion to such suffering). However, Jesus foresees his suffering in other texts Mark uses plus some other texts across the tradition (Mark: Mark 9:31 = Matt. 17:22-23 = Luke 9:44; Mark 10:33-34 = Matt. 20:18-19 = Luke 18:31-33; Mark 10:45 = Matt. 20:28; Mark 2:20 = Matt. 9:15 = Luke 5:35; Mark 14:7 = Matt. 26:11; Parable: Mark 12:1-12 = Matt. 21:33-46 = Luke 20:9-18; L: Luke 13:32-33; 17:25; 24:7, 21, 46).[13] Thus, the theme of Jesus' suffering is multiply attested, while the memory of Peter making a key declaration has what could be called "soft" multiple attestation because of John's account.

---

12. Meier, *A Marginal Jew*, (New York: Doubleday, 2001), 3:235-36, says treating the declaration of Peter "necessarily entails" treating its aftermath found in Jesus' remarks on suffering. Meier accepts some of this event as being Mark's creation, including what is called Mark's "messianic secret." We examine this claim in detail in the section on objections.

13. For a defense of the core authenticity of this category of texts, Hans Bayer, *Jesus' Predictions of Vindication and Resurrection: The Provenance, Meaning, and Correlation of the Synoptic Predictions*, WUNT 2.20 (Tübingen: Mohr Siebeck, 1986).

Palestinian Environment

Caesarea Philippi is not a natural locale for this event, although its place in first-century geography is well known. In fact, if one visits the Holy Land today, this is one of the tourist spots. What one finds is a location just outside of ancient Galilee. The key locale for the site involves a sheer cliff running up several hundred feet. Carved into the rock at various spots are niches that held idols tied to temples that were located by the waters that ran near the base of the cliff. Some of the niches were carved after Jesus' time, but the character of the location dates back to before his time. These niches tell us that this locale was home to many temples. The god Pan and the emperor Augustus are among the more prominent figures honored here. So central was Pan that the alternate name of the site is Paneas. The worship of Pan here looks to reach back to the period after Alexander the Great's conquest of the area. In other words, this is the most prominent locale for worship of multiple gods in the region. It is about as un-Jewish a spot as one could have found in the ancient land.

Now, some wish to argue this setting is a later creation because of its connection to Hellenistic religion and its implicit argument that Jesus is superior to their gods, including the emperor. However, the presence of this place's name appears in a locale uncommon for Mark's naming of locations. The locale is too specific for the kind of transition taking place here (compare Mark 1:21; 2:1; 3:1, 20; 5:1; 6:16; 7:24). Mark speaks of the "villages of Caesarea Philippi," so he does not evoke this specific temple locale but merely an association with the site. This more implicit connection reads more ambiguously than an explicit location. It has less the feel of a created event. More than that, the expression is not like other settings in Mark's Gospel; Mark tends to refer to a region or district in such descriptions ("region of Geresenes," 5:1; "their region," 17; "region of Tyre," 7:24, 31; "district of Dalmanutha," 8:10).

In addition, the locale is out of character with much of Jesus' ministry, which focused on Jewish concerns and preaching to the nation. The events described and the moment of the great declaration are not associated with Jewish imagery. Nor do the gospel writers name a setting like the edge of Jerusalem or the singular temple, but the most contrastive religious environment of polytheism. Yet this is evoked only indirectly by the use of a town's name. The scene has the feel of a distinctive memory.[14] When Jesus was in these regions, he is not described as going into the cities, but as staying on the outskirts or in villages. That part of the story then fits Jesus' ministry practice elsewhere in the region. A made-up story may have made more explicit some of the associations of the location and made the challenge to polytheism more explicit. Even more, a story created in line with the rest of Mark's story would have had a more Jewish focus than this locale does. Why not have situated this central declaration in a more Jewish locale, since one can place it anywhere if the story is made up? Why not as Jesus draws near to Jerusalem or in the context of his ministry near his home and the Sea of Galilee?

Yet another detail here is that the placement of this event comes at a time just after John the Baptist has been beheaded. This may explain a sojourn north of his jurisdiction and away from danger for a time. Antipas is alluded to as knowing about Jesus in Mark 6:14. Jesus is next described in places as diverse as Tyre and Sidon, the Decapolis, and Bethsaida, as well as in Caesarea. All these locations are outside the jurisdiction of Antipas.

Embarrassment

All of the Palestinian background points to a real event, and the timing fits as well. The scene may also be considered with reference to the criterion of embarrassment. Peter challenges Jesus when Jesus mentions his approaching suffering right after this declaration. Jesus replies to Peter, telling him, "Get behind me Satan!" (Mark 8:33 = Matt. 16:23). The detail is shocking enough that Luke omits it. This strong rebuke is not likely to be part of a story the church creates. It ends up having one of its key leaders severely rebuked, not exactly the way to commend your leadership to a public already raising questions about what you believe. This is a classic example of the criterion of embarrassment. Why would the church create a story that embarrasses one of its leaders this way? The embarrassing detail must be in the story because it was a part of the event. It strains credulity to see this story created with this unflattering picture of Peter and retained in the church's tradition about him, when those who kept this tradition had a high regard for Peter.[15] The reason such a detail would be retained was that the event made a deep impression on community memory.

14. Dunn says, "There are several indications that Mark has been able to draw on a well-rooted memory, with variations between the Synoptists characteristic of performance flexibility." *Jesus Remembered*, 644. What Dunn means by performance flexibility is that with gospel material rooted in oral tradition, accounts were retold but not always in the same words. What was retained was the gist of the story. Dunn responds to the claims of Bultmann that the scene is a transposed Easter story resurrection appearance retrojected back into the ministry. Dunn responds that that no appearance is portrayed as taking place so far north. Dunn asks two important questions: (1) Why would the disciples be here after the crucifixion? (2) Why have an appearance attributed to this region? Bultmann, *History of the Synoptic Tradition*, (New York: Harper & Row, 1968), 259; Dunn's response is in *Jesus Remembered*, 644–45.

COHERENCE

The final criterion to consider is coherence. Now, it must be acknowledged that this criterion is one of the most subjective in the list. Coherence can be in the eye of the beholder. Working backward from Jesus' execution ordered by Rome, we know that Jesus had to be seen as some type of insurrectionist in their eyes, because that was the reason one was publicly executed. A claim to be Messiah, a leader of the people in deliverance, fits this category better than being a nonviolent prophet. Working forward from John the Baptist, one recalls that Jesus' ministry evoked the eschatological hope of deliverance for the nation. We see the Twelve being selected, pointing to a reconstituted people of God with Jesus at its head. The kind of activity Jesus engages in reads like the hope expressed in a text from Qumran (4Q521). Here God will perform marvelous acts in the decisive deliverance: "for he will heal the badly wounded and will make the dead live, he will proclaim good news to the meek, give lavishly [to the need]y, lead the exiled and enrich the hungry."[16] Earlier in the text, in line 1, there is mention of at least one messianic figure, so it is not hard to think that the Messiah could be the one through whom God works these acts, or at least that God's activity is associated with the eschatological period that includes Messiah or some prophetic-like, end-time figure.[17] The expectation for those who held

---

15. Meier argues that the Satan remark is historical but cannot be connected credibly to a larger context to get its full sense. *A Marginal Jew* 3:236–38. We shall argue that if the "messianic secret" misleads us to think of this theme as Markan, then we regain the historical context for this remark. This will be the point of our discussion in the objections section.

16. The brackets indicate a break in the manuscript where text is missing. The sense is supplied by the context.

17. In line 1 of 4Q521, there is discussion whether one or more messianic figures are in view, as well as whether the stress is on a messianic or prophetic figure as the one through whom God works. John Collins opts for a prophet who is like the anointed figure of Isaiah 61 versus a royal messiah. Collins, *The Scepter and the Star: The Messiahs of the Dead Sea Scrolls and Other Literature* (New York: Doubleday, 1995), 205–6. Martin Hengel and Anna Maria Schwemer see a singular reference to a messianic figure here, but they do not discuss the kind of messiah in view. Hengel and Schwemer, *Jesus und das Judentum* [Jesus and Judaism] (Tübingen: Mohr Siebeck, 2007), 332–33. Florentino García Martínez sees a reference to the "davidic Messiah." Martínez, "Messianic Hopes in the Qumran Writings," *The People of the Dead Sea Scrolls*, ed. Florentino García Martínez and Julio Trebolle Barrera (Leiden: Brill 1995), 168–69. The kind of figure in view in the 4Q521 text is not clear, as the debate shows. This is not an unusual situation, as this text is fragmentary, so we do not have a full context to understand it completely. It may be more important to see the text as not telling us who the end-time figure is, but the activity points to the eschatological period of God's decisive deliverance.

to such a hope is that God would act and do so through some commissioned figure.

Everything around Jesus points in a messianic direction. John 6:14-15 says the people wanted to make him king. Jesus refused (for reasons we are about to discuss). Our only point here is that Jesus' actions evoked such hope. This is clearly the case in the new community that preached Jesus after his death. The new community rooted in his ministry preached him as the Messiah, even calling him Jesus Christ, where the second name is not a last name but the attaching of a central title to identify him. This hope is expressed in texts from L in Luke 19:11 and 24:21, where the disciples express either that the kingdom is arriving or that they had hoped Jesus was the Messiah. If Jesus had not presented himself in such a light to some degree (and in fact had refused to accept such a title, as some scholars claim), then it is very unlikely his later followers would have placed him in such a category as a central way to see him. If Jesus evoked such hope generally, then he almost certainly did so among his own disciples. The fact we know they believed this and died for that belief adds to the likelihood such an understanding was rooted in things Jesus did and said. Dunn argues that Peter's being the one to "blurt out their common hope" fits with the character we have of Peter elsewhere.[18] We are either dealing with a figure who presented himself as an eschatological prophet or one who acted as the end-time deliverer, that is, the Messiah. The claims of authority already traced in the gospels through the meals, the handling of the Sabbath, and exorcisms cohere with a figure who sees himself as more than a prophet.

OBJECTIONS TO THE SCENE'S AUTHENTICITY

So multiple attestation, Palestinian environment, embarrassment, and coherence speak for this event. If so, however, there is a surprising element in this authenticated event that also needs attention. It is Jesus' command of silence following Peter's declaration. Here some raise an objection, arguing as did William Wrede in 1901, that this "secrecy" was actually substantially a product of Mark's creative presentation of Jesus to cover up what had been a nonmessianic ministry of Jesus and give it an air of credibility. Those after Wrede took his theory and turned it into a full denial of a messianic understanding for Jesus. This idea has become exceedingly popular in New Testament studies. If it is true, then the scene involving Peter is a construction

---

18. Dunn, *Jesus Remembered*, 645.

of the early church and not a historical clue about Jesus, his ministry, and the belief of the earliest disciples during that time.

Here we run into one of the major objections to this scene, if not to the entire gospel portrait of Jesus' ministry. The tension within the event is summarized in this question: Why would Jesus elicit a declaration of who he is only to silence that recognition? In other words, is this event a piece of early church apologetics projected back on Jesus to make his ministry *appear* messianic when it was not? Is Jesus' hesitation about the title actually a reflection of his having rejected the title? To get at this objection, we have to discuss the varieties of Jewish messianic hope that existed in the period and why one had to be careful about what one evoked in appealing to this title. We also need to examine objections to the idea of a later messianic secret as well.

Oddly enough, perhaps the most powerful challenge to the idea of the secret comes from its originator, William Wrede. For in a little-known fact, he articulated before his death in a personal letter to Adolf von Harnack that he no longer could hold to a nonmessianic view of Jesus with certainty. Written in 1905, about a year before his death, the relevant part of the letter reads, "I am more disposed than I used to believe that Jesus saw himself as the chosen Messiah." This change of opinion is crucial, because Wrede cannot say this without denying the gist of his earlier view. His original claim was that the call for the disciples to be silent was a secret Mark created. In other words, the secret covered up the messianic belief of the community that came to them without historical roots from Jesus. The messianic position of Jesus was a completely later theological idea.[19]

The most outstanding historical reason for rejecting this view is that a belief in resurrection would not in itself be a sufficient cause for messianic faith. Wrede's original explanation of the secret requires that a belief in resurrection could lead the community to deduce and conclude that Jesus is the Messiah, since Jesus did not teach a messianic belief himself. However, there was no precedent in Judaism for teaching that the Messiah would be raised. So if the church came to believe Jesus was raised (whether for historical reasons or not),

---

19. Martin Hengel reports on this letter in "Jesus, the Messiah of Israel," in *Studies in Early Christology* (Edinburgh: T & T Clark, 1995), 16. Details about this letter appear in Martin Hengel and Anna Maria Schwemer, *Der messianische Anspruch Jesu and die Anfänge der Christologie: Vier Studien* [The messianic claim of Jesus and the beginning of Christology: Four studies] (Tübingen: Mohr Siebeck, 2001), ix. This book is a full defense of the messianic claim of Jesus. For this discussion, as well as the German and English of the key part of the letter, see Wilkins, in Darrell. L. Bock and Robert L. Webb, eds. *Key Events in the Life of the Historical Jesus* (Grand Rapids: Eerdmans 2010), 333, n. 143. For Wrede's earlier view, see his *The Messianic Secret* (London: Clarke, 1971, trans. of the 1901 work), 67–69, 218–20.

that belief in itself would not lead them to take a nonmessianic Jesus and make him messianic. There was no need or precedent within Judaism to go there. Some pondered if John the Baptist had been raised without making him Messiah (Mark 6:14). Other Jewish figures exalted to heaven get there without a messianic tag being attached to them (Moses, Elijah, and Isaiah). So we know that the belief in Jesus' messianism is reflected in the earliest phase of the life of the new community, and we may reason that this messianic view of Jesus preceded his death and resurrection, since the resurrection itself would not have generated it. Dunn says it this way: "The messiahship of the crucified Jesus is the *presupposition* of the scriptural apologetic mounted by the first Christians, not its achievement; 'the title "Messiah" was inseparably connected with the name of Jesus because Jesus was condemned and crucified as a messianic pretender.'"[20]

There is another problem with arguing that Mark created this scene. It is not clear why Mark would focus the confession on Jesus being the Messiah, when Son of God and Lord were more important and central titles for the early church. The ambiguity with which this title is placed on the table for consideration in Mark makes it more likely that this is a text rooted in Jesus than from the early church.[21]

So if the secret as a church production cannot explain Jesus' call to silence, then what can?[22] Would Jesus really tell them to say nothing? Why would he do this? To answer this question, we need to consider why Jesus would call his disciples to say nothing yet about this role. This involves interpreting whether Jesus' reaction is an unqualified endorsement of the declaration, a denial of it, or a qualified acceptance of it.

That Jesus is not rejecting the saying in a call to silence has already been treated. First, a created event cannot explain the early faith of his followers and their willingness to die for this belief. If Jesus had denied he was Messiah, as soon as persecution against the disciples rose to the level of threatening the key leaders with death, they would have simply stepped back from this belief. Second, if Jesus denied Peter's reply, we have the strange result of a turning-point remark in a key event that ends up being denied. However, this would leave us with no declaration at all that Jesus affirms! This kind of empty

---

20. Dunn, *Jesus Remembered*, 626–27, presents this argument. The citation is from 627, and the emphasis is his. The embedded citation in the sentence is from Nils A. Dahl, "The Crucified Messiah," in *Jesus the Christ: The Historical Origins of the Christological Doctrine*, ed. D. H. Juel (Minneapolis: Fortress Press, 1991; repr. of a 1960 article), 39–40.

21. This point is made most clearly in Hengel and Schwemer, *Jesus und das Judentum*, 521–22.

22. Wright calls the secret, if it goes back to Mark, a "Markan trick." *Jesus and the Victory of God*, (Minneapolis: Fortress Press, 1996), 529. He also argues that this explanation of its origin cannot work.

ending makes no sense for the importance given to the passage here. Third, Mark shows he is comfortable with the title and its discussion elsewhere (14:61; 15:32). A similar silence command appears in Mark 9:7-9, where the confession is not to be rejected. Rather, the call for silence is to prevent a misunderstanding of what it means. Finally comes the silencing of demons in 1:34, where the confession is silenced, even though 1:34 says the demons "knew" him (a similar command for silence appears in 3:11). Mark's theme of silence is not because what is said is wrong, but because the remark is either ill timed, misunderstood, or sourced in less than credible witnesses.

That Jesus is not accepting the title without qualification is shown by his own hesitancy to use the title and his switch to Son of Man when he speaks of himself. There are only two Marcan passages where this title is prominent in Jesus' discussion. One is in the Olivet discourse about the end, when he notes many will claim the Messiah has come, but they are not to listen (Mark 13:21 = Matt. 24:5, 23). This remark has nothing directly to do with Jesus. The second text is when Jesus asks why Jewish hope calls the Christ David's son, when David calls him Lord (Matt. 22:41-42 = Mark 12:35 = Luke 20:41). This is only a generalized discussion of Messiah. Beyond this, the only other use that points to Jesus in a presentation of his own use is Matt. 23:10. All other uses, but one very late in Luke 24:46, are of people commenting about Jesus (narrative comments from Matthew in Matt. 1:1, 16-18; Herod on the Christ's location of birth in 2:4; John the Baptist in 11:2; a question at his Jewish examination in 23:63 = Mark 14:61 = Luke 22:68; Pilate during deliberation over the release of Jesus or Barabbas in Matt. 27:17, 22; a narrative remark by Mark in Mark 1:1; mocking from the scribes observing his death in Mark 15:32 = Luke 23:35; angels in Luke 2:11; Simeon in 2:26; demons in 4:41; Jewish leaders bringing a charge to Pilate in 23:2; a criminal from the cross in 23:39; a disciple on the road to Emmaus in 24:26; and Jesus in 24:46). Jesus' lack of explicit use of the title does suggest an element of hesitancy about it.

What is a key to unraveling this scene is the relationship between "Messiah" in this text and "Son of Man" in the prediction about suffering that follows. The same kind of exchange happens at the Jewish examination by Jesus. Someone says "Messiah" or "Christ," while Jesus responds by discussing "Son of Man." Son of Man is multiply attested and is a title only Jesus uses, never appearing independently of Jesus in any epistle in the New Testament.[23] This lack of usage in the letters shows it was not a title the early church used as a confessional term. Unlike Messiah, it is an empty term, in that it is an idiom for a human. It can also picture an authoritative figure who rides the clouds like transcendent beings as Dan. 7:13-14 shows, but the allusion appears only in a few texts. Up to Jesus' time, it was not a technical term of any kind, unless one includes the use of the title in a work like *1 Enoch*.[24] Often in the gospels, Jesus uses this term in contexts pointing to his authority—for example, "the Son of Man is Lord of the Sabbath" (Mark 2:28). It is his preferred title. He also uses it in this declaration scene to announce his coming suffering. This is a new take on the Messiah Peter just confessed. This prediction of suffering Peter initially cannot accept, because for him, Messiah is a figure of power, not humility.

Here is a major clue that Jesus accepts but qualifies this messianic understanding of Peter. The disciples do not yet understand all that Jesus sees himself as being as the decisive delivering figure. They still have some things to learn, especially about his coming suffering. The same would be true of the crowds if Jesus were openly proclaimed to be Messiah. So the disciples are to wait on making this proclamation until they get it.

Yet another factor is that if Jesus were publicly proclaimed Messiah (or king, as John 6 says it), this would place him at immediate risk before Rome. These gentile rulers of Israel preferred to appoint and recognize who was king. Rome would have seen this outright claim as a direct challenge.

A look at the variety of Jewish expectations on Messiah shows what would have been expected had Jesus gone public with this title.[25] There was no single understanding of this figure, but all the options had a powerful figure who did not suffer. *Psalms of Solomon* 17–18 was written in the century before Christ, probably after Pompey took Rome in 63. It has a political and militaristic Messiah who conquers the nations. The parables of *1 Enoch* (chs. 37–71) have a long discussion of a more transcendent delivering figure. As just noted, this work likely also was written in the later part of the century before

---

23. There are probably fifty-one distinct Son of Man sayings in the tradition (out of the eighty-two uses present; reuse in a parallel does not count in getting to the smaller number). Fourteen of these are from Mark, and ten are from Q. Every source has such sayings, so it is multiply attested. Raymond Brown, *The Death of the Messiah*, 2 vols. (New York: Doubleday, 1994), 1:507. Outside the gospels, the title does appear in the sermonic letter Heb. 2:6 (where Psalm 8 is being cited and the reference is to humanity), Acts 7:56, and Rev. 1:13; 14:14.

24. The date of this work is debated. Many place it around the time of Jesus, if not slightly later, because the section containing the title was not found among the copies of *1 Enoch* at Qumran. But the majority of Second Temple scholars place it at the end of the previous century or early in the first century. James Charlesworth and I are currently editing a book, *Parables of Enoch: A Paradigm Shift* (London: T & T Clark, 2013), that takes a close look at this book's date and argues for the earlier setting.

25. Excellent summaries can be found in Collins, *The Scepter and the Star*; and Jacob Neusner, William Green, and Ernest Frerichs, eds., *Judaisms and Their Messiahs at the Turn of the Christian Era* (Cambridge: Cambridge University Press, 1987).

Christ or early in the first century of his birth. This messianic figure judges with God from heaven and exercises power from God's side. The messianic expectation at Qumran was of two messianic figures, a political deliverer and a priestly Messiah, with the priestly figure having the prominent role (1QS *Rule of the Community* 9:11). Another figure at Qumran is the mysterious Melchizedek, who looks like the transcendent figure in *1 Enoch* in many ways (11Q *Melchizedek*). We also have the prophet-like Moses figure, a leader-prophet, as presented in other texts from Qumran (4Q *Testimonia* 1–8). In this same *Testimonia* text, we also see described a kingly star who crushes enemies, like the *Psalms of Solomon* portrait of a military hero (4Q *Testimonia* 9–13). This figure appears alongside a priestly Levi figure (4Q *Testimonia* 14–22). So to utter "Messiah" to a Jewish public in the first century would generate one of these powerful images and potentially produce a Roman pushback. Given the variety of messianic conceptions, the exclusive emphasis on power, and height of expectation coming with the title Messiah, Jesus preferred to speak of the Son of Man and teach his disciples about the prospect of suffering they had not anticipated.

So we are arguing that Jesus accepted this title in a qualified way. In it, Jesus accepted the idea that he was more than a prophet. This is the only way to make sense of Peter's declaration that Jesus is Christ in contrast to the public's view that he is some kind of a prophet. In saying this, Peter saw Jesus standing in the center of God's delivering program. Jesus was not ready yet to make a full public disclosure, so he waited to use it or associations with it until he was ready to press matters at the end of his public ministry. He also waited to use the title extensively in public until the disciples were in a better position to begin to appreciate the suffering that would come with Jesus' activity. So first, Jesus used caution in allowing messianic associations with his public work, at least in much of his public activity. He was careful because the disciples, crowds, Jewish leadership, and Rome might mistakenly think Jesus was out to establish a strictly political-military rule. Second, Jesus also needed to qualify Peter's understanding so that the suffering Jesus attached to his mission could be incorporated into the appreciation of this title. Jesus was to be a different kind of Messiah than the populace and disciples had anticipated. The disciples struggle to get this even up to the end of Jesus' public ministry. Only with his rejection, death, and resurrection are they able to make full sense of this piece of the puzzle.

The important difference in Matthew's presentation fits in here. Matthew's account is less ambiguous about the title and is clear that Jesus embraced the title. Matthew has additional remarks from Jesus to Peter, stating that Peter has received a revelation from God. This full embrace of the title is the result of where one ends up when one looks at the career of Jesus as a whole. Jesus affirmed this title, provided it is understood in the sense of Jesus being Messiah, sufferer, and even Son of God. If Mark had intended a denial of the title, it is hard to see how Matthew, not to mention the early Christian community that confessed Jesus as the Messiah, could end up where they do. It is hard to see a later community putting a response seen as negative from Mark alongside a clearly positive one from Matthew in the same Jesus collection. The issue was too central to bring together such disparate ideas.

One final objection might be that Jesus' ambiguous response led the disciples to think he responded positively, when his response was really ambivalent. The disciples are then said to have made more of his reply to Peter than Jesus really intended and built on it in the early church period. But this argument also has problems. Do we really think it *more* likely that these disciples would have spent the time they did with Jesus and made what was ambiguous into a core point about him if he did not accept such an idea? Is it not more likely (all we can do historically) that they got the point (and connected it to other events like the entry, which if authentic, in its core shows that this response was not a denial but merely a hesitation about being properly understood, as well as a concern about the time when the claim would be made because of the reaction it could generate from Rome?

Another element is that this event is also part of a sequence that makes the point that Jesus acted in a messianic manner in other authentic scenes. This macro argument is also a part of the case for authenticity.[26]

It is one thing to grant that a scenario is plausible (and recognize different people weigh these plausibilities differently), but to weigh it as more likely means to suggest at least that a case for authenticity has some ground to stand on—maybe even better historical ground than the other candidates. (Weighing does not mean precluding; it means suggesting why one scenario may be more coherent than another without appealing to scriptural authority.)

One thing that has troubled me in many historical-Jesus discussions is why people in discussions like this can say things like "The question of Jesus' messiahship came up during his lifetime" and "He did not completely deny such an identification because of such texts" but then step back from thinking maybe that text got the connection right. A scenario that says Jesus was ambiguous and the disciples misread it has the look of a *via media*, but if a text does this

---

26. The claim that there is a core messianism that has a depth coherence across events is one of the burdens of the entire volume, Bock and Webb, *Key Events in the Life of the Historical Jesus*.

well, might it not have the setting right? I think it is here the macro argument alongside the argument about the scene's own details can help us so we do not get too isolated in what we consider relevant. In light of this combination, it is likely this scene is authentic in its core. The disciples read Jesus right when they came to confess him as Messiah, by which is meant that he stands at the center of God's salvation program and that the category of prophet is not adequate to describe Jesus or who he thought himself to be.

Now, it is key to understand what I am arguing for in this defense of authenticity. I am not arguing for every detail but for the core authenticity that the scene gives solid evidence that Jesus did accept a messianic designation with the qualification that there were still things the disciples needed to understand about the kind of Messiah Jesus would be. It is the nature of the corroborative process that is part of historical-Jesus discussion that the support for authenticity in an event often is a general support. It is also important to say that showing this with criteria that are aligned skeptically is important. To fail to meet criteria in a corroborative model does not mean the events did not happen, only that one cannot give corroborative reasons for it having taken place. That is another important limitation to realize about the method, but when the bar is crossed, as it has been set so high, it is a significant result. This important event fits that description and meets the standard.

All of this speaks to the core authenticity of this scene, which if authentic, tells us significant things about how Jesus saw his mission. It places Jesus in a messianic eschatological context, in contrast to many historical-Jesus presentations that see his self-understanding as limited to a prophetic category. It also provides a solid link between the historical Jesus and the Christ of faith, who, as the late George Caird, formerly of Oxford, reminded us, are not as distinct as many historical-Jesus scholars argue.[27]

Conclusion

In sum, our essay has argued that those with a confession can make contributions to historical-Jesus studies. Their position of faith does not disqualify them from speaking to these issues historically, provided they use

---

27. Caird calls the separation of these two categories one of the cardinal errors of method in much historical-Jesus study. Caird, *New Testament Theology*, ed. Larry Hurst (Oxford: Clarendon, 1994), 351–56. The two are distinct, but the question is whether they are connected or the result of an unbridgeable ditch, to use Lessing's metaphor. In saying this, I am not claiming a psychoanalysis of Jesus that crawls into his mind. I am arguing that we can read his intentions by his acts and words, something Ben Meyer argued is a part of historical analysis. Meyer, *The Aims of Jesus* (London: SCM, 1979).

arguments and methods all share. The issue is not their faith position, as many claim in dismissing their work, but the quality of the specific argumentation they bring to the discussion. That is what I have tried to show in this essay.

The historical arguments show Jesus accepted in a qualified way the claim he was Messiah. The rest of his ministry shows how he filled this expectation out, by speaking of his suffering and waiting to go public with such an idea until he forced issues when he came to Jerusalem the final time. The claim for authenticity fits a method of historical verification and source assessment, making the case on those kinds of terms. The example of Peter's declaration shows how that is done within the kinds of parameters historical-Jesus discussion entertains.

A confessional voice belongs at the table, because it has important issues to raise about the connection of the historical Jesus and the Christ of faith for all who participate in the conversation. As long as the reasons are historically rooted, the claims deserve a fair hearing and direct engagement that does not use the writer's confession as an excuse not to engage or as a means to be dismissive.

7

The Historical Jesus from the Synoptics and the Fourth Gospel?
Jesus the Purifier

Craig L. Blomberg

The Third Quest of the historical Jesus continues unabated. Of course, the media give more attention to the idiosyncratic, whether to the Jesus Seminar or the Gnostic Gospels or the supposed discovery of the Jesus-family tomb in Jerusalem. Even in the academy, creative new portraits of a Jesus radically different from Christian orthodoxy still regularly garner disproportionate amounts of attention at the expense of less "exciting" but more responsible research.[1] Fringe participants in Jesus research revive long-outworn theories of Greco-Roman background and influence on the Jesus "myth"[2] that fly in the face of most everything we know about early first-century Judaism and the congruence of the canonical Gospels' portraits of Jesus with a credible picture of a self-styled Jewish rabbi, ministering in Israel in the light of issues and debates central to the core of what Jacob Neusner likes to call the "Judaisms" of Jesus' era.[3]

Representative of the studies that reflect the true *statis questionis* across a broad middle ground of scholarship today are summaries like James Charlesworth's slim 2008 volume on *The Historical Jesus: An Essential Guide*,

---

1. See esp. Philip Jenkins, *Hidden Gospels: How the Search for Jesus Lost Its Way* (Oxford: Oxford University Press, 2001).

2. E.g., Robert M. Price in numerous publications, conveniently summarized in his "Jesus at the Vanishing Point," in *The Historical Jesus: Five Views*, ed. James K. Beilby and Paul R. Eddy, 55–83 (Downers Grove: InterVarsity, 2009).

3. Out of seemingly endless possible examples, see Jacob Neusner, *Judaism When Christianity Began: A Survey of Belief and Practice* (Louisville: Westminster John Knox, 2002), 4–6.

which asks and answers twenty-seven central questions about the discipline today.[4] Even more recent still is the published form of the first Princeton-Prague Symposium on Jesus Research in 2005, released just last year, edited by Charlesworth and Petr Pokorný, entitled *Jesus Research: An International Perspective*, with studies on topics as diverse as the criteria of authenticity; Jesus in Galilee; paradigm shifts concerning Judaism; the water-into-wine miracle; Jesus as itinerant teacher, as teller of parables, and in contrast with John the Baptist; the implicit Christology in Jesus' sayings about life and kingdom; how Jesus understood his death; his "subversive" interpretation of Scripture; and his inverse strategy for eschatological cleanliness—a contagious purity.[5]

Voluminous in the primary and secondary literature canvassed is Craig Keener's *The Historical Jesus of the Gospels*, which appeared late in 2009, with especially helpful reflections on what did and did not constitute good, reliable historiography and biography in Jesus' world and an assessment of the canonical and noncanonical gospels in light of those criteria, as well as application of the criteria of authenticity to each major segment of the Synoptics' Jesus-portraits.[6] Appearing for the first time at the Institute of Biblical Research's (IBR's) 2009 November meetings in New Orleans was the multi-author volume in the first *Wissenschaftliche Untersuchung zum Neuen Testament* series from Mohr Siebeck on a dozen of the most compellingly authentic portions of the Jesus tradition in the Synoptics.[7] This tome is the fruit of a ten-year project of the IBR's historical-Jesus study group, with meticulously researched and repeatedly revised chapters on Jesus' baptism by John, exorcisms and the kingdom, Jesus and the Twelve, Jesus' table fellowship with sinners, the Sabbath controversies, Peter's declaration concerning Jesus' identity, the royal entry into Jerusalem, the temple incident, the Last Supper, blasphemy and the Jewish examination of Jesus, the Roman examination and crucifixion, and Jesus' empty tomb and appearance in Jerusalem. Also worthy of mention and even more wide-ranging in perspectives represented are James Dunn's and Scot McKnight's coedited anthology of excerpts of classic and contemporary writers, entitled *The Historical Jesus in Recent Research*, published in 2005 by Eisenbrauns,[8] and

---

4. James H. Charlesworth, *The Historical Jesus: An Essential Guide* (Nashville: Abingdon, 2008).

5. James H. Charlesworth and Petr Pokorný, eds., *Jesus Research: An International Perspective* (Grand Rapids: Eerdmans, 2009).

6. Craig S. Keener, *The Historical Jesus of the Gospels* (Grand Rapids: Eerdmans, 2009).

7. Darrell L. Bock and Robert L. Webb, eds., *Key Events in the Life of the Historical Jesus* (Tübingen: Mohr Siebeck, 2009).

8. James D. G. Dunn and Scot McKnight, eds., *The Historical Jesus in Recent Research* (Winona Lake, IN: Eisenbrauns, 2005).

Routledge's 700-plus-page *Encyclopedia of the Historical Jesus*, edited by Craig Evans and released in 2008.[9]

What one almost never finds in any of these works, however, or in any of the other major historical-Jesus books of recent vintage, is anything more than a token nod to the possibility of the Fourth Gospel contributing to our understanding of the Jesus of history. The reasons are well known: John is so much more different from the Synoptics overall than each of the first three Gospels is to the other two. John seems much more overtly theological and has the consistently highest Christology of the four. And his was probably the last of the four to be written, perhaps by a sizable interval, and thus the most chronologically removed from the life of the Nazarene. Even thoroughly Evangelical historical-Jesus books, like Keener's and the Bock and Webb anthology, or nearly Evangelical treatments, like N. T. Wright's large *Jesus and the Victory of God*[10] and James Dunn's even larger *Jesus Remembered*,[11] do next to nothing with the Fourth Gospel, recognizing the uphill battle they would have to fight. More surprisingly still, when past Evangelical Theological Society President Darrell Bock produced his large volume *Jesus according to Scripture*, which was virtually a commentary on a harmony of the Gospels, he separated out all of the Johannine material for separate treatment, rather than attempting any integration with the Synoptic texts.[12]

Alongside the Third Quest, nevertheless, one may observe a continuing proliferation of works in keeping with the spirit of what John A. T. Robinson dubbed "the new look on John" already in the late 1950s—recognizing the authenticability of a significant core of distinctively Johannine material, especially in light of how thoroughly Jewish the background, contents, and setting of the Fourth Gospel actually are.[13] I attempted a "maximalist" treatment, drawing on the full range of studies available to me by the end of the twentieth century, in my *Historical Reliability of John's Gospel*, released in 2001, to see just

---

9. Craig A. Evans, ed., *Encyclopedia of the Historical Jesus* (London: Routledge, 2008).

10. N. T. Wright, *Jesus and the Victory of God* (London: SPCK; Minneapolis: Fortress Press, 1996).

11. James D. G. Dunn, *Jesus Remembered* (Grand Rapids: Eerdmans, 2003).

12. Darrell L. Bock, *Jesus according to Scripture: Restoring the Portrait from the Gospels* (Grand Rapids: Baker, 2002).

13. John A. T. Robinson, "The New Look on the Fourth Gospel," *TU* 73 (1959): 338–50. Robinson himself became a major contributor to this new look with his posthumously published book, *The Priority of John*, ed. J. F. Coakley (London: SCM, 1985; Oak Park, IL: Meyer-Stone, 1987). While this "new look" still finds numerous adherents, trends in Johannine research today subdivide into more conflicting diversity than ever. For a representative sampling, see Francisco Lozada Jr. and Tom Thatcher, eds., *New Currents through John: A Global Perspective* (Atlanta: Society of Biblical Literature, 2006).

how far this case might be pushed, using the standard criteria of authenticity along with the newer criterion of double similarity and double dissimilarity.[14]

Over the nine years since, Mohr Siebeck has released *Challenging Perspectives on the Gospel of John* in 2006, edited by John Lierman, which includes reassessments of the authenticity of the Johannine sayings, messianism according to the Fourth Gospel, the theme of the temple, the relationship of John to Luke, "the myth of Orthodox Johannophobia" in the second century, and the Mosaic pattern of John's Christology, along with more literary- or narrative-critical studies.[15] Richard Bauckham's 2007 work, *The Testimony of the Beloved Disciple*, gathers together a number of his previously published studies now in revised form on "narrative, history, and theology in the Gospel of John," as his subtitle phrases it.[16] And the second volume of the "John, Jesus, and History" Seminar of the Society of Biblical Literature, published in 2009, moves sequentially through the Fourth Gospel with twenty-nine separate contributions on aspects of historicity in each section.[17] Also significant for the question of Johannine historicity are major sections of Bauckham's *Jesus and the Eyewitnesses: The Gospels as Eyewitness Testimony* (2006)[18] and Robert Gundry's *The Old is Better: New Testament Essays in Support of Traditional Interpretations* (2005), especially his substantial essay on "the apostolically Johannine pre-Papian tradition concerning the Gospels of Mark and Matthew."[19] Given Gundry's detailed iconoclastic commentaries on Matthew and Mark,[20] moreover, one can scarcely accuse him of being one naturally to gravitate to traditional interpretations.

---

14. Craig L. Blomberg, *The Historical Reliability of John's Gospel* (Downers Grove: InterVarsity, 2001). Gilbert Van Belle cites my work in some detail and reproduces in his footnotes long lists of like-minded sources but also observes the full spectrum of scholarship on the topic and ultimately decides that we simply cannot know if John is historical or not. Van Belle, "The Return of John to Jesus Research," *LS* 32 (2007): 23–48.

15. John Lierman, ed., *Challenging Perspectives on the Gospel of John* (Tübingen: Mohr Siebeck, 2006).

16. Richard Bauckham, *The Testimony of the Beloved Disciple: Narrative, History, and Theology in the Gospel of John* (Grand Rapids: Baker, 2007).

17. Paul N. Anderson, Felix Just, and Tom Thatcher, eds., *John, Jesus, and History*, vol. 2, *Aspects of Historicity in the Fourth Gospel* (Atlanta: Society of Biblical Literature, 2009).

18. Richard J. Bauckham, *Jesus and the Eyewitnesses: The Gospels as Eyewitness Testimony* (Grand Rapids: Eerdmans, 2006), 358–471.

19. Robert H. Gundry, *The Old Is Better: New Testament Essays in Support of Traditional Interpretations* (Tübingen: Mohr Siebeck, 2005), 49–73.

20. Robert H. Gundry, *Matthew: A Commentary on His Handbook for a Mixed Church under Persecution*, rev. ed. (Grand Rapids: Eerdmans, 1994); idem, *Mark: A Commentary on His Apology for the Cross* (Grand Rapids: Eerdmans, 1993).

Methodologically, however, pride of place in the new look on John must go to Paul Anderson's tireless campaigning for what he calls a "bi-optic" perspective on Jesus—a historical reconstruction based on the most solid data from both the Synoptics and John.[21] In his one book-length treatment of the topic, he ably surveys what he terms the unjustified "de-historicization of John" and the "de-johannification of Jesus." He delves in detail into what he deems to be "interfluential, formative and dialectical" relationships between John and the Synoptics and the oral and written sources that preceded each. He goes so far as to list all the common pericopes between John and the Synoptics, forty-four "memorable sayings common to John and Mark," and thirteen "possible contacts between the Johannine and Q traditions."[22]

From all this, Anderson derives eight major topics that he believes John can contribute to depictions of the historical Jesus, which are normally not adequately treated: Jesus' association with John the Baptist at the beginning of his public ministry, Jesus' calling of disciples as "a corporate venture," an attempted "revolt in the desert" in conjunction with the feeding of the five thousand and its aftermath, the centrality of Jesus' healings on the Sabbath, Jesus' sense of prophetic agency from the Father and resistance from key branches of the Jewish leadership, Jesus' inaugural temple cleansing, significant details in the passion of the Christ, and further attestations to resurrection appearances at the beginning of the Jesus movement. From these flow also the likelihood of Jesus' travel to and from Jerusalem during a multiyear ministry, the probability of John correctly including additional events early in Jesus' ministry, his favorable receptions in Galilee among Samaritans, women, and gentiles, and Jesus' teaching about the "way of the Spirit" and "the reign of Truth."[23]

What has yet to be undertaken, however, is a synthetic study of the historical Jesus incorporating these or similarly derived elements alongside the most securely historical pieces of information inferable from the Synoptics. Anderson concludes his volume by observing, "If gospel historiography can be seen as a more dialogical enterprise—from epistemic origins to tradition-critical

---

21. Paul N. Anderson, "John and Mark: The Bi-optic Gospels," in *Jesus in Johannine Tradition*, ed. Robert T. Fortna and Tom Thatcher (Louisville: Westminster John Knox, 2001), 175–88; idem, "Interfluential, Formative, and Dialectical: A Theory of John's Relation to the Synoptics," in *Für und wider die Priorität des Johannesevangeliums*, ed. Peter Hofrichter, 19–58 (Hildesheim: Georg Olms, 2002); and idem, "Aspects of Historicity in John: Implications for the Investigations of Jesus and Archaeology," in *Jesus and Archaeology*, ed. James H. Charlesworth, 587–618 (Grand Rapids: Eerdmans, 2006).

22. Paul N. Anderson, *The Fourth Gospel and the Quest for Jesus: Modern Foundations Reconsidered* (London: T & T Clark, 2006), 43–99, 101–26, 131–32 and 134–35, respectively.

23. Ibid., 135–45, 154–72.

analyses—the John *versus* Jesus dichotomy might yet be supplanted by a more conjunctive and nuanced approach." He then adds, "Might this lead us to a *fourth* quest for Jesus? Only time will tell."[24]

For the rest of this paper, I would like to take one tiny step in that direction. If one proceeds through the Fourth Gospel, major pericope by major pericope, isolating those portions, if any, that commend themselves as the most historically probable, do any *consistent patterns* of Jesus' teaching or activity emerge that could be used to supplement the standard historical-Jesus portraits (based on the Synoptics alone) in ways that neither essentially replicate those portraits (suggesting the redundancy of the exercise) nor inherently contradict them (suggesting that we do indeed have to choose one or the other, rather than some form of synthesis)? In making his foray into this minefield, Anderson, like a handful of others who have tried something similar, isolates seemingly unrelated passages or themes.[25] Recurring themes are typically chalked up to Johannine redaction, and often rightly so. But among the portions of John that historical investigation can authenticate with the greatest probability, is there any theme or motif that unites these passages but does not stand out as an obvious major candidate for Johannine redaction because it does not surface consistently or emphatically elsewhere in the Gospel? Is it a theme or motif that perhaps we have often missed because we have not asked this specific question in exactly this way? It appears to me that at least one such significant pattern of Jesus' activity does result from studying the relevant texts with these questions in mind.

It is widely agreed that the Fourth Gospel's distinctive portrait of Jesus' early ministry overlapping and intersecting with that of John the Baptist stands a strong chance of being accurate. Later Christians would not likely have depicted Jesus' first followers and even to some degree Jesus himself emerging out of the orbit of John's ministry (John 1:29-51). If John must decrease so that Jesus can increase (3:30), then initially John may have been more prominent and influential.[26] The Fourth Gospel also is the only one to note that Jesus

---

24. Ibid., 192.

25. Cf., e.g., E. Earle Ellis, "Background and Christology of John's Gospel," in *Perspectives on John: Method and Interpretation in the Fourth Gospel*, ed. Robert B. Sloan and Mikael C. Parsons, 1–25 (Lewiston: Mellen, 1993); David Wenham, "A Historical View of John's Gospel," *Themelios* 23, no. 2 (1998): 5–21; Francis J. Moloney, "The Fourth Gospel and the Jesus of History," *NTS* 46 (2000): 42–58; D. Moody Smith, *The Fourth Gospel in Four Dimensions: Judaism and Jesus, the Gospels and Scripture* (Columbia: University of South Carolina Press, 2008), 81–111.

26. See esp. John P. Meier, *A Marginal Jew: Rethinking the Historical Jesus*, vol. 2, *Mentor, Message and Miracles* (New York: Doubleday, 1994), 100–30.

himself encouraged baptism, even while clarifying that baptism was performed by means of his disciples (4:1-2). Given the centrality of baptism in John's ministry and in subsequent Christian ministry, this is historically probable but hardly an emphasis even in John.[27] Keeping these ritual lustrations in their Jewish context, and drawing on Joan Taylor's detailed study of the Baptist, we may suggest a title for Jesus not regularly applied to him, namely, the "purifier." What Taylor concludes concerning John's "immersion" may well have been true of Jesus' practice as well:

> [It] was wholly in keeping with other Jewish immersions in having to do with ridding the body of uncleanness, but it also entailed the different idea that previous immersions and ablutions were ineffective for Jews without the practice of true righteousness. Immersion itself could not be used as a method of exhorting God for forgiveness. . . . It had its own integrity and followed on from people turning back to the way of God, just as becoming clean followed on from people's acceptance into Israel as God's obedient servants.[28]

Leaving completely to one side the question of the miraculous in the first Cana episode (John 2:1-11), what strikes the student of the Synoptics most is the close correlation between the account of water become wine and the little parable or metaphor of new wine requiring new wineskins in Mark 2:22 and parallels. I argued more than twenty years ago that the most authenticable portion of the Johannine miracle account by the standard criteria was the enacted object lesson of Jesus teaching that his ministry was bringing "new wine" against the "old water" of at least some forms of the existing Judaism of his world.[29] But once we realize this, John 2:6 fairly jumps off the page at us—the jars containing the transformed water were used for ritual purification. Why in the world does the Fourth Evangelist tell us this, when he makes nothing more of it? His redactional emphasis is clearly disclosed in verse 11: this was the first of Jesus' signs meant to lead people to belief in him.[30] But if Jesus was a purifier, then we see him here purifying the water already used for another kind of purification

---

27. Ibid., 122, applying the criterion of embarrassment (Jesus using a ritual so indebted to John). Cf. D. Moody Smith, *John* (Nashville: Abingdon, 1999), 110.

28. Joan E. Taylor, *The Immerser: John the Baptist within Second Temple Judaism* (Grand Rapids: Eerdmans, 1997), 99–100.

29. Craig L. Blomberg, "The Miracles as Parables," in *Gospel Perspectives*, vol. 6, *The Miracles of Jesus*, ed. David Wenham and Craig Blomberg, 333–37 (Sheffield: JSOT, 1986).

30. Cf. Robert Kysar, *John, the Maverick Gospel*, rev. ed. (Louisville: Westminster John Knox, 2007), 95–102.

by transforming it into something altogether different—wine, which regularly symbolized joy and gladness (cf. Sir. 31:27-28; Ps. 104:15; and Judg. 9:13)—an apt pointer to the "new joy of the kingdom."[31] This motif now closely matches the major theme of the arrival of the kingdom, which dominates the Synoptics and is regularly seen as historically trustworthy and central to Jesus' ministry.[32]

The next passage in John has traditionally been called the "temple cleansing" (2:13-25). As applied to the Synoptic narrative of Jesus' demonstration in the temple the last week of his life, it is better labeled a "clearing," portending the temple's destruction, or, following Ben Witherington's predilection for punning, Jesus' "temple tantrum"![33] But in the Johannine context, as an inaugural event, cleansing—purification—makes better sense. Here Jesus is upset with the *corruption* of the temple merchants, an item not found in the Synoptics, and something he could hope would change by their returning to pure, unadulterated practices. In John, the only predicted destruction is that of his body (v. 19). The Fourth Evangelist's theological emphasis is clearly this post-resurrection understanding of Jesus' cryptic words about destroying the metaphorical temple and raising it in three days.[34] But the purification theme continues, in the background, and very plausible in the context in which it appears.

John 3 introduces us to Jesus' dialogue with Nicodemus (vv. 1-15 or 21). If there is a historical core here at all, it is, as Barnabas Lindars points out, in the pair of double-Amen sayings (vv. 3 and 5) that resemble the Synoptic logion about entering the kingdom as a little child (Matt. 18:3-4).[35] John's discourses may well have regularly been built up from such core metaphorical sayings,[36]

---

31. Cf. Colin G. Kruse, *The Gospel according to John* (Leicester: InterVarsity, 2003; Grand Rapids: Eerdmans, 2004), 91–96.

32. Still definitive is George R. Beasley-Murray, *Jesus and the Kingdom of God* (Exeter: Paternoster; Grand Rapids: Eerdmans, 1986).

33. Ben Witherington III, *The Christology of Jesus* (Minneapolis: Fortress Press, 1990), 107.

34. Even this is best understood as traditional, given the chronology that makes it virtually impossible to place "forty-six years" after the beginning of the rebuilding of the temple (John 2:20) to a date any later than 28 CE, and given the garbled reference to 2:19 in Mark 14:57-58 and parallels, better understood if it were now at least two years later than when Jesus first spoke of the destruction of "this temple." See further Richard Bauckham, "John for Readers of Mark," in *The Gospels for All Christians: Rethinking the Gospel Audiences*, ed. Richard Bauckham (Grand Rapids: Eerdmans, 1998), 159–61.

35. Barnabas Lindars, *The Gospel of John* (London: Marshall, Morgan & Scott, 1972; Grand Rapids: Eerdmans, 1981), 150. See even Rudolf Bultmann, *The Gospel of John* (Oxford: Blackwell; Philadelphia: Westminster, 1971), 135, n. 4.

36. Barnabas Lindars, "Discourse and Tradition: The Use of the Sayings of Jesus in the Discourses of the Fourth Gospel," *JSNT* 13 (1981): 83–101.

in this case on the need to be born again, which is interpreted as being born of "water and the Spirit." We need not detain ourselves with the debate over whether literal baptism is in view here or not; either way, the water imagery suggests purification, most likely with Ezek. 36:25-27 in the background: "I will sprinkle clean water on you, and you will be clean; I will cleanse you from all your impurities and from all your idols. I will give you a new heart and put a new spirit in you; I will remove from you your heart of stone and give you a heart of flesh. And I will put my Spirit in you and move you to follow my decrees and be careful to keep my laws"[37] (NIV here and throughout).

Water imagery continues with the long dialogue in John 4 between Jesus and the woman at the well (4:4-42). One could argue that this is John's theological overlay, especially given the prominent role of "living water" in the narrative. But unlike the seven christologically distinctive "I am" sayings in the Fourth Gospel, Jesus never actually calls himself living water here. His claims are more indirect, like the more implicit Christology of the Synoptics that more readily satisfies the criteria of authenticity.[38] Clear Johannine emphases are Jesus' self-revelation as Messiah, the belief of Samaritans, and the still-coming but already-present age of Spirit and truth. Purification is not a major emphasis of the passage as John presents it. But it is unambiguously present nevertheless in Jesus' offer to the woman of water that will forever slake her spiritual thirst *and* become in her "a spring of water welling up to eternal life" (vv. 13-14). As Keener explains, "'Living,' that is, fresh, running or flowing, water was essential for purification in strict Jewish tradition." Moreover, "'Living waters' would flow from Jerusalem in the end time (Zech 14:8), and it would be natural . . . to connect this passage midrashically with Ezek 47, where this river brings life (Ezek 47:9). This water would also purify from sin (Zech 13:1; cf. John 3:5)."[39]

John 4:43-54 impinges on purification only to the extent that a man is physically healed, also clearing up whatever ritual impurities may have attached themselves to his maladies. Chapter 5:1-15 narrates a second healing, of a paralyzed man, by the pool of Bethesda. Here water reappears, not as a means of healing, but as a foil for Jesus' healing the individual apart from the water. The purification Jesus provides is superior to the pool's miraculous powers in which the man, thus far in vain, had been trusting.[40] But John's main interest lies with the timing of the miracle—the Sabbath—and the conflict it generates, which in

---

37. Of many recent authors who concur, see, e.g., Andrew T. Lincoln, *The Gospel according to Saint John* (London: Continuum; Peabody, MA: Hendrickson, 2005), 150.

38. Cf. Craig L. Blomberg, *Jesus and the Gospels: An Introduction and Survey*, rev. ed. (Nashville: B & H; Nottingham: InterVarsity, 2009), 467-70 and the literature there cited.

39. Craig S. Keener, *The Gospel of John: A Commentary* (Peabody, MA: Hendrickson, 2003), 2:604-5.

turn triggers Jesus' discourse that dominates the rest of the chapter (vv. 19-47). Still, purification is what started it all.

John 6 comprises the feeding of the five thousand, the subsequent walking on the water, and the bread-of-life discourse and its aftermath, provoked by the feeding miracle. Now John's focus is on bread—literal and metaphorical. Yet what is often forgotten is the almost-certain ritual impurity of at least some in a crowd of this size, spontaneously following Jesus into the wilderness, which he deliberately organizes into a giant banquet—table fellowship without the table! Mark goes so far as to use the plural of the word for "symposium" (*sumposion*, usually translated blandly as "groups"; Mark 6:39). What is more, no facilities would enable appropriate hand washing. Ritual purists would have objected on multiple counts. As Wilson Poon phrases it, "The good news of God's unconditional acceptance of sinners is *materially fulfilled* by all kinds of 'undesirables' without regard to the meal conventions of the Pharisees."[41] For Jesus, however, the spiritual sustenance he offers more than outweighs the realities of ritual impurity.[42]

Chapters 7-9 are tied together by the setting of Jesus in Jerusalem at *Sukkoth*, the festival of tabernacles. The motif of Jesus as the light of the world unifies these chapters. At the beginning of chapter 7, Jesus' brothers, whether sincerely or mockingly, are telling him to leave Galilee and go up to Jerusalem so that people there will see his works. They contrast secrecy and public disclosure, the very items that darkness and light regularly represent in John (vv. 2-4). Jesus does eventually go but not until halfway through the feast (v. 14). On "the last and greatest day of the festival" (v. 37a), Jesus announces in one of his classically Johannine "I am" sayings that he is "the light of the world" (8:12). The claim would have stood out in bold relief against the backdrop of the service in the temple on the last evening of the festival. After a week of lighting four huge lamps to accompany joyful singing and dancing, on the last night the main candelabrum was left unlit as a reminder that Israel had not yet experienced full salvation (see esp. *Sukk.* 5.2-4).[43] Chapter 9 applies the motif of literal light by narrating Jesus' healing of the man born blind, giving him literal sight. In between Jesus' initial self-disclosure and the healing of the blind man,

---

40. See esp. Steven M. Bryan, "Power in the Pool: The Healing of the Man of Bethesda and Jesus' Violation of the Sabbath (John 5:1-18)," *TynB* 54 (2003): 7–22.

41. Wilson C. K. Poon, "Superabundant Table Fellowship in the Kingdom: The Feeding of the Five Thousand and the Meal Motif in Luke," *ExpT* 114 (2003): 226.

42. See further Craig L. Blomberg, *Contagious Holiness: Jesus' Meals with Sinners* (Downers Grove: InterVarsity, 2005), 103–8.

43. Cf. further George R. Beasley-Murray, *John*, rev. ed. (Nashville: Nelson, 1999), 126–28.

a dialogue with the crowds escalates into a conflict, culminating in the most astonishing "I am" statement of them all in John 8:58, the probable allusion to the divine name of Exodus 3:14: "Before Abraham was, I am."[44]

All this represents the Johannine emphasis. But initially, Jesus again refers to living water, again not in the form of an actual "I am" statement (7:37-39). In fact, interpreters dispute whether there is much Christology here at all, or whether the point of the metaphor is primarily pneumatological: the rivers of living water stand for the Spirit that comes from Jesus to empower his followers.[45] Of course, the coming role of the Spirit *is* a major Johannine emphasis, but primarily in the Farewell Discourse, where he is known as the Paraclete, and water imagery is absent altogether. Nothing more is made of these rivers of living water in either chapter 7 or chapter 8, but it is probably not coincidental that water reemerges in chapter 9 in the context of Jesus' healing the blind man.[46] Unlike the healing by the pool of Bethesda, here Jesus sends his "patient" directly to a pool—the pool of Siloam—to wash in it. The water becomes the immediate agent for the man's physical purification, the washing that forms a key prerequisite before he can be ritually purified as well. This is scarcely John's redactional emphasis; that would be the concluding contrast between the literal sight of the once-blind man and the spiritual blindness of the Pharisees with whom he is debating (9:35-41).[47] We have all the more reason, then, to see the underlying purification motif as part of the historical core of these chapters.

Neither water nor purification more generally appears explicitly in John 10. This chapter is unified by the theme of Jesus as the Good Shepherd. Still, the correlation continues between Jesus' claims and their settings, which began with his Sabbath healing and the defense of his working as his Father does in chapter 5, continued with the bread-of-life discourse corresponding to Passover in 6:4, and most recently disclosed him as the light of the world near the time of the service of darkness during Tabernacles.[48] Here the temporal indicator

---

44. The Greek *egō eimi* ("I am") could also derive from texts such as Isa. 41:4 or 43:10, in which Yahweh emphatically declares, "I am he." Cf. esp. Catrin H. Williams, *I Am He: The Interpretation of 'Anî Hû' in Jewish and Christian Literature* (Tübingen: Mohr Siebeck, 1999).

45. Cf. Keener, *Gospel of John*, 2:728-29.

46. It was this very pool—Siloam—from which water was drawn by priests, who then processed with it to the temple on each of the first seven days of the festival (Sukkot 4.9, 5.1), forming the backdrop to Jesus' earlier teaching in John 7:37-38 on living water.

47. For fullest detail, see Matthias Rein, *Die Heilung des Blindgeborenen (Joh 9): Tradition und Redaktion* (Tübingen: Mohr Siebeck, 1995).

48. Cf. Francis J. Moloney, *The Gospel of John* (Collegeville, MN: Liturgical, 1998), 164.

appears in verse 22. It was the festival of Dedication—Hanukkah. The very holiday during which Jews celebrated the riddance from the land of Israel of the evil Seleucid shepherds, epitomized by Antiochus IV, and their replacement by the good Maccabean shepherds (see especially Ezekiel 34 for the link between shepherd and ruler) was the time that Jesus claimed to be his people's noble[49] shepherd. But, of course, the main event that the feast of Dedication celebrated was the purification of the temple itself in 164 BCE. If Jesus is walking about the temple precincts declaring, in essence, to be the fulfillment of Hanukkah,[50] just as he did with Sukkoth, Pesach, and Shabbat, then beneath whatever explicit theological overlay we may choose to attribute to the Fourth Evangelist lurk implications for purification. The Gospel writer may be stressing Jesus as the Good Shepherd, but implicitly Jesus himself was claiming to provide an even greater purification than the purification of the temple almost two hundred years earlier.

John 11 turns to the resurrection of Lazarus. There can be no greater physical cleansing than reawakening from the dead—the restoration of life, not to mention the removal of the defilement of corpse uncleanness. But explicit discussion of purity plays no integral role in the chapter. However, reminiscent of 2:6, John 11:55 refers to ritual purification completely tangentially, by describing those who went up to Jerusalem just before Passover to be ceremonially cleansed in preparation for the festival.[51] Verse 56 explains the Evangelist's reason for including this remark: it accounts for why people started looking for Jesus even before the feast itself got under way. But why would they expect him to arrive early, unless they suspected he would participate in (or perhaps challenge) the forms of ritual washing that others adopted? If he were known to be a purifier, even an unconventional one, everything falls into place.

John 12 comprises the anointing of Jesus at Bethany, the so-called triumphal entry, and the discussions that ensued from these events. Neither water nor purity concerns figure directly in the chapter, but Mary's pouring a pint of pure nard over Jesus' feet and wiping them with her hair (v. 3a), understood by Jesus as preparation for his burial (v. 7), is certainly one kind of

---

49. For this translation of *kalos* and its significance, see Jerome H. Neyrey, "The 'Noble Shepherd' in John 10: Cultural and Rhetorical Background," *JBL* 120 (2001): 267–91.

50. For the fullest treatment of possible allusions to Ezekiel 33–37 in John 8–11, see Mary K. Deeley, "Ezekiel's Shepherd and John's Jesus: A Case Study in the Appropriation of Biblical Texts," in *Early Christian Interpretation of the Scriptures of Israel*, ed. Craig A. Evans and James A. Sanders, 252–64 (Sheffield: Sheffield Academic, 1997).

51. The reference to ceremonial cleansing supports the authenticity of the setting. See Josephus, *War* 1.229; *Pesach* 9.1; originally based on Num. 9:6-13).

purification. Perfume applied to mitigate some of the odor of decaying corpses, here used even before Jesus has died, spreads a sweet fragrance throughout the house (v. 3b). The reason for the anointing is the same in Mark 14:8, so this is scarcely a redactionally created emphasis. Jesus the purifier is himself being purified ahead of time, in light of the agony and ignominy he is about to experience.[52]

The foot washing that dominates John 13 is much more clearly a purification. Verses 10-11 clarify that it symbolizes spiritual cleanliness. The shocking nature of a master washing his disciples' feet and the humiliating position it puts Jesus in combine to make it unlikely that any other later Christian would have invented this story. As he characteristically does, the Fourth Evangelist distinguishes between the event itself and later theological insight into it (v. 7), insight that, in context, will surely include Judas' role in Jesus' betrayal, and possibly additional reflection on the meaning of baptism as a once-for-all washing versus repeated "toppings up" of subsequent spiritual cleansing. The disciples would also need more time to learn what it meant for them to wash others' feet. But Jesus as foot washer, as purifier, seems securely anchored to the historical bedrock of the chapter.[53]

The Farewell Discourse of chapters 14–16 has the least amount of material pertaining to our topic of any section of comparable length thus far. Not surprisingly, it is also the segment that brings together the greatest number of key Johannine themes. However one understands the composition of these chapters, whether as a single discourse of Jesus,[54] a combination of two or more segments of his teaching,[55] or more predominantly Johannine invention,[56] it makes sense that in this last sustained address attributed to Jesus, in which he prepares his disciples for his departure, the densest cluster of the major themes

---

52. James F. Coakley demonstrates that, though rare, anointing of a guest's feet with oil or perfume did at times occur as a special gesture of hospitality. Coakley, "The Anointing at Bethany and the Priority of John," *JBL* 107 (1988): 246–48.

53. The fullest relevant study is John Christopher Thomas, *Footwashing in John 13 and the Johannine Community* (Sheffield: JSOT, 1991). More recently and succinctly, cf. Jay J. Kanagaraj, "Johannine Jesus, the Supreme Example of Leadership: An Inquiry into John 13:1-20," *Themelios* 29 (2004): 15–26.

54. See esp. L. Scott Kellum, *The Unity of the Farewell Discourse: The Literary Integrity of John 13.31—16.33* (London: T & T Clark, 2004); cf. John C. Stube, *A Graeco-Roman Rhetorical Reading of the Farewell Discourse* (London: T & T Clark, 2006).

55. See esp. Francisco Segovia, *The Farewell of the Word: The Johannine Call to Abide* (Minneapolis: Fortress Press, 1991); and George L. Parsenios, *Departure and Consolation: The Johannine Farewell Discourses in Light of Greco-Roman Literature* (Leiden: Brill, 2005).

56. See esp. Christina Hoegen-Rohls, *Die nachösterliche Johannes: Die Abschiedsreden als hermeneutischer Schlüssel zum vierten Evangelium* (Tübingen: Mohr Siebeck, 1996).

of his ministry should appear. The structure of the final form of these three chapters defies consensus, but a good case can be made for a broadly chiastic arrangement. Wayne Brouwer's proposal is as compelling as any, with the climactic center becoming part or all of John 15:1-17, the segment of text often entitled "the vine and the branches."[57]

At the beginning of this segment, we also encounter the lone reference to cleansing in this discourse. Verses 1-3 read, "I am the true vine, and my Father is the gardener. He cuts off every branch in me that bears no fruit, while every branch in me that does bear fruit he prunes so that it will be even more fruitful. You are already clean because of the word I have spoken to you." The word translated "prunes" is καθαίρει, which also means "he cleans."[58] To prune a plant involves cleaning it by removing dead wood, cutting it back, and preparing it for greater growth in the next season. The location of this motif, coupled with its lack of reuse elsewhere in the discourse suggests its authenticity. If the sermon was built up secondarily from its core, this pruning/cleansing would have been there from the start. If the sermon was built up by combining chapter 14 with chapters 15–16, due to the awkward seam, "Rise, let us go hence," at the end of 14, the pruning/cleansing appears at the beginning of the originally second discourse, a non-inversely parallel structure presumably built up from its initial metaphor.[59] And if these three chapters formed a unity from the beginning, then we have here a central element but not the most important one, because it does not reappear in the parallel halves that lead up to and away from it.[60] By now, the frequency of "Jesus the purifier" occupying an important, probably historical position in a pericope, but not so central a one as to make us suspect Johannine overlay, has proved striking indeed. If the Gospel ended at this point, we could conclude with confidence that we had discovered the pattern of consistent activity for which we were looking that reflected a significant but neglected contribution of the authentic Johannine material to the quest of the historical Jesus.

But there is more. John 17, often called Jesus' high-priestly prayer, contains parallels to every petition of the Lord's Prayer in Matt. 6:9-13, all but one in the identical order.[61] If there is a historical core to this chapter, it will include these

---

57. Wayne Brouwer, *The Literary Development of John 13–17: A Chiastic Reading* (Atlanta: Society of Biblical Literature, 2000). Brouwer also surveys other chiastic proposals.

58. BDAG, 387.

59. Cf. Christian Dietzfelbinger, *Der Abschied des Kommenden: Eine Auslegung der johannischen Abschiedsreden* (Tübingen: Mohr Siebeck, 1997).

60. See, e.g., Mark W. G. Stibbe, *John* (Sheffield: JSOT, 1993), 164.

61. William O. Walker Jr., "The Lord's Prayer in Matthew and in John," *NTS* 28 (1982): 237–56.

multiply attested parallels, including the appeal for the disciples' sanctification (John 17:17), conceptually similar to their forgiveness and deliverance from evil in Matthew. Such consecration makes us again recall our leitmotif of purification. Christ's sanctification leads to his followers' sanctification. Just as Christ was sent into the world, so he sends his followers into the world now in this condition (vv. 18-19). Just as we pray for our sins to be forgiven, we pledge to forgive others (Matt. 6:12; cf. Luke 11:4). As I wrote once before, "Given the theological problems that Christianity would later wrestle with, in the light of its conviction of the relationship between Father and Son not always being transferrable to the relationship between Jesus and the disciples, one wonders if verses like these," in either Matthew or John, "could have been created without foundations in the utterances of the historical Jesus."[62]

Specific references to purification or its conceptual equivalents prove scarcest of all in the Johannine passion and resurrection narratives. We read, and only in the Fourth Gospel, that the Jewish leaders wanting to meet with Pilate on the morning of the crucifixion avoid entering his palace to avoid ceremonial uncleanness (18:28).[63] This will not be a concern for Jesus as Pilate proceeds to interrogate him, but then he apparently had no choice as to where he would be held and questioned. Water reappears in 19:34 in the outflow of water and blood from Jesus' body after the spear thrust confirming his death. Yet, despite a venerable history of seeing symbolism here somehow related to baptism and the Lord's Supper, this is much more likely just a part of John's emphasis on Jesus' full humanity and completely genuine human death, probably against docetic if not fully gnostic counterclaims.[64] John 19:39-40 describes Joseph of Arimathea and Nicodemus preparing Christ's body for burial and laying it in the tomb, in keeping with their burial customs. We recall here Mary of Bethany's prior actions and thus can envision a certain purifying objective, but it is more simply a gesture to slow or mask putrefaction for a time. It was certainly not sufficient under Jewish law to prevent the ritual impurity that anyone subsequently touching the corpse would contract.[65] Finally, there is one more appearance of water, in 21:1-14, as the resurrected Lord appears to the disciples on the shore of the Sea of Galilee, after enabling Peter and company

---

62. Blomberg, *Historical Reliability of John's Gospel*, 223.

63. On the chronological problems raised here and in related passages in John, see esp. Barry D. Smith, "The Chronology of the Last Supper," *WTJ* 53 (1991): 29–45.

64. See, e.g., Charles H. Talbert, *Reading John* (New York: Crossroad, 1992), 245; F. F. Bruce, *The Gospel of John* (Basingstoke: Pickering & Inglis; Grand Rapids: Eerdmans, 1983), 376.

65. On this incident, see further Dennis Sylva, "Nicodemus and His Spices (John 19:39)," *NTS* 34 (1988): 148–51.

to haul in a miraculous catch of fish. One might imagine that by pointing the disciples to the place in the water where their earlier futile fish-catching attempts could be more than compensated for, Jesus was somehow purifying the water, but this would be a stretch that the text in no way sanctions.

On the other hand, while no unambiguous references to Jesus as purifier appear in the closing four chapters of the Gospel of John, the entire combination of crucifixion and resurrection that dominates this narrative clearly had a purifying intent. Jesus' death would atone for humanity's sins, while his resurrection would vindicate his earlier teaching and testimony, showing him indeed to be the Risen Lord. It is regularly pointed out that atonement is less a Johannine emphasis than in most other portions of the New Testament, but it is still present (see esp. John 1:29, 32, esp. in light of 1 John 1:7; 2:2; and 4:10), all the more probably authentic for its muted role.[66] John 20:22-23 associates the ministry of the Spirit with the disciples' ability to forgive (or deny forgiveness for) the sins of others, again recalling the petition of the Lord's Prayer about forgiveness (cf. also Matt. 16:19; 18:18).[67] If Christ had to go away (i.e., be killed) for the Spirit to come (John 16:7), if when the Spirit comes he will make forgiveness possible, and if forgiveness is linked with sanctification/purification in John 17, then there is a continuation of the motif of purifying even in the passion and resurrection narratives, however subordinated it may be to other, more distinctively Johannine emphases.

I propose, then, that the upshot of our survey is that at least one important but often-neglected[68] christological thread running throughout the Fourth Gospel, not easily attributable to later conscious Christian invention, and consistently located in contexts and given meanings both of which support authenticity, is Jesus as purifier—the washer, cleanser, or renewer of those who will come to him. The language of purity, especially of clean and unclean, is noticeably more frequent in the Synoptics but still not pervasive, but it also aptly sums up a commonly noted and very central practice of Jesus in the first three Gospels—his meals with sinners.[69] In an entire monograph on this subject,

---

66. See esp. Bruce Grigsby, "The Cross as an Expiatory Sacrifice in the Fourth Gospel," *JSNT* 15 (1982): 51–80; and Max Turner, "Atonement and the Death of Jesus in John," *EQ* 62 (1990): 99–122.

67. Steven E. Hansen stresses that John's and Matthew's teaching on this topic belong together as two parts to one unified whole. Hansen, "Forgiving and Retaining Sin: A Study of the Text and Context of John 20:23," *HBT* 19 (1997): 24–32.

68. E.g., in the *New Interpreter's Dictionary of the Bible*, Hannah K. Harrington has, under her section on the New Testament, discrete subsections on the Synoptic Gospels and Acts and on the Pauline Literature, but nothing on the Johannine material. Even in her final subsection, labeled "Other NT Texts," she mentions only John 15:3 from the Fourth Gospel. Harrington, "Clean and Unclean," in *New Interpreter's Dictionary of the Bible*, ed. Katharine D. Sakenfeld, 1:681–89 (Nashville: Abingdon, 2006).

I have argued, following ideas sparked by Marcus Borg more than twenty-five years ago,[70] that the entire contrast between Jesus' convictions and those of most of the rest in his Jewish world, both then and earlier, was that Jews were concerned primarily about the unclean defiling the clean, whereas Jesus believed the holy could purify the unclean. In other words, he saw holiness as more contagious than impurity. For all sorts of reasons, this theme passes the historical tests of authenticity with flying colors.[71]

The results of our investigation of John, then, are not to suggest a new or unrelated theme to be added to those already known from the Synoptics. However, its recurring presence in John suggests that perhaps the Third Quest has not traditionally paid enough attention to this particular theme as one of the very central pieces of the historical Jesus' ministry. Certainly one does not find the quantity of literature on Jesus' table fellowship, apart from the Last Supper and its unique significance, than one does, say, on the kingdom, parables, healings and exorcisms, ethical teachings, Sabbath controversies, road to the cross, or messianism. Christianity over the centuries has not dwelt often enough on the ways in which Jesus' followers can permeate society to help purify it, cleanse it, and make it less corrupt, more filled with love of God and neighbor, more distinguished by care for the neediest, and more characterized by integrity in every area of life. Rather, it has often reverted to its Jewish roots with a greater concern about becoming corrupted than about providing a winsome antidote to corruption. By way of application, it is often uncomfortable to suggest that "contagious holiness" may be more at the heart of the agenda of the historical Jesus then we have typically recognized, because it implies it should be more at the heart of what his followers are about. But if that is the case, then this exercise has been all that much more warranted and worthwhile.

---

69. For the most thorough, recent study, see János Bolyki, *Jesu Tischgemeinschaften* (Tübingen: Mohr Siebeck, 1998).

70. Marcus J. Borg, *Conflict, Holiness, and Politics in the Teaching of Jesus* (New York: Mellen, 1984).

71. Blomberg, *Contagious Holiness*. Cf. idem, "Jesus, Sinners and Table Fellowship," *BBR* 19 (2009): 35–62; idem, "The Authenticity and Significance of Jesus' Table Fellowship with Sinners," in Bock and Webb, *Key Events in the Life of the Historical Jesus*, 215–50.

8

Critical Blindness, Wise Virgins, and the Law of Christ
Three Surprising Examples of Jesus Tradition in Paul

David Wenham

"Bear one another's burdens, and so [you will] fulfil the law of [the] Christ." So says Paul in Galatians 6:2.[1] Critics have agonized over his meaning and particularly over his reference to "the law of Christ." Some have suggested that he is referring to the Old Testament law "love your neighbor as yourself," others that he has in mind the self-giving attitude that characterized Jesus in his ministry and crucifixion. Many have been uneasy about his choice of words: why does Paul speak of "the law" of Christ?

Remarkably, almost no scholar even considers that there might be a connection with John 13:34-35, where Jesus says, "A new commandment I give to you, that you [should] love one another; even as I have loved you, that you [should] also love one another. By this all men [sic] will know that you are my disciples, if you have love for another." Although both the Pauline text and the text in John's Gospel speak of supporting/loving "one another," and although they both identify this specifically as a command/law of Jesus/Christ, scholars have apparently not even thought there could be a connection.[2]

This could be because they are so clear that there is another good explanation of Gal. 6:2, though the amount of scholarly ink the phrase has evoked shows that scholars find the phrase puzzling. But even if a satisfactory

---

1. Throughout this chapter, I primarily have used the RSV, with some modifications, marked in brackets.

2. An honorable exception is R. Y. K. Fung in his *The Epistle to the Galatians*, The New International Commentary on the New Testament (Grand Rapids: Eerdmans, 1988), 288–89. Also C. Stettler, "The 'Command of the Lord' in 1 Cor 14,37: A Saying of Jesus," *Biblica* 87 (2006): 50.

other solution had been found, it is still surprising that almost no one observes the possible connection, even if only to dismiss it.

The reasons for this omission are, however, easy to identify: First, most scholars do not see much evidence of Paul drawing on Jesus traditions in his letters. Second, Galatians is usually dated relatively early (by some as the earliest of Paul's letters at around ad 48), whereas John's Gospel is usually dated late, perhaps in the 90s. So the idea that Paul could be quoting this "Johannine" tradition does not even enter the mind. Finally, although John might conceivably have retained an early tradition, the absence of this "new commandment" of Jesus in the Synoptics (which have Jesus calling for love of neighbor and love of enemy, but not for love of "one another") makes this an unlikely explanation. And indeed, John's rather insular version of the command has been seen to reflect his sectarian context and outlook at the end of the first century, and has a poor claim to historical authenticity.

So the idea of a connection is not made, even, interestingly, by conservative scholars, who may have a relatively high view of John's historical value. However, this failure to make the connection illustrates how scholarly theories and a scholarly consensus can have a baneful effect and prevent us from even exploring interesting possibilities that are "out of the box"—in this case, the box of scholarly theories. Of course, all scholars will come to particular issues with presuppositions and existing ideas, and there is nothing wrong with that. In this case, I am inclined to agree with those who date Galatians before the Synoptic Gospels and the Synoptics before John. But the problem comes when particular presuppositions are so rigidly or narrowly held that they become blinkers that prevent us from seeing things.

One of the major blinkers that have affected much scholarly thinking over the past century has been a failure to reckon with the importance of oral tradition in early Christianity. This failure has been challenged in recent years by significant scholars, such as S. Byrscog, James Dunn, and Richard Bauckham. But the blinkers still remain on in much scholarly thinking and writing, and the fact—I choose the word advisedly—that there was strong oral tradition alive and well in the earliest days of the church is often not reckoned with. In particular, it does not seem to cross the mind that later writers, such as Matthew and Luke (in relation to Mark) or John (in relation to the Synoptics), will very likely have known and used plenty of such traditions.

The "Word of the Lord" in 1 Thess. 4:16

Before examining Gal. 6:2 with some care, we will illustrate the point about scholarly oversight with another example, from 1 Thessalonians 4. First Thessalonians is widely recognized as one of Paul's earliest letters, perhaps to be dated around ad 49. In chapter 4, Paul famously says to the Thessalonian Christians who are mourning members of the congregation who have died before the Lord's return, "For this we declare to you by the word of the Lord, that we who are alive, who are left until the coming of the Lord, shall not precede those who have fallen asleep. For the Lord himself will descend from heaven with a cry of command, with the archangel's call, and with the sound of the trumpet of God. And the dead in Christ will rise first; then we . . . shall be caught up together with them in the clouds to meet the Lord in the air; and so we shall always be with the Lord." (4:15-17). These verses pose an intriguing puzzle for scholars: what is the "word of the Lord" to which Paul is referring?

There is not any known word of Jesus that seems quite to fit the bill and that addresses the question of "the dead in Christ." So commentators have suggested various other possibilities: maybe it is a saying of Jesus that has not come down to us, or maybe it was a word of prophecy delivered by a charismatic prophet, or maybe Paul is simply speaking out of his own authority—he is delivering a word from the Lord. All these are possible.

However, the preferable view is the first—namely, that "the word of the Lord" in question is a reference to a saying, or sayings, of Jesus found in the gospels. It is true that there is no direct reference in Jesus' teaching to the position of the "dead in Christ" at the time of the Parousia. But what scholars have almost always missed is the possibility that Paul has in mind the parable of the Wise and Foolish Virgins. Four considerations favor this view:

First, there are a lot of possible and some probable echoes of Jesus' eschatological teaching in 1 Thessalonians 4 and 5.[3] Immediately after his "This we declare to you [tell you] by the word of the Lord," Paul goes on to describe the Lord's coming from heaven in ways that are strikingly similar to the description of the coming of the Son of Man in Mark 13/Matthew 24: he comes from heaven, with a sound of a trumpet, with clouds, with angels, to

---

3. This has often been recognized by scholars. Thus, recently C. Wanamaker and B. Witherington III both comment on the parallels between 1 Thessalonians and Matthew 24, but neither considers the possible link between the parable of the virgins in Matthew 25 and 1 Thessalonians. Wanamaker, *The Epistle to the Thessalonians* (Grand Rapids: Paternoster, 1990), 170–71; Witherington, *1 and 2 Thessalonians* (Grand Rapids: Eerdmans, 2006), 135–36. See also the important monograph of Christian Stettler, *Das Letzte Gericht: Studien zur Endgerichtserwartung von den Schriftspropheten bis Jesus* (Tübingen: Mohr, 2011), 233–66.

gather his elect.⁴ We are certainly in the same world of thought as the synoptic eschatological teaching of Jesus.

A few verses later in 1 Thessalonians, Paul speaks of the Lord's coming as like that of a thief coming in the night (5:2). This is a striking parallel to Jesus' parable of the Thief, which is found in both Matthew's Gospel (in 24:42-44 in the same context as the other eschatological teaching about the Lord's coming) and in Luke (12:39-40). Paul says the Thessalonians "know well [accurately] that the day of the Lord will come like a thief in the night," and the probable reason for that knowledge is that it was a Jesus tradition they had been taught. There is every likelihood that the parable goes back to Jesus, not just because it is recorded in Matthew and Luke, but also because it is highly unlikely that the early Christians would have come up with the comparison of their master to a thief.

Scholars have often recognized this likely allusion, helped by the fact that the parable being found in Matthew and Luke is what scholars call "Q tradition." Such tradition is conventionally seen as some of the earliest Jesus tradition in the New Testament. So it is entirely possible that Paul might have known it.

But if that is a relatively easy assumption, because of a particular widely held scholarly view, the idea that Paul might be alluding to the parable of the Wise and Foolish Virgins when he speaks of "the word of the Lord" is much less easy, even though it is found adjacent to the parable of the Thief in Matthew's Gospel. It is only found in Matthew's Gospel and so is often seen as relatively late tradition, without a very strong claim to historical authenticity.⁵

However, if we look out from the blinkers of a narrowly applied scholarly theory, the idea that Paul is alluding to the Wise and Foolish Virgins is a rather good one.⁶ Three further things favor it.

The second of our four considerations is the otherwise puzzling phrase "the word of the Lord," as we have previously discussed."

---

4. The trumpet is only in Matthew's version of the discourse, but the other elements are in all three gospels.

5. But Luke does have something slightly reminiscent of the parable also adjacent to the parable of the thief, "Let your loins be girded and your lamps burning" (12:35).

6. In the early church, the parable of the virgins was regularly related to Christians dying and to 1 Thessalonians 4, e.g., by Methodius, Chrysostom, and Augustine. See A. C. Thiselton, *1 & 2 Thessalonians through the Centuries* (Chichester: Wiley-Blackwell, 2011), 123–28. W. Schenk argues for Paul knowing a version of the parable, though a significantly different one from that in Matthew. Schenk, "Auferweckung der Toten oder Gericht nach den Werken: Tradition und Redaktion in Matthäeus xxv 1-13," *NovT* 8 (1966): 223–34.

Third is some of the vocabulary used: In the parable, the wise and foolish virgins fall asleep, and Paul speaks of the Christians who have died as "asleep." The bridegroom's coming is announced with a shout inviting the virgins to "meet him"; they rise up, and the wise are ready to go into the wedding feast "with him." Paul similarly speaks of the Lord coming with a cry of command and the archangel's call, of the dead in Christ rising up "to meet" the Lord (the same Greek phrase), and of them then being with the Lord.

Fourth, and finally, is the appropriateness of the parable for Paul's point. At first sight, it may seem unlikely—perhaps exegetically irresponsible, given the focus of the parable on the different preparedness of the wise and the foolish virgins—that Paul would use the picture of the virgins "rising up" to make a point about resurrection. Yet the parable is about people falling asleep when the bridegroom did not come as quickly as they hoped, and that picture was, in fact, very apt for Paul in addressing the Thessalonians, who were worried about their loved ones who had "fallen asleep" before the Lord's return.[7]

In making his point, Paul was not just drawing on the parable—he is not a naive proof-texter! We have seen that there are a number of parallels to the teaching of Jesus about the Son of Man's coming on the clouds to gather his elect, and in addressing the Thessalonian worries about those who have died before the Parousia, he is drawing creatively and intelligently on those traditions, with the parable of the virgins being one key ingredient, because it speaks of "those who sleep."[8]

Whether or not that explanation of the "word of the Lord" is right, at least it is a serious possibility, which has largely been ignored by commentators, who have been influenced banefully by critical assumptions.[9] At least it deserves consideration.

But the main focus of this article makes that point even more clearly.

---

7. On this, see my *Paul: Follower of Jesus or Founder of Christianity?* (Grand Rapids: Eerdmans, 1995), 305–11. Various of the ideas discussed in this article develop points noted in my book.

8. The parallels between the Matthean form of Jesus' teaching and Paul's teaching in 1 and 2 Thessalonians have led some, notably M. Goulder, to argue that the direction of dependence is from Paul to Matthew, not from Jesus to Paul. Goulder, *Midrash and Lection in Matthew* (London: SPCK, 1974), 154. This is an example of thinking that is influenced by particular scholarly consensuses about the dates of New Testament books and traditions. But the unlikelihood of Paul inventing the idea of Jesus' coming being thief-like and also the Pauline reference to "the word of the Lord" point to the direction being from Jesus to Paul, not from Paul to Matthew.

THE LAW OF CHRIST IN GAL. 6:2

In Gal. 6:2, Paul's injunction to the Galatian Christians to "bear one another's burdens, and so [you will] fulfil the law of [the] Christ"[10] has given rise to much scholarly discussion. Obvious questions are, what does Paul mean by "the law of Christ," and why does he use this phrase to make his point?

Paul has described the "works of the flesh" and the "fruit of the Spirit" in the second half of Galatians 5. He follows those descriptions with a positive exhortation to the Galatians to walk by the Spirit, and then with the negative side of the coin says, don't be big-headed, provoking one another and envying one another. He then moves on to another aspect of responsibility within the Christian community, giving instruction to the Christian "brothers" about how to deal with someone who falls into sin: "you who are spiritual should restore him in a spirit of gentleness. Look to yourself [yourselves], lest you too be tempted" (6:1). This then leads into the words about bearing each other's burdens and fulfilling the law of Christ. This is followed by another warning against big-headedness: "If any one thinks he is something, when he is nothing, he deceives himself" (v. 3).

The general drift of Paul's thought is clear: he wants the Galatian Christians to display in their community the gifts of the Spirit—notably, to relate well to "one another" in humility and mutual support. But why does he say that such behavior serves to "fulfil the law of Christ"?

---

9. M. W. Pahl in his recent doctoral thesis, *The "Word of the Lord" in 1 Thessalonians 4:15* (London: T&T Clark, 2009), acknowledges the use of Jesus' eschatological tradition in 1 Thessalonians but doesn't recognize the parable of the virgins, speaking of "the relative lack of significant and verbal agreement between that parable and 1 Thess. 4.16-17a" (18). He argues instead that "the word of the Lord" is the gospel message about the Lord, which Paul proclaimed. John Nolland in his commentary takes more seriously the striking parallels, but he concludes that the differences (e.g., in Matthew, all the virgins rise, not just the righteous) point to the conclusion that the similarities are "nothing more than a curious coincidence." Nolland, *The Gospel of Matthew* (Grand Rapids: Eerdmans; Bletchley: Paternoster, 2005), 1007; similarly, W. D. Davies and D. Allison, *A Critical and Exegetical Commentary on the Gospel according to Saint Matthew* (Edinburgh: T&T Clark, 1997), 3:398. But it is one thing to conclude that the Matthean parable may not have resurrection in mind—though see K. P. Donfried, "The Allegory of the Ten Virgins (Matt 25:1-13) as a Summary of Matthean Theology," *JBL* 93 (1974): 415–28; it is another thing to conclude that Paul might not have seen it as highly pertinent to the current question. But scholars tend not to think of the possibility that Paul might be referring to a "Matthean" saying of Jesus.

10. The future indicative "you will fulfill" (*anaplerosete*) has good textual attestation, but so does the alternative use of the aorist imperative, *anaplerosate*. However, the argument of this article is unaffected by the textual variant.

THE WAY AND EXAMPLE OF CHRIST

A good number of commentators have argued that Paul is referring quite simply to the example of Christ and to his self-giving.[11] There is probably some truth in this view, but still it seems a little odd to speak of Christ's example as "the law" of Christ, not least in a letter where Paul has been speaking about how Christ has brought freedom from the law, and where he has warned strongly against those who "desire [want] to be under law" (4:21).

But perhaps the oddity of the phrase can be exaggerated: could Paul have used the phrase precisely because "the law" has been such an important theme in the letter? He is not playing with words in a trivial sense, let alone suggesting that conversion to Christ is just swapping one oppressive law for another. On the contrary, the law of Christ and the Spirit is freedom compared with slavery. But he uses the word deliberately to refer to the Christian way of behaving, because "the law" has been such an important theme in his letter. He would not normally speak in that way of Christ's way, but in this context, it makes sense.[12]

Something rather similar may be true of 1 Cor. 9:19-20, where we find the nearest parallel in Paul's letters to the idea of "the law of Christ." He speaks there of himself not being "under the law," i.e., the law of the Jews, but then he says he is "not being without law toward God but under the law of Christ" (v. 21). Paul is not "God's lawless one"; he is, in fact, "Christ's enlawed one" (my translations). The Greek is difficult to interpret exactly, let alone to translate into English. But his point is clear enough: his relationship with Christ is one that is the opposite of lawlessness. So here, where Paul is thinking primarily about relationship to the Jewish law, he coins a phrase to express the fact that, as a Christian, he is not lawless. In 1 Corinthians he speaks of being "enlawed of Christ," in Galatians of fulfilling the "law of Christ."[13]

In other words, Paul means "and so you will be living in Christ's way," but he uses "fulfilling the law" language because of the main theme of Galatians.[14] He has talked a great deal about the Old Testament law in the first part of the

---

11. E.g., B. Witherington III, *Grace in Galatia* (Edinburgh: T&T Clark, 1998), 422–26.

12. Paul is very emphatic that going back under the law of Moses would be spiritually disastrous and a betrayal, but he is not neurotic or negative about the whole notion of the law. Indeed, he can speak, in this very context, of Spirit-inspired love being the "fulfilment of the law" (5:13). He uses the same language in Rom. 13:8-10, in a letter where he has spoken of the law as "holy and just and good" (7:12).

13. I speak of Paul "coining the phrase" as though he may have invented it de novo in this context. However, if my proposal about Gal. 6:2 is correct, and there was a well-known idea of there being a "law of Christ," then Paul's phraseology is not so innovative. See further on 1 Corinthians 9 in my discussion of 1 Cor. 14:37, later in this chapter.

14. "Fulfilling the law" is a phrase he used earlier in the letter when speaking of the Old Testament law (5:14; compare Rom. 13:8-10).

letter, but now he has come on to explain the Christian alternative to living by the law, i.e., living in Christ's humble and caring way, or as he puts it, living by "Christ's law."

This could be the simple explanation of the phrase. But the niggling feeling remains that "the law of Christ" is a surprising way to speak of living in Christ's way at the end of a letter where there has been so much emphasis on Christ bringing freedom from law. First Corinthians does not have that emphasis, and Paul's used of the phrase "Christ's enlawed one" in 1 Cor. 9:19 may be difficult to translate, but it makes perfect sense in the context, as a contrast to being "God's lawless one." That is not the case in Galatians 6, and Paul could easily have chosen another phrase to express what he wants to say about burden carrying being Christ-like and spiritual (e.g., "as is fitting in the Lord Jesus").

The suspicion remains that by using the phrase "and so [you will] fulfil the law of Christ [literally, the Christ]," Paul is referring to something rather specific that the Galatians will know about, not just referring to the example or way of Christ.

Paul's Opponents' Phrase

An alternative but not entirely dissimilar view is that it was a phrase known to the Galatians, because it was originally used by Paul's Jewish-Christian opponents, who used it to identify Jesus as someone upholding the law (or bringing a new Messianic Torah). Paul has taken their phrase but uses it polemically, investing it with new meaning in line with his understanding of faith (in Christ) working through love and so fulfilling the Old Testament law.[15] But although it is not impossible, the phrase is not a very obvious one for his shadowy opponents to have used, and it is hardly the most straightforward way for Paul to proceed, to adopt the phrase of those he has been denouncing so vehemently and to use it with a quite different meaning.

The Law "Taken in Hand" by Christ: Love Your Neighbor as Yourself

A popular and reputable view is that Paul has in mind "the Law as it has been taken in hand by Christ."[16] This is attractive, in that Paul has been talking about love and living by the Spirit as the fulfilling of the law. He has specifically quoted the command "love your neighbor as yourself" with approval and as

---

15. See H. D. Betz, *Galatians* (Philadelphia: Fortress Press, 1979), 300–1, citing H. Georgi. Against this view and questioning the idea of the Messianic Torah, see also Witherington, *Grace in Galatia*, 422.

16. So J. L. Martyn, *Galatians* (New York: Doubleday, 1997), 547–49, 554–58.

relevant to the Galatians (5:14), and this Old Testament command is one that Jesus in the gospel tradition discusses, endorses, and interprets more than any other verse from the Old Testament (so Matt. 5:43; 19:19; 22:39; Mark 12:31; Luke 10:27).[17] So it might make sense to call this a "law of Christ." And it is easy enough to see how "bearing one another's burdens" in Gal. 6:2 is indeed a fulfillment of the command to love one's neighbor as oneself.

This view is clearly plausible.[18] Yet "the law of Christ" remains a less-than-obvious way of speaking of the Old Testament law, albeit adopted and reinterpreted by Jesus. As for "you shall love your neighbor as yourself," it is hard to see how this could be called the law of Christ. It is an Old Testament law from Lev. 19:18—a law of Moses, in other words—and that is explicitly said by Paul in Gal. 5:14. Yes, it might be possible to argue that Jesus adopted it to such an extent that it could be described as his law, the Messiah's law. But even that is not so evident from the gospel texts: in some at least, Jesus appears to find the Levitical law lacking, so in Matt. 5:43, he offers "love your enemies" as his love command, over against "love your neighbor," and something similar is true of Luke 10, where the parable of the Good Samaritan sets out Jesus' ideal of love of enemies in response to the lawyer's question about love of neighbor. Of course, Jesus is not questioning the Old Testament law, not at all. But it is not obvious that the distinctive "law of the Messiah" is the neighbor-love command of the Old Testament, which indeed Jesus' Jewish contemporaries are as capable of quoting as Jesus himself.[19] As for Paul, what he says explicitly about "You will love your neighbor as yourself" is that the whole of the Old Testament law is fulfilled in those words, not that it is the law of Christ.

The Love Command in John's Gospel

How then is Paul's phrase "so [you will] fulfil the law of [the] Christ" to be explained? The remaining and normally ignored option is that Paul is referring to Jesus' "new commandment" as recorded in John's Gospel, first in John 13:34-35, where, following the account of Jesus washing his disciples' feet, Jesus says, "A new commandment I give to you, that you love one another; even as I

---

17. Arguably, it also lies behind the so-called Golden Rule of Matt. 7:12; Luke 6:31. James's reference to it as the "royal law" in 2:8 might also be seen as supporting this view, if the "royal" comes from Jesus' kingdom teaching.

18. J. D. G. Dunn speaks attractively of Torah as interpreted by the love command in the light of the Jesus tradition and the Christ event, so combining this view with the first view we noted. Dunn, *The Epistle to the Galatians* (London: Continuum, 1993), 93.

19. To judge from Matt. 19:19, Mark 12:33, and Luke 10:27.

have loved you, that you also love one another. By this all men [sic] will know that you are my disciples, if you have love for one another." This command is reiterated in John 15:12 and 17.[20]

In favor of this view are the following points:

> 1. Paul speaks—rather puzzlingly, as we have seen—of "the law of Christ." John in his gospel specifically has Jesus give a "new" command to his disciples, and Jesus identifies it as something that will distinctively identify his followers.[21]
> 2. Paul speaks of "bearing *one another's* burdens" as fulfilling the law of Christ. The new commandment in John is all about loving "one another," the same Greek word.
> 3. It is obvious that bearing another's burdens, as urged by Paul, might be seen as a way of fulfilling the command to love another.
> 4. Paul's exhortation comes in the context that begins (arguably) in 5:13 and 14, where Paul moves from his discussion of the law and of Christian freedom into his discussion of Christian conduct. He says, "For you were called to freedom, brothers. Only do not use the freedom as an opportunity for the flesh, but *through love be servants/ slaves to one another*. For all the law is fulfilled in one word, "Love your neighbor as yourself" (5:14, my translation). The central and keynote exhortation is "Through love be servants/slaves to one another."

What is striking about this from our point of view is first that Paul begins this section of ethical exhortation with a reference to loving one another, and second that he combines the idea of loving one another with the idea of serving or being a slave to one another.[22] John 13 has just the same combination of ideas: Jesus speaks of "loving one another, as I have loved you" only a few verses after the story of his washing his disciples' feet. That action was shocking to the disciples, because Jesus was taking the role of a family slave in what he did. But

---

20. And it is echoed in 1 John 3:23, "And this is his [God's] command that we should believe in the name of his Son Jesus Christ and that we should love one another, as he gave command to us."

21. Michael Thompson in *Clothed with Christ: The Example and Teaching of Jesus in Romans 12.1— 15.13* (Sheffield: JSNT, 1991), 30–36, has a useful discussion of how to recognize Pauline references to traditions of Jesus and speaks of "tradition indicators" (which indicate that a tradition is being used). An example of such would be "This we tell you by a word of the Lord" in 1 Thess. 4:15, as already discussed. In Gal. 6:2, "the law of Christ" could easily be something similar, certainly something important that he expects the Galatians to understand.

22. Thirdly, we observe that the Old Testament command to love the neighbor is not the command given by Paul, but is quoted in support of Paul's keynote call "through love be servants/slaves to one another."

Jesus went on to tell his disciples that they similarly should wash "one another's" feet (John 13:14), before later going on to give his new command about loving one another "as I have loved you."

All this adds up to a strong case for believing that Paul's law of Christ is to be identified with the new commandment of Jesus in John's Gospel. His exhortation "Through love be servants/slaves to one another" is plausibly seen as his version of that law.

This argument is supported by the strong attestation elsewhere in Paul's letters of both those themes: loving one another and being slaves to others.[23] What we do not find in Galatians 5 and 6 is a clear equivalent of the Johannine reference to Jesus as the model of the love that Paul calls for: "love one another as I have loved you."[24] But what we do find in Galatians is the striking reference by Paul to "the Son of God who loved me and gave himself [up] for me" (2:20). And elsewhere in Paul's writings, he often connects his exhortations to generosity and humility with Christ's example. The closest parallel in Paul's letters to Gal. 6:2 is Rom. 15:1-3: "We who are strong ought to bear the weaknesses of those who are not strong, and not to please ourselves. Let each of us please our neighbor for his good to build him up. For Christ also did not please himself. But as it is written, 'The reproaches of those who reproach you fell on me'" (my translation). But the most striking example of such a christological connection is in Phil. 2:5-11, which like Gal. 6:2 comes in the context of an exhortation to humility.[25] Scholars have from time to time compared Philippians 2 with the account of Jesus' washing of the feet in John 13, and that comparison is the more plausible when it is observed that these passages share not just the themes of extreme humility and service, but also the theme of Jesus' death as exemplifying this humble service. In Philippians, that is on the surface; in John 13, it is implied by the way John puts the story in the context of Jesus' coming death and comments "he loved them [his own] to the end" (vv. 1-3) and by the strong hints that his action is parabolic and will only be understood after his death, which will effect the cleansing of his disciples (vv. 6-7).

The thesis that "the law of Christ" in Gal. 6:2 is the "new commandment" of Jesus in John's Gospel is much the most plausible explanation on offer. Or it

---

23. Notably in Rom. 13:8; 1 Thess. 3:12; 4:9; 5:15; 2 Thess. 1:3; Col. 3:12-14; Eph. 4:32; Rom 15:7-8; 1 Cor. 9:19, 22; 2 Cor. 4:5.

24. But the reference in Gal. 6:17 to "bearing in my body the marks/*stigmata* of Jesus" is interesting and possibly significant, not least as it follows so soon after 6:2.

25. But see also Rom. 15:7; 2 Cor. 8:9.

would be unless the obvious objections that we noted at the beginning of the article carry weight.[26]

OBJECTIONS AND RESPONSES

The objections boil down to the following points:

> 1. Galatians was written by Paul in the 50s (some of us put it even in the late 40s).
> 2. John was written, according to most scholars, in the 90s or perhaps a little later.
> 3. John is very different from the Synoptic Gospels and is very widely seen as a relatively late theological reinterpretation of the story of Jesus, which reflects John's own context and interests, and which is relatively unhistorical.
> 4. The command to "love one another as I have loved you" is found only in John, not in the more trustworthy Synoptics. It is unthinkable that Jesus could have emphatically given a new commandment about what should distinguish his disciples, without the Synoptics recording it.
> 5. The Synoptics have Jesus teaching about love of neighbor and, strikingly, about love of enemy. John's teaching about the disciples loving one another is quite a different kettle of fish and probably reflects the sectarian nature of John's church at the time the gospel was written, certainly not the more open attitude of Jesus.[27]

So Paul cannot have had the "Johannine" love command of Jesus in mind when referring to the "law of Christ."

Only the last two points in that apparently formidable case need addressing seriously. It is possible to dispute the dating of John's Gospel but not necessary to do that. As for the view that John is a relatively late and unhistorical gospel, that might be the case,[28] but still, many scholars have recognized that there is a

---

26. With rather little prompting, some nonacademic colleagues and friends, when asked what "the law of Christ" might be, have answered in terms of the love command. But scholars have not even considered the "obvious" idea, because of the world of scholarly ideas that they inhabit!

27. Another possible objection could be that the word *law* (*nomos*) in Galatians 6 is broader than the word *commandment* (*entole*) used in John's Gospel. However, we have already argued that Paul seems to be referring to something relatively specific and identifiable, and in any case, the words are very closely related, and Paul can hop from one to the other without embarrassment, e.g., in Rom. 7:7-11. In 1 Cor. 14:37, he speaks of the "commandment of the Lord," arguably in the same connection as Gal. 6:2 (see discussion below).

28. There are strong arguments for not thinking it to be the case.

good case for believing there are some early independent traditions of Jesus in John's Gospel that have not come to John from the Synoptics. The question is whether the love command is one of them, or whether this is something that comes from John and his context, not from Jesus.

What cannot be doubted is that John does have a particular fondness for the love/*agape* group of words and a particular interest in the unity of the Christian community (see chapter 17). So does the first letter of John, and that may offer an explanation of the Johannine emphasis, since it describes an unhappy schism in the church and "antichrists" having gone out from us (2:18-19). The christological focus of the gospel and the epistle, as well as the emphasis in both on the importance of unity and "loving one another," may well be explained in that way. That does not, however, mean we should too readily accept the idea that the author of the gospel (or whoever the author was) could or would have invented de novo the new commandment, putting it very emphatically on the lips of Jesus, when it had no basis in tradition.[29]

But what of the most substantial problem with recognizing the Johannine love command as historical Jesus tradition—namely, its supposed absence in the Synoptic Gospels? Our contention is that it is not absent at all, or at least only in the sense that the precise wording "love one another as I have loved you" is absent.

What is strongly present in the synoptic tradition is an emphasis on Jesus' followers as his family and as brothers and sisters to each other (Mark 3:31-35; Matt. 12:46-50; Luke 8:19-21). They are called to behave as a family, resolving their disagreements, not causing others to fall, caring for each other, forgiving each other. So in Matt. 5:21-25, the call is to "be reconciled to your brother," and in Matt. 18:6-35, the call is to strive for agreement and reconciliation, and so "you have gained your brother" (v. 15). In Mark 9:42-50, the very strong warning against causing a brother to fall is followed by the intriguing "Have salt in [among] yourselves, and be at peace with one another." Luke 17:1-4 is parallel to Mark 9 and Matthew 18, and the same message is conveyed.[30]

But the most significant synoptic evidence is the Lord's teaching to the disciples on serving one another. This occurs at various points in the Synoptic

---

29. The explanation that it fits John's supposedly sectarian tendencies—in particular his late-first-century context, when church and synagogue decisively split—is vulnerable to all sorts of criticism. There are serious doubts about whether there was such a split at the end of the first century. The idea that John is sectarian is questionable; John 3:16 and 20:31 suggest a rather different picture. And if the emphasis on loving one another is an indication of sectarianism, then the earliest Christian church was as guilty of such an outlook as the Johannine church, as is evident from Paul's emphasis on loving one another, among other things.

Gospels: in Mark 9:35, where the disciples are discussing who is the greatest; in Matt. 23:11, where Jesus is telling his disciples not to seek top seats and titles; and most importantly, in the parallel passages in Matt. 20:20-28//Mark 10:35-45 and the differently located and differently worded Luke 22:24-27.[31] Although the Lukan passage is different from that of Matthew and Mark, all three passages have several things in common:

> 1. The context is a dispute among Jesus' disciples about their importance. In Matthew and Mark, James and John ask for top seats in Jesus' kingdom, to the annoyance of their colleagues. In Luke, it is simply said that they were disputing about which of them was the greatest.
> 2. Jesus goes on to describe how gentile rulers like to exert their authority over others.
> 3. Jesus says to his disciples, "Not so . . . among you," and he says that "the greatest among you" or "the one who wants to be great among you" must be your servant (Matthew and Mark: "servant" and "slave").
> 4. Jesus refers to his own role. In Matthew and Mark, he says, "The Son of Man did not come to be served but to serve," and in Luke, he says, "I am among you as one who serves."
> 5. Matthew and Mark have Jesus go on to refer specifically to his death "and to give his life a ransom for many." Luke does not, but his location of the saying in the passion story implies the same understanding.[32]

---

30. Matthew 18 is of particular interest in that it discusses dealing with "your brother" who has fallen into sin (so also Luke 17:3), which is exactly what Paul addresses in Gal. 6:1, just before his statement about "the law of Christ." Paul may well have this Jesus tradition in mind in 1 Cor. 5:1-5 and perhaps also in 2 Cor. 2:5-11: in both, Paul speaks of handling brothers who have sinned. The possibility that Paul could be drawing on the traditions found in Matthew 18 is one that scholars do not easily contemplate, because of the widespread view that the relevant parts of the chapter in Matthew are Matthean redaction (though those who believe in Q may pause to note that Luke 17:1-4 has things in common with Matthew and not just with Mark). But it could be that Matthew is drawing on non-Marcan traditions in chapter 18, which Paul knows. It could be that the "law of Christ" in Gal. 6:2 is precisely a reference to these traditions. The parallel between 1 Cor. 5:1-5 and Matthew 18 is discussed in my *Paul: Follower of Jesus or Founder of Christianity?*, 210–13. Various ideas in this article were suggested in that book, though not all developed as here.

31. The differences between the Lukan passage and the Matthew/Mark passage are plausibly taken to indicate Luke's use of a different source. But it is not necessary for our present purposes to try to determine the history of the different traditions. However, their occurrence in several different contexts may be evidence of its importance for the evangelists.

The relevance of this to our discussion of "the new commandment" of John should be clear. Here we have in the Synoptic Gospels an important tradition that relates very closely to the new commandment:

> 1. In both, it is a question of relationships/status/greatness among the disciples.
> 2. In both, Jesus offers a style of behavior that is to mark out his followers as distinctive. In the Synoptics, the contrast is specifically with the behavior of worldly leaders. In John, it is more simply said that this will be how Jesus' disciples will be recognized.
> 3. In both, Jesus calls for—indeed, commands—humble serving of others. John has Jesus say, "love one another," not "serve one another," but the love has been illustrated by the preceding washing of the feet. It is love through self-sacrificial service of others, not some vague sort of emotional love.
> 4. Finally, in both, Jesus offers himself (especially his death) as the model of such service.

It is clear from this that the Johannine love command is not a Johannine eccentricity or the creation of an introverted Johannine community at the end of the first century. It is a particular expression of an important tradition of Jesus that goes back as early in the gospel tradition as we can go.[33]

At this point, we can return to Paul and the "law of Christ," and our problem with identifying this with the "new commandment" of Jesus in John's Gospel has been eliminated. We have found the roots of that new commandment going back into the earliest Jesus traditions we have. And the

---

32. Scholars have seized on Luke's "omission" of the ransom saying as evidence that Luke is not into the idea of Jesus' atoning death. This, however, is another example of scholarly hypotheses misleading: the hypothesis in this case is that Luke is using Mark, and the conclusion is that he has deliberately left out the reference to Jesus' atoning death. But Luke shows every sign of having an independent version of the tradition here—hence the different location and wording. John perhaps reflects this same tradition, since he has Jesus at the Last Supper "among them as one who serves," washing the disciples' feet. And in any case, Luke's location of the tradition in the context of the Last Supper and the passion of Jesus indicate that he relates the serving to the passion, and it is no accident that Luke is the only evangelist to have a specific reference to Isaiah 53 in his passion narrative, at 22:37. The idea that Luke is not into the atonement fails to take into account the powerful narrative theology that is implied in the words of Jesus on the cross found in Luke 23:34, 39-43.

33. It is interesting that John does not use the wording of *service* or *slave* when referring to the disciples' relationships with each other, and he has Jesus say, "I no longer call you slaves . . . but I have called you friends" (15:15). It may be that John has deliberately avoided that terminology, using "love one another" by preference, but John 13 makes clear that he sees this "loving" in terms of the most humble and costly service.

conclusion that this is Paul's "law of Christ" is strengthened by our earlier suggestion that Gal. 5:13 is his version of the law "through love be slaves to one another." The bringing together of the themes of love and service is exactly what we have witnessed in our discussion of John in particular.[34] This conclusion is also strengthened by the possible evidence of Paul's familiarity with—and fondness for—Jesus' teaching about self-sacrificial service. Most striking is 1 Cor. 9:19, "Though I am free from all men [sic] I have made myself a slave [enslaved myself] to all, that I may win the more," which is very reminiscent of Mark 10:44, "Whoever would be first among you, must be [shall be] slave of all."[35] This last Pauline text comes, interestingly, immediately before Paul's reference to himself as *ennomos Christou*, "Christ's enlawed one," the possible parallel to Gal. 6:2 that we noted. It is also interestingly similar to Gal. 5:13, "Do not use your freedom as an opportunity [excuse] for the flesh, but through love be servants [slaves] of one another," which comes shortly before Gal. 6:2. The convergence of similar ideas and even phraseology is striking.

This observation brings us back to our starting point and enables us to conclude with some confidence that Paul's reference to the "law of Christ" in Gal. 6:2 is to be identified with the new commandment of John 13, "love one another, as I have loved you."[36] This conclusion does not exclude all of the other interpretations: Those who have seen the "law of Christ" as referring to Christ's self-giving example are partly right, because the new commandment is "as I have loved you." Those who have seen it as having to do with the fulfillment of the Old Testament law also are partly right, in that Paul does see the law of Christ as fulfilling the Old Testament law.[37] The suggested interpretation of the "law of Christ" thus embraces those insights, but the specific reference

---

34. The Synoptics do not use the terminology of *love* when referring to the death of Jesus, but there can be no doubt that this is precisely how they do view it. Luke's description of Jesus' death with his words of forgiveness and hope to his executioners and to the repentant criminal is just one illustration.

35. Paul in that saying expresses his hope/ambition that he will "gain the more," which is not a million miles away from Mark 10:45, where Jesus speaks of his death as giving his life as "a ransom for many." At the end of that section of 1 Corinthians, Paul speaks of seeking the good "of many" and then concludes, "Be imitators of me, as I am of Christ." For a wider discussion of these and related texts, see my *Paul: Follower of Jesus or Founder of Christianity?*, 255–71.

36. We do not find the actual words "love one another" in the Synoptic Gospels; love is a particular favorite word of John's Gospel. But we certainly find the concept in the Synoptics, and there is every possibility that Jesus himself spoke of loving *and* serving one another, as does Paul in Gal. 5:13.

37. Just a few verses later in Galatians, Paul speaks of "doing good to all, but especially to those of the household of faith" (6:10), indicating his awareness of the Christian's responsibility to his or her brothers and sisters in faith (the "law of Christ"?), being a particular subset within a broader responsibility to society ("love your neighbor"?).

to the new commandment has almost always been missed because of particular scholarly perspectives, which have a blinkering effect on those working with them.[38] But the conclusion is well based, as we hope we have shown.

The "Command of the Lord" in 1 Cor. 14:37

The final puzzling Pauline text, which we will treat much more briefly, is 1 Cor. 14:37.[39] Here, following his highly controversial and much-debated teaching on women keeping silence in church, Paul says emphatically, "If anyone thinks that he is a prophet, or spiritual, he should acknowledge that what [the things] I am writing to you is a [or the] command of the Lord (*kuriou entole*)."[40] The question is, why does Paul use this phrase here? H. Conzelmann in his commentary asks precisely that question and comments that "It is not clear how Paul grounds his assertion that his exposition is a command of the Lord himself."[41]

It could be simply a rather authoritarian statement, with Paul invoking dominical authority for his controversial teaching, reminding us of the tongue-in-cheek advice sometimes given to speakers: when the argument is weak, shout louder! However, an alternative is that it is parallel to the "law of Christ" in Gal. 6:2, which we have just studied at length, and that Paul is referring to the same Jesus traditions about loving and (especially) serving. C. K. Barrett summarily dismisses the idea that Paul might be quoting Jesus here, but he

---

38. In his Word commentary, R. N. Longenecker refers to the John commandment. Longenecker, *Word Biblical Commentary 41: Galatians* (Nashville: Thomas Nelson, 1990), 283. But even he does not make the connection in his discussion of "the law of Christ," which he takes to mean gospel principles. Ibid., 275–76.

39. I am grateful to my brother Gordon for asking me about the possible relevance of this text.

40. There is a textual question here (as well as about the preceding verses and what they say about women), with some manuscripts omitting the word *command* (*entole*). The case for retaining the word is quite good; see the comments of B. M. Metzger, *A Textual Commentary on the Greek New Testament* (London: UBS, 1973), 566. But my argument still has some force if the word is omitted, since Paul still insists that his teaching is "of the Lord." It is just possible that some scribe(s) omitted the word because they could not identify the "command" of the Lord.

41. *1 Corinthians* (Philadelphia: Fortress Press, 1975), 246.

does not note the arguments that might favor that view.[42] These include the following:

> 1. There is the fact that the phrase is problematic and needs some explaining. It will hardly do to claim that Paul is shouting loud to defend a weak argument.
> 2. The genitival phrase "command of the Lord" is similar to "law of Christ" (Gal. 6:2; cf. 1 Cor. 9:21).[43] And it is reminiscent of those places where Paul clearly refers to Jesus traditions as coming from "the Lord," i.e., 1 Cor. 7:10, 12; 9:14; and arguably 1 Thess. 4:15).
> 3. The overall context of the phrase is the preceding discussion of spirituality and worship (and notably the use of prophecy and tongues in worship), as is highlighted by the words "If anyone thinks that he is a prophet, or spiritual, he should acknowledge that what [the things] I am writing to you is a [or the] command of the Lord (*kuriou entole*)." He speaks generally about the practice of worship in verses 26-33 and then particularly about women in church worship in verses 33-35.[44]

In both sections, Paul emphasizes the importance of "being in submission." So Paul says, "the spirits of prophets are subject [submit] to prophets" and the women "should be subordinate [in submission]" (vv. 32, 34).

Submission (*hupotassein*) for Paul did not have the demeaning connotations that it almost invariably has for modern readers, but is frequently a positive term expressing the practical "ordering oneself" under another or giving precedence to another (so Rom. 13:1 in connection with the governing authorities, 1 Cor. 15:28 of Jesus putting himself under his Father). If we were to paraphrase it

---

42. These arguments have been ably explored and presented by Christian Stettler in "The 'Command of the Lord' in 1 Cor 14:37: A Saying of Jesus," *Biblica* 87 (2006): 42–51. He notes many of the connections we have been exploring in our discussion of Gal. 6:2, though in the article he sees that text as referring to Jesus' summary of the whole law, rather than to the specific command to the disciples about serving each other.

43. The word *command* is different from the word *law*; "the law of the Messiah" is arguably somewhat more general than "a command of the Lord." But as we have already observed, the terms are very closely related, being used almost interchangeably in some contexts by Paul. There is no problem at all in thinking that Paul would have seen loving service as the "law of the Messiah" but also would have seen "love one another as I have loved you" (or "serve one another through love") as the specific command of the Lord at the heart of that law.

44. Unless these verses are deemed to be an interpolation, a view for which there is no clear manuscript evidence, however much modern critics might wish there to be such evidence. Our argument is not seriously affected if the verses are viewed as an interpolation, since the "subjection" theme is strong in the preceding verses.

"letting another/others be first" and relate it to humility,⁴⁵ then the connections to Paul's teaching elsewhere are obvious (e.g. Philippians 2).

It is also worth noting that the overriding concern of Paul in the whole of 1 Corinthians 12–14, where this teaching is found, is for love in the community and for building up the community. The "submission" comes in that context and, we might say, under that rubric.⁴⁶

It is clear how very closely related Paul's teaching on "submission" (and order and peace) in 1 Corinthians 14 is to the teaching of Jesus about following his example of servanthood within the fellowship of his followers, which we have already explored when discussing Gal. 6:2. In Matthew, Mark, and Luke, the teaching comes in the context of Jesus' disciples vying for and squabbling about position. The various Pauline passages that we have noted have something rather similar: in Galatians 5 and 6, as we saw, the immediately preceding context is "Let us have no self-conceit, no provoking of one another, no envy of one another" (5:26), and the immediately following context is "For if any one thinks he is something, when he is nothing, he deceives himself" (6:3). In 1 Corinthians 9, the reference to being "Christ's enlawed one" and to making myself a "slave to all" is in the overall context of tensions between "strong" and "weak" Christians, and Paul concludes the section with "I try to please all men [everyone] in everything I do, not seeking my own advantage, but that of many, that they may be saved. Be imitators of me, as I am of Christ" (10:33—11:1). In Philippians 2, the example of Christ's humility follows Paul's words "Do nothing from selfishness [rivalry] or conceit, but in humility count others better [more significant] than yourselves. Let each of you look not only to his own interests, but also to the interests of others. Have this mind among yourselves, which is yours [you have] in Christ Jesus" (2:3-4).⁴⁷ First Corinthians 14 makes sense as another passage reflecting the same range of ideas: the context is divisions in the church and especially in worship over spiritual gifts; the message is love, building others up, and putting oneself last.⁴⁸

We conclude that it is entirely feasible that "It is a command of the Lord" (or even simply "it is from the Lord") in 1 Cor. 14:37 is a reference to the Jesus

---

45. See G. Delling in *TDNT* 8:45, noting how important and distinctive the idea is in the Christian tradition and comparing 1 Peter 2, where reference is made to Christ leaving us an example through his suffering on our behalf.

46. The centrality of 1 Corinthians 13 makes that point, as does the emphasis on "building up." See also Stettler, "The 'Command of the Lord,'" 45.

47. If our argument is correct, then when Paul refers to "the mind of Christ," he is reflecting quite probably not only on the humility of Jesus' actions, but also on his specific commandment to the disciples.

tradition, such as we find it in Mark 10. It looks rather as though "the law of Christ" in Gal. 6:2, the "command of the Lord" in 1 Cor. 14:37, and "being Christ's enlawed one" in 1 Cor. 9:19 may all be related to the same tradition and saying of Jesus.

The argument regarding 1 Cor. 14:37 may score slightly less in terms of probability than the preceding arguments about 1 Thess. 4:15 and Gal. 6:2, but it is at least a real possibility to be reckoned with and not dismissed. And it is a significant argument in that Paul turns out not to be speaking with an exaggerated sense of his own authority, but as someone who is echoing the teaching of Jesus about servant leadership and applying it to the practicalities of worship in Corinth.

Concluding Observations

I suggest—and hope—that this article has achieved three things. First, that it has thrown light on three of the vexed exegetical questions from Paul's letters: What is the "word of the Lord" to which Paul is referring in 1 Thess. 4:15, when he speaks about Christians who have died? What is the "law of Christ" to which he refers in Gal. 6:2? And why does he refer to the "command of the Lord" in 1 Cor. 14:37?

Second, I hope it has supported the view that Paul draws significantly on the traditions of Jesus in his letters. Some scholars have been very cautious about recognizing Jesus traditions in Paul's writings, allowing in not much more than Paul's reference to the Lord's Supper in 1 Cor. 11:23-25, plus 1 Cor. 7:10-11, where Paul quotes the Lord on divorce, plus 1 Cor. 9:14 on the Lord's workers being paid for their work. But there are numerous other examples of possible or probable echoes, of which we have just discussed three.

Third, I hope it has made out a good case for Matthew in his own non-Marcan traditions ("M" material, as scholars label it) and for John in his gospel having very early Jesus traditions. Scholars have too often been locked into an academic straitjacket, which has blinded them or at least prejudiced them against certain possibilities (including that Paul might be referring to the non-Marcan non-Q texts we have been discussing). But even if Marcan priority is correct (as I suspect) and John's Gospel is relatively late (as I suspect), this does

---

48. If Eph. 5:21 is Pauline in some sense at least, then it is notable that it speaks of Christians in general "submitting to one another out of reverence for Christ" and then a few verses later speaks of husbands loving their wives "as Christ loved the church and gave himself up for her" (v. 25). We see the ideas of submission, love, and the example of Christ and his sacrifice all come together here.

not mean they did not have very early traditions of Jesus in addition to Mark. On the contrary, it is a priori extremely likely that they did.

Scholars are beginning to wake up again to the fact that the stories and sayings of Jesus first circulated orally in the early church; they were "passed down" and "received," as Paul puts it.[49] So when Matthew, Luke, and John came to write their gospels, they may have had Mark as a written source, but they did not learn about Jesus first from Mark but from oral tradition. Instead of Marcan priority, we might appropriately speak of oral-tradition priority. Paul had access to that tradition and saw it as the "word of the Lord," to which he and others should give the greatest attention.[50]

---

49. That there may also have been very early written traditions of Jesus is another real possibility that has largely been discounted by modern scholars, despite Luke 1:1 and the New Testament letters showing that the Christian community was a writing community. On such possibilities, see E. E. Ellis, *Christ and the Future in New Testament History* (Leiden: Brill, 2001), 212–41. My father, John Wenham, in his *Redating Matthew, Mark and Luke* (London: Hodder, 1991), 230–38, argued for a very early date for all of the Synoptic Gospels, and he revived the early-church view that Luke was "the brother whose praise is in the gospel" (my translation) in 2 Cor. 8:18 and that Paul was referring to his work as a gospel writer (noting also 1 Tim. 5:18). Stewart Lauer in his 2011 PhD thesis for the University of Wales, "Traces of a Gospel Writing in 1 Corinthians: Rediscovery and Development of Origen's Understanding of 1 Corinthians 4:6B," argues for Paul's reference being to Matthew's Gospel. Even without coming to that startling conclusion, one might agree that "what is written" in 1 Cor. 4:6 could be Paul's earlier letter or another Christian writing, perhaps including instruction about the law of Christ. But it is always important to beware of parallelomania and of imagining significant parallelism where there is none.

50. It is notable that Paul refers to "fulfilling the law of Christ" in a way that is reminiscent of how he and others speak of the "fulfillment" of the Old Testament law (e.g., Gal. 5:14).

Index

Adam, 43, 58, 63
Alexander the Great, 33, 53, 150
Ananias, 73
Anderson, Paul, 146n10, 166n17, 167–68
anthropology, 19, 26n106, 66
anti-Italianism, 53
anti-Semitism, 53
aphorisms, 26, 28, 115, 117–18, 122
apocalyptic, 15, 27, 29, 37–38, 42, 48, 65, 96, 97n10, 118–19
apologetics, 6, 147, 154
Armstrong, Neil, 70
Augustine of Hippo, 41, 184n6
Augustus, Caesar, 31, 35, 63, 68–69, 74, 95, 150

Babylonians, 32, 33, 53
Bardo Museum, 31
Barret, C. K., 87n23, 197
Barth, Karl, 18
Bauckham, Richard, 166, 170n34, 182
Baur, F. C., 8
Beasley-Murray, George R., 78n1, 170n32, 172n43
Berakot, 106
Blomberg, Craig L., 103n33, 105n39, 163–79
Bock, Darrell L., 59–60, 141–62, 164n7, 165, 179n71
Borg, Marcus, 179
Bornkamm, Günther, 20
Brosend, William, 97n12, 109
Brouwer, Wayne, 176
Bousset, Wilhelm, 16–17
Brooten, Bernadette, 95n5
Brown, Raymond, 29, 156n23

Bultmann, Rudolf, 17–19, 21, 22, 30, 151n14, 170n35
Buttrick, David, 103n32, 105–6
Byrne, Brendan, 103n33, 104
Byrscog, Samuel, 182

Caiaphas, 73
Caird, G. B., 41, 42n6, 160
Caligula, 35, 52
Campolo, Tony, 96
Capernaum, 34, 35, 39, 67, 90, 98, 126–27
Challenging Perspectives on the Gospel of John (Siebeck), 166
Charlesworth, James, 143n4, 146n10, 157n24, 163–64, 167n21
Chilton, Bruce, 78n2, 81n6, 81n7, 88n25
Christian Empire, 56
Christian tradition: Eastern, 58–59; Western, 2, 58–59
cleanup, great/divine/God's, 34, 37, 39, 40
Constantine, Donation of, 2
Conzelmann, Hans, 20, 197
Court of the Gentiles, 73
Crosby, Michael H., 94n4, 102n28
Crossan, John Dominic, 22n88, 23–26, 28, 30, 31–76, 78n2, 93n1, 94n3, 102n30, 116n1
cynic, Jewish, 24; preacher, 28

demythologization, 18–19
Descartes, Rene, 2; *Cogito*, 2
Dibelius, Martin, 17
Docetism, 19, 41, 177
Dodd, C. H., 80, 116n2
Downing, Gerald, 28

Dunn, James D. G., 4, 22, 78n2, 119, 144n7, 151n14, 153, 155, 164, 165, 182, 189n18

Ebeling, Gerhard, 20
Ecclesiastes Rabbah, 107
empire, 25, 32–34, 36, 37, 51, 53–56, 61, 93
Enlightenment, 15, 94, 142; post-Enlightenment, 67, 69; pre-Enlightenment, 68–69
1 Enoch, 30, 74, 97n10, 157–58
Epictetus, 122–23
eschaton, 32–34, 36, 38
eschatological: conclusions, 21; Jesus, 14n59; kingdom of God as, 14n59; as mind-set of Jesus, 6; transformation, 40
eschatology, 22; as motif, 14n59; thoroughgoing, 16, 21, 22
Evans, Craig A., 77–91, 165, 174n50
Evangelical Theological Society, 165
exile, 35, 46–48, 152
existentialism, 19, 30
exodus, the, 32, 38, 51, 173
4 Ezra, 30

feminist, feminism, 95n9, 106, 147
fides quaerens intellectum, 71
Ford, Richard Q., 98n15, 108
form criticism, 13n54, 17–21, 30
France, R. T., 80, 81n7
Francis of Assisi, 95
Fredrikesen, Paula, 40
Fuchs, Ernst, 20
Funk, Robert, 22, 116nn1–2

Galilee, 34–39, 51, 55, 62, 66, 94, 95, 97, 98, 126–27, 150–51, 164, 167, 172, 177
Gnostic Gospels, 163
God's Son, 27, 30, 136
Good Shepherd, 44, 173–74
Gospel of Thomas, 116–19

Gundry, Robert, 166

Habermas, Gary R., 4n7
Harnack, Adolf von, 11, 13n54, 18n75, 154
Hasmoneans, 35
Hegel, 8–10
Heidegger, 18
Hellenism, 1
Herod Agrippa I, 35
Herod Antipas, 34–39, 51, 66, 95, 98, 151
Herod the Great, 35, 62
Herzog, William, 57, 98n15, 99–100, 102n29, 103n31, 108n48
historical monograph, 66
Holtzmann, Heinrich Julius, 10–11
Holy Spirit, 38, 60
Homer, 31
Hooker, Morna D., 81n6, 87n23
Hoppe, Rudolf, 97n11
Horsley, Dick, 55, 93n1
Hultgren, Arland, 97n13, 101n25, 102n27, n29, 107n38, 109, 111n54
Hurtado, Larry, 42

imperium, 32

Jackson, Shelly, 50
Jerusalem, 52, 54, 62, 65, 79–80, 127–29, 138, 150–51, 161, 163, 164, 167, 171, 172, 174; destruction of, 43, 47, 88; temple of, 67, 88, 109–10
Jerusalem Talmud, 106–7
Jesus Seminar, 22, 163
Johannine tradition, 48, 165–73; 175–78, 182, 191–93, 195
Josephus, 52, 54, 82n12, 109–10, 174n51
Julius Caesar, 68

Kähler, Martin, 16–17, 19, 30, 143n3
Käsemann, Ernst, 19–20, 143n2

Keck, Leander E., 4n8, 7n20, 8n27, 14n59
Keener, Craig S., 104n34, 109n51, 164–65, 171, 173n45
kerygma, 19–20
Kierkegaard, 18
King of the Jews, 35
Kingdom of God, 6, 11, 14, 25, 26, 33, 34, 36, 37, 38, 45, 48, 50, 53, 66, 77, 78n1, 79, 115, 117, 120, 170
Kingdom of heaven, 37, 95, 97, 102
Kleinman, Arthur, 25
Kloppenberg, John, 123
koinonia, 50

Lachmann, Karl, 10
Lamech, 60–61
land of Israel, 45, 54, 174
Language of the Gospel: Early Christian Rhetoric, The, 115, 121
Lessing, G. E., 4, 5n11, 160n27
Levinas, Emmanuel, 99, 100n20
Levine, Amy-Jill, 58, 78n2, 93–113
liberal, 5, 11, 12, 16, 18n75, 30, 93, 94
Liebenberg, Jacobus, 116n1, 117
Lindars, Barnabas, 170
Loader, William, 105–6, 112n55
Loisy, Alfred, 50
Luke, 21n85, 35, 37–40, 42–44, 48, 62, 66, 67, 74, 78–80, 83, 88–90, 95, 109, 116–20, 122, 128, 136, 143n3, 148, 149, 151, 153, 156, 166, 172n41, 178, 182, 184, 189, 193, 194, 195n32, 196n34, 199, 201
Luther, Martin, 2, 18n75

m. Baba Metziah, 99
Macedonians, 53
Matthew, 20n85, 37, 49, 60–62, 66, 67, 74, 83n15, 84n18, 94n4, 95, 100, 102, 103n33, 104nn34–35, 105nn38–39, 105n41, 105n43, 108, 109, 110nn51–52, 111n54, 117, 119, 122, 125–39, 148, 156, 158, 159, 166, 176–78, 182, 183, 184, 185, 186, 193, 194, 199–201
matrix, 28, 32–33, 53, 63, 67, 71–72, 75, 78
McKnight, Scot, 78n2, 164
Medes, 32, 53
Meier, John P., 22–23, 149n12, 152n15, 168n26
Melchizedek (11Q), 158
Meyer, Ben F., 9, 12, 22, 143n2, 144n6, 160n27
Messiah, Jewish, 54, 135
messianic consciousness, 13n55, 14
messianic light, 27, 46
messianic secret, 12–14, 115, 148, 149n12, 152n15, 154
miracles, 6, 8, 9, 25, 28–29, 35, 48, 67, 68, 69, 74, 75, 168n26, 169n29
Micah, 34, 81n8, 131
Midrash Psalms, 111
Midrash Tanhuma Ki Tissa, 107
Migdal, new synagogue in, 51
Miller, Robert J., 125–39
Mosaic Law, 49
Muir, John, 41
Mystery of the Kingdom of God, The, 14, 115

Narrative, The Grand, 50
Nazareth, 4, 22, 28n110, 34, 39, 40, 52, 89, 126, 127
Neill, Stephen, 10, 22
Nicaea, council at, 63
Nietzsche, 14, 15
nonviolent resistance, 25, 39–40, 52
nonviolent revolutionary, 51, 54
North Africa, 51

open commensality, 25

Pahl, M. W., 186n9
Pan, 150

Parables, 26, 28, 42, 44–48, 51, 57, 93–113, 115–24, 135, 143n2, 157, 164, 169n29, 179; of the sower, 45–48, 115, 122; of the lost coin, 48; of the lost sheep, 48; of the mustard seed, 47; of the pearl of great price, 48; of the seed growing secretly, 48; of the treasure in the field, 48
Parousia, 183, 185
Patterson, Stephen J., 61, 115–24
Pauline literature, 178n68
Pax Americana, 93
Pax Romana, 93
Perrin, Norman, 20, 85n20
Persians, 32, 33, 53
Pfleiderer, Otto, 12
Pharisees, 73, 104, 105, 120, 135, 172, 173
Philo, 52, 110n52, 123
Pilate, 38, 40, 52, 53, 64, 65, 156, 177
Pokorný, Petr, 164
Poon, Wilson, 172
pre-Enlightenment world, 68–69
privatization of sin, 56
prophecy, 6, 43, 46n12, 75, 111, 118n7, 125–39, 183, 198
prosperity gospel, 96
Psalms of Solomon, 157–58

Q, 83, 119, 120, 123n16, 131, 168, 184, 194n30, 200
Queen of the South, 43
Quest: Jesus, 1–30, 142–43, 163, 165, 167n22, 168, 176, 179; New, 19–21, 30; Renewed New, 22, 30; Third, 22, 30, 143, 163, 165, 179
Qumranites, 52

redaction criticism, 13n54, 14, 20, 30
reign of God, 29, 78–79
Reimarus, H. S., 2–6, 9, 10, 15, 21, 30
Reiser, M., 78n1
Religionsgeschichtliche Schule, 14, 16
Ritschl, Albrecht, 11, 14

Robbins, Vernon, 28, 95n6
Robinson, James M., 20
Robinson, John A. T. (Bishop), 82, 83, 165
Rollman, Hans, 13n55
Roman Empire, 51, 53, 54, 63, 68, 72, 93n1
Rome, 32, 35–40, 51, 52, 53, 56, 58, 60, 61, 65, 66, 67, 82n12, 93n1, 98n15, 104, 119, 152, 157, 158, 159
Rule of the Community (1QS), 158
Rütenik, K. A., 7

sages, 27, 38, 42
Sanders, E. P., 22, 23, 88, 90n26
Satan, 42, 56, 63, 64, 78, 151, 152n15
Schleiermacher, Friedrich Daniel Ernst, 6–8, 10, 30
Schmidt, K. L., 17
Schweitzer, Albert, 4, 14–16, 19, 21, 22, 29, 142
Semachot de Rabbi Chiyah, 110
separation of church and state, 56
Sepphoris, 36, 52, 53, 61, 95n5, 98
Shinall, Myrick C., Jr., 93–113
Sitz im Leben, 18, 85n19, 87
Snodgrass, Klyne R., 97n13, 98, 101n24, 106, 107n45
social dimensions, 55, 66
social gospel, 55
social implications, 54, 55
social location, 61, 62, 66
source criticism, 11, 30
Son of David, 43
Son of Man, 27, 30, 33, 37, 43, 48, 50, 51, 53, 83–89, 118, 119, 156–58, 183, 185, 194
sovereignty of God, 54, 88
Spinoza, Baruch (Benedict), 2, 3
Stewart, Robert B., 1–30, 75, 76
Strauss, David Friedrich, 8–10, 12n49, 30
Sukkoth, 172, 173n46 (as Sukkot), 174

Sung, Lilias, 25
symbolic actions, 27
Synoptic Gospels, 10, 18n74, 81, 178n68, 182, 192, 193, 195, 196n36, 201n49
synoptic problem, 10
Syr. Baruch, 30
Syrians, 53

Tatum, W. B., 4n9
Taylor, Joan, 169
Tekton, 61–62
Testimonia (4Q), 159
Testimony of the Beloved Disciple, The (Bauckham), 166
textual retrofitting, 130
theology, dialectical, 19
Tiberias, 34, 36, 98
Tiberius, 35, 38, 52
Torah, 28, 41, 43, 82n12, 88, 89, 99n17, 104, 107, 120, 188, 189n18
Tosefta, Bava Metzia, 101
Tractatus Theologico-Politicus, 2
Troeltsch, Ernst, 16, 17
Tutu, Desmond, 41
Twelftree, Graham H., 79n3

Übermensch, 14
Urmarcus, 10
Urmatthäus, 10

Valla, Lorenzo, 2
Virgil, 31, 32, 61
virginal conception, 74–75

Wachsmann, Shelley, 36
Weisse, Christian Hermann, 10
Wenham, David, 168n25, 169n29, 181–201
Wesley, John, 55, 104
Wilder, Amos, 115, 116n1, 121
Wisdom, 27, 28, 30, 45, 46, 49, 79, 83, 84, 96, 116, 122, 123n16
Witherington, Ben, III, 22, 26–30, 41–50, 51–58, 58–67, 69–71, 73–75, 93n2, 99n17, 170, 183n3, 187n11, 188n15
Wrede, William, 4n8, 12–15, 19, 21, 22, 153, 154
Wright, N. T., 10n36, 21, 22, 24, 25n100, 44, 45, 46, 48, 155n22, 165n10

Xavier, Hieronymus, 4n10

Yodfat, 51

Zarephath, 43
Zealots, 52
Zeira, Rabbi, 106

www.ingramcontent.com/pod-product-compliance
Lightning Source LLC
Chambersburg PA
CBHW051942290426
44110CB00015B/2074